Truth by Analysis

TRUTH BY ANALYSIS

GAMES, NAMES, AND PHILOSOPHY

Colin McGinn

OXFORD
UNIVERSITY PRESS

Oxford University Press, Inc., publishes works that further
Oxford University's objective of excellence
in research, scholarship, and education.

Oxford   New York
Auckland   Cape Town   Dar es Salaam   Hong Kong   Karachi
Kuala Lumpur   Madrid   Melbourne   Mexico City   Nairobi
New Delhi   Shanghai   Taipei   Toronto

With offices in
Argentina   Austria   Brazil   Chile   Czech Republic   France   Greece
Guatemala   Hungary   Italy   Japan   Poland   Portugal   Singapore
South Korea   Switzerland   Thailand   Turkey   Ukraine   Vietnam

Published by Oxford University Press, Inc.
198 Madison Avenue, New York, New York 10016

www.oup.com

Oxford is a registered trademark of Oxford University Press.

Library of Congress Cataloging-in-Publication Data
McGinn, Colin, 1950–.
Truth by analysis : games, names, and philosophy / Colin McGinn.
    p. cm.
Includes bibliographical references (p.).
ISBN 978-0-19-985614-5 (hardcover : alk. paper)
1. Philosophy.   2. Analysis (Philosophy)   I. Title.
B53.M38   2012
101—dc22   2011013650

1 3 5 7 9 8 6 4 2

Printed in the United States of America
on acid-free paper

Contents

Preface

This book had an improbable gestation. A couple of years ago I decided to teach a class on philosophy and sport. The idea was to combine intellectual work with actual athletic activity—mainly tennis. My role as teacher was to teach people how to think and how to play a game. To my knowledge, such a class had never before been attempted (it was a notable success). I needed some texts for the class and happened across a book I had not heard of before, having not had an active interest in philosophy of sport—*The Grasshopper: Games, Life and Utopia*, by Bernard Suits. Apparently, it had some reputation in philosophy of sport circles. It lay around in my study for a while unread, slim and unassuming, with a photograph of a big bright grasshopper on the cover, with big black eyes. As the time for the class approached, I started to read it: a curious text, written as a Platonic dialogue between insects, with the eponymous grasshopper about to die, quite willingly. The author, speaking in the persona of his wise insect, announces his intention of defining the concept of a game. I shook my head: *that* isn't going to fly (or hop). For a good thirty-five years I had followed the conventional wisdom that Wittgenstein had shown that the concept *game* is not definable by means of necessary and sufficient conditions. Moreover, when I first read the purported definition I felt unconvinced, suspecting counterexamples by the bushel. The book pressed on, bringing up and defusing one putative counterexample after another, making sound and sensible points. Still I was not convinced—I just needed to think harder to find devastating counterexamples. After a second reading, and then a third, I gave up the fight: games had been defined! This came as quite a shock to the system—physiologically and doctrinally. Now the search for definition—for conceptual analysis—seemed like not such a misguided enterprise, even for the most recalcitrant of cases. Suits had changed my philosophical worldview. I proceeded to teach people how to play the game of tennis while now possessing a penetrating analysis of the nature of games.

It was natural, some time later, to teach a class on meta-philosophy, with *The Grasshopper* as one of the set texts. This I did with Mark Rowlands in the spring semester of 2009. We read a number of distinguished authors who discuss the nature of philosophy, covering the linguistic turn, naturalism, philosophical explanation, subjective and objective, puzzles and problems, linguistic therapy, and intuitions. The consensus at the end was that Suits stood up better than all the rest. My faith in conceptual analysis had been restored (and I always had a hankering for it). I took to describing those who shared my newfound methodological conviction as "the Miami Analysts." This group holds a distinctive set of positions, to be adumbrated in the course of this book. We oppose the idea of the linguistic turn, holding that language has no special role within philosophy. We also deny that philosophy is *about* concepts. But we also reject, yet more vehemently, the kind of naturalism that is commonly traced back to Quine: we do not see philosophy as "continuous with science." Philosophy, for the Miami Analysts, is not an empirical subject at all. Positively, we maintain that philosophy deals with what I shall unabashedly call the "intelligible world"—that is, the world as it is revealed to pure unaided reason. Thus there are two principal parts to this meta-philosophy: (a) philosophy is about ordinary non-linguistic reality; and (b) philosophy proceeds by using pure reason to elucidate the world. Part (a) distances philosophy from linguistic studies, formal or informal (except where the topic is explicitly language); part (b) distances philosophy from the sciences—physics, biology, and psychology. The position is quite traditional, holding that philosophy is a special and distinctive mode of intellectual inquiry and that its subject matter is simply the whole of reality (the same reality as that investigated by empirical science, as well as history, geography, criminology, and music theory). We set out to analyze the world by unaided reason. We deplore and resist any "turn" away from that traditional task, whether it is toward language or science. We also believe that it is important to insist on this methodological stance, because philosophy, to thrive, needs a sound meta-philosophy to guide it. We detect symptoms of the loss of confidence that has lately afflicted philosophy— a kind of desperate search for some sort of respectable self-conception, with the options narrowly constrained. There are many who apparently feel that if it isn't ordinary language (supplemented perhaps by some technical language) then it must be science. The Miami Analysts identify and occupy a different intellectual location: the intelligible world as revealed by reason—the analysis of objective reality, undertaken conceptually.

There is another theme that grows out of Suits's work: the contrast between play and labor—and the different value of both sorts of activity. Play has intrinsic value, being undertaken for its own sake; but labor has instrumental value, as a means for achieving an independently desired goal. Where does philosophy fall? In this book, I maintain that philosophizing is an intrinsically valuable activity, not justified by any goal that exists outside itself—as is also true of game playing. Scientific investigation, by contrast, is an activity directed to a goal external to the activity itself—like other forms of labor, such as digging ditches. Philosophy, therefore, has a special nature as a form of human activity: it has intrinsic value, not merely instrumental value. Philosophy can thus be aptly described as the "play of reason"—though with the deadly serious aim of discovering truth (about the world beyond us). Again, it is helpful to make this explicit, because it provides a self-conception that can clarify the status of philosophy as a form of human activity: philosophy is not a form of labor, but a form of leisure—something done for its own sake. As the ancients might put it, in philosophy man finds true happiness, because his action is inherently valuable to him. The exercise of pure reason produces happiness because such exercise is undertaken for its own sake and not for the sake of the external goods it may bring. The philosopher can be a type of hedonist (not so the scientist).

In addition to this uplifting stuff, the book contains discussions of family resemblance, the paradox of analysis, logical form, the problem of definitional sufficiency, the analytic-synthetic distinction, proper names, varieties of analysis, the perils of ontology, the logic of instantiation, and other such familiar topics. It aspires to be a complete defense of conceptual analysis as constituting the nature of philosophy. (I am, of course, under no illusions as to how this will be received in some quarters.)

I would like to thank Mark Rowlands, Harvey Siegel, Otavio Bueno, Amie Thomasson, and Jane Casillo for helpful comments. E. J. Lowe, Uriah Kriegel, and Ernest Sosa also provided thoughtful and encouraging reports for the press.

Colin McGinn

December 2010
Miami

Truth by Analysis

1 Philosophy and Analysis

The main thesis of this book can be stated succinctly: philosophy is the a priori search for essences, undertaken in a spirit of play. The first part of the thesis will have a familiar ring, but the second part will doubtless strike a discordant note. Indeed, the second part will seem in tension with the first part: searching for essences sounds serious and weighty, while playing is deemed light and frivolous. That there is no tension will not become clear until Chapter 10, when I consider the question of the value of philosophy as an activity—then it will become clear that I attach a special value to philosophy. But for now I shall concentrate on the first part of my guiding thesis: the contention that the goal of philosophical activity is to discover the essences of things by means of a priori investigation. By "essence," here I understand roughly what Aristotle meant by the phrase "the what it is to be" of a thing: so philosophy is concerned to discover what it is to be a certain kind of thing—what being of a certain kind *consists in* (in that indispensable philosophical phrase).[1] Moreover, it is

[1] The *Oxford English Dictionary* defines "essence" as "the intrinsic nature or indispensable quality of something, which determines its character" and "a property or group properties of something without which it would not exist or be what it is." The word is from the Latin *essentia*, from *esse*, "be." Apparently Aristotle never used a simple Greek word synonymous with "essence," preferring the cumbersome "what it is to be"; his Latin translators, baffled by his usage, supplied the word "essence," so that we now speak of "Aristotelian essence." It is worth bearing Aristotle's original phrasing in mind when hearing the word the "essence," and I use the two interchangeably in the course of this book: it reminds us that we are not speaking of anything particularly esoteric or technical—merely the idea of what is involved in something being the kind of thing it is. As Aristotle says, in philosophy we are concerned with "being *qua* being," i.e., things considered in their essence—their what-it-is-to-be. By contrast, natural science is concerned with things in relation to their causes and effects (roughly).

concerned with essence *qua* essence—with the necessity of that which constitutes the what-it-is-to-be of a thing. And note the reference to *things* here: we seek the essence of things or beings, not the essence of concepts or ideas or words. We want to know what makes something the thing it is—what constitutes its being as the kind of being it is. To introduce an allied concept: we are after the *definitions* of things—the results of philosophy are definitions, and the method of philosophy is defining. As Aristotle says, "a definition is an account (*logos*) that signifies an essence."[2] To spell it out: a definition is a piece of discourse that expresses or articulates the essence of a thing or a kind of thing—so definition is a relation between language (or possibly just thought) and something beyond language (or thought), namely, reality, being, existence, the objective. Things have essences independently of language, and our task is to formulate in language what those essences are—*qua* essences. Thus modality is central to philosophical investigation—as is definition. The natural and mathematical sciences may also be in the business of discovering essences (chemistry, geometry), but they are not concerned, as sciences, with the modality of what they discover. Philosophy is. Philosophy is also, according to the thesis, an a priori investigation: it is not a species of empirical inquiry, and it is not methodologically comparable to the natural sciences (though it is comparable to the formal sciences). It seeks the discovery of essences by a priori means alone—not by experiment or observation or experience.[3] It operates "from the armchair": that is, by unaided (usually solitary) contemplation. Its only experiments are thought-experiments, and its data are possibilities (or "intuitions" about possibilities). Thus philosophy seeks a priori knowledge of objective being—of non-linguistic and non-conceptual reality. We are investigating being as such, but we do so using only a priori methods.

My conception of philosophy is thus resolutely old-fashioned; indeed, it is up to its gills in notions and commitments that many view as having been refuted. And let me now add another controversial ingredient to this antiquated picture: conceptual analysis. For I shall also contend that the proper method for uncovering the essence of things is precisely conceptual analysis. Analysis is the method, and analyses are the results. I shall have much to say about the nature of analysis as we proceed, but by way of preliminary orientation, two aspects of it may be mentioned: the provision of necessary and sufficient conditions, specified without circularity; and the operation of decomposition or dismantling, or breaking down

---

[2] The phrase occurs in *Topics*, Book I, Chapter 5. An alternative translation is "a phrase signifying a thing's essence." This brings in the reference to *things* explicitly, but "account" seems better than "phrase," because it suggests something positively theoretical. I take it that a decent paraphrase, capturing Aristotle's intentions, would be this: "a linguistic formula that signifies (refers to) the essence (what-it-is-to-be) of a thing or kind of thing." Thus a definition takes as its object a non-linguistic entity and renders its essence in words.

[3] This does not preclude philosophical reflection on the natural sciences, as distinct from common sense—hence on what has been discovered by empirical or experimental means. Nor does it rule out revisions of common sense, as we shall see later.

into parts. An analysis (at least one central kind of analysis) consists in breaking a concept down into its conceptual components and showing how they are severally necessary and jointly sufficient for the original concept to apply. The *analysandum* is a complex concept, consisting of a cluster of sub-concepts, and the *analysans* is a specification of its conceptual parts that provide necessary and sufficient conditions for the concept analyzed. The analysis is both known a priori and a necessary truth. We arrive at the analysis by considering possible cases and asking ourselves whether the concept applies or not in these cases—that is, by consulting our "intuitions." I use quotation marks for the word because I prefer to speak of our *judgments* about possible cases—our reasoned, rational, and justified judgments. The concept of intuition has other irrelevant connotations, of groundless stabs in the dark or peculiar premonitions; I am speaking of a certain kind of rational belief that we have about possible situations—about a certain type of *knowledge*. Thus, confessedly, I am a completely unrepentant proponent of conceptual analysis in the most unapologetic sense: a priori, decompositional, necessarily true, non-circular, supplying necessary and sufficient conditions, and the aim of philosophy. Philosophy consists centrally of breaking complex concepts down into simpler concepts, until the primitive concepts are reached (though I broaden analysis in certain important ways in Chapter 7). I hold that there is nothing wrong in principle with this basic picture, despite the widespread impression that such a picture has been radically undermined. My view combines classical Aristotelian metaphysics with the methods of early analytic philosophy: the essence of reality uncovered by the method of conceptual analysis. We discover the essential structure of reality—what the world is like in itself—by analyzing our concepts; or better (for reasons that will become clear later), we discover the essences of things by *conceptually* analyzing those things. Concepts are not the *object* of our interest—things are—but our *method* is to view things conceptually, that is, as we conceive them. The range of our interest can be enormous and enormously varied: science and common sense, ethics and metaphysics, epistemology and philosophy of mind, aesthetics and mathematics, logic and the meaning of life. In each area, however, our philosophical method is conceptual analysis, directed ultimately at worldly essences: philosophy has a very heterogeneous range of interest, of subject matter, but its method is uniform and unvarying. It is therefore a unified field, not a patchwork of unrelated investigations. The *essence* of philosophy is the search for essences carried out by means of conceptual analysis (and undertaken in a spirit of play).

This type of view, so baldly stated, may be found suspect, or even shocking, today, but it was really the standard conception for most of the history of the subject, in one form or another. Essences have been around forever, as have analyses of them. Let me swiftly and superficially survey the history of philosophy from this perspective. First, we have Aristotelian essence and Platonic definition: the essences of things, the definition of words or concepts. Man is a "rational animal"; knowledge is "true belief with an account."[4] Aristotle seeks the essential nature of different categories of things, and Plato is forever asking for the meanings of words like "justice," "piety," "the holy," "knowledge." But actually they were not the first: before them we have the figures of Pythagoras and the pre-Socratics. Euclid's *Elements* is all about definition and essence, and breaking the complex down into the simple; and it is a commonplace that Plato and Aristotle were greatly influenced by early Greek geometry. Geometric figures are the paradigms of the definable, the composite, the resoluble—they have analyses in the plainest sense. The pre-Socratics too were concerned with questions of essence: the essential nature of reality is air, or water, or fire, or atoms in the void. Reality is in its essence stable and permanent, or it is essentially volatile and changeable (Parmenides, Heraclitus). Plato and Aristotle continue the tradition, seeking essences, definitions, and conceptual breakdowns. Later philosophy followed in their footsteps, with logic attaining prominence in the Middle Ages—the analysis of propositions and their logical interrelations. Indeed, the scholastics might be said to be obsessively definitional and text-bound. In the modern period, we find Locke's concern with simple and complex ideas, and reducing the complex to the simple, along with analyses of such things as personal identity and "mixed modes";[5] Hume's attempt to define causation by means of necessary and sufficient conditions, as well as his Lockean picture of the composition of concepts; Descartes' emphasis on "clear and distinct ideas," his definition of matter and mind in terms of extension and thought, his conceptual reduction of geometry to arithmetic; Leibniz's analysis of modality in terms of possible worlds and his concern with "truths of reason"; Berkeley's definition of physical objects as ideas in the mind of God; Kant's introduction of the analytic-synthetic distinction and his a priori analysis of human reason; and innumerable other early analytic enterprises. All of these philosophers took it for granted that things had essences and that it was their job to discover them by fundamentally a priori methods. And there was no doubt that human thought consists of a hugely complex system of ideas with a basically compositional structure, capable of rational analysis.

[4] Plato's idea that knowledge is true belief ("correct judgment" in standard translations) accompanied by an "account" is in the *Theaetetus*, perhaps the first major work of analytic epistemology. Of course, the notion of an "account" needs elucidation, a point pressed by Socrates. To my mind, Plato's three-part definition is very much on the right lines here: see Chapter 3. In general, the dialectical form of Plato's texts well captures the Socratic method of extracting necessary and sufficient conditions for concepts by cross-questioning. Among the early triumphs of the method we must include Plato's "Euthyphro" argument, showing that we cannot define the holy as what the gods love: by asking a question of definition, Socrates here undermines the whole idea that divine will can be the basis of morality. This was no small achievement and it arose from straightforward philosophical analysis.

[5] See especially Locke's *Essay*, Book II, Chapter XII. Locke stresses the active powers of the mind in forming complex ideas (simple ideas he takes to arrive passively): we have a faculty that enables us to *construct* complex concepts from simpler components. To suppose that all our ideas are simple would be to slight that constructive power. Analysis of ideas is thus insight into the active or synthesizing powers of the mind. Given that the mind has such creative powers, the existence of complex ideas susceptible of analysis is virtually guaranteed.

But it was not until the twentieth century that philosophers started to become more self-conscious about analysis as a method, and to develop specific conceptions of the aims and procedures of analysis.[6] In this they reverted to a previous, less self-conscious era, that of the empiricists and rationalists of the seventeenth and eighteenth centuries, and away from the anti-analytic temper of the time. I am thinking particularly of Russell and Moore and their early influences. They were in reaction against the neo-Hegelian idealism of Bradley and others, then the orthodox position at Cambridge and elsewhere, with its stringent monism, its doctrine of "internal relations," and its general hostility toward resolution into parts (the "organic whole," etc.). It seemed like liberation to Russell and Moore to be able to say that propositions might be analyzable into components and that the world might consist of separable things. They accordingly found inspiration in the conceptual atomism of the old empiricists and in Leibniz's logical metaphysics. Moore began to declare that philosophy is not about whether our commonsense propositions are true or justified, but about what they mean, about their correct analysis; and his celebrated denial that Good can be analyzed was part of this new analytic orientation (Good was the *exception* to general analyzability). Russell's newfound logicism, his universal symbolic language, his theory of descriptions, his atomistic empiricism—all led to a belief in analysis as the way forward. The philosophy of Logical Atomism was the natural outcome: analyzing the world into complex and simple facts that mirror structured propositions, with specific recommendations for rectifying misleading aspects of ordinary language, and a powerful new logical language to articulate the results. Wittgenstein's *Tractatus* embodies that same viewpoint in a particularly pure form: ordinary language and thought can be analyzed into underlying logical forms, with simples and complexes, modes of compounding, atomic propositions, logical particles, ultimate names. The search was on for "completely analyzed propositions." Frege had already analyzed sentences of arithmetic into logical language, devising a new symbolic notation for the purpose, and analyzed propositions ("thoughts") into the function-argument structure; quantification, in particular, provided an insightful analysis of ordinary statements involving generality. In this heady period, logical analysis promised to inaugurate great strides forward, and to provide continuity between traditional philosophy and the new methods. It offered rigor, clarity, and a sense of mission. It also offered a metaphilosophy. The purposes of analysis might be various, and the exact form of the analytic scaffolding might be in dispute, but the idea of a resolution into parts by supplying necessary and sufficient conditions was common ground. Maybe we need to correct the blemishes of ordinary language, maybe we need to revise our basic ontology; or alternatively, we should just seek to describe and record our ordinary thought and talk—in either case, we are in the business of supplying equivalents of our ordinary sentences that serve to articulate and clarify the import of those

---

[6] See Soames, *Philosophical Analysis in the Twentieth Century*, for a solid historical survey.

sentences. Whether revisionary or descriptive, analysis was the preferred method, and the form in which philosophical results were to be stated.[7]

Nor was this outlook confined to the English-speaking countries, with their characteristic historical concerns. Husserl's phenomenology is likewise conceived as the search for essences by means of "phenomenological intuition"—the attempt to discover the essential character of this or that act of consciousness. Husserl conducts his phenomenological inquiries from the armchair, seeking conceptual insight, dissecting and analyzing. He suspends "the naturalistic standpoint."[8] Even Sartre's existentialism can be aptly seen as an exercise in conceptual analysis: consciousness (the "for-itself") is to be defined as essentially Nothingness, while "things" (the "in-itself") is defined as Being. Sartre is giving us the essence of the twin poles of his ontology, and he does so by analyzing concepts—particularly, the concept of intentionality. Consciousness is to be analyzed by means of intentionality, and intentionality is to be analyzed as a relation between the nothingness of consciousness and the being of the world. (Empirical science plays no role here.)[9] Both Husserl and Sartre are, in effect, engaged upon a search for the a priori essence of things (probably Heidegger too, but I know less about his philosophy). You don't need to be an "analytic philosopher" in the narrow sense in order to be concerned with analysis and essence.

Logical positivism also was invested in analysis: there was Carnapian "explication," as well as the reductive analysis of Carnap's *Aufbau*; Ayer's phenomenalist translations of material object statements; behaviorist analyses of psychological concepts; operationalist analysis in physics; emotivist analysis in ethics; analysis of natural laws into statements of constant conjunction; and so on. Then too, we had so-called ordinary language analysis: Strawson's analysis of definite descriptions, as against Russell's analysis; Austin's analysis of speech acts into locutionary meaning, illocutionary force, and perlocutionary effect, as well as his correspondence analysis of truth; Ryle's analysis of mental talk into subjunctive conditionals and his analysis of subjunctives into "inference tickets"; and so on. In addition, we find the kind of analyses proposed by Grice: of perception, of meaning, of different types of "implication." Grice's method was precisely to propose necessary and sufficient conditions guided by intuitions about possible cases, showing great ingenuity in the production of counterexamples, and in the

[7] See Urmson, *Philosophical Analysis: Its Development Between the Two World Wars*, for a detailed and enlightening account of the history of analysis in the early twentieth century. Urmson sees debates about the nature of analysis to be the prime shapers of the course of analytical philosophy.

[8] Here I may be forgiven for citing (for the first time) my first published article, "Mach and Husserl," which tries to find a *rapprochment* between positivism and phenomenology. (The article was written when I was twenty-two and is based on an undergraduate dissertation that I wrote as a psychology student at Manchester University in the late 1960s and early 1970s.)

[9] Let me also cite my article on Sartre for the *Oxford Companion to the Mind*, edited by Richard Gregory. So I am not favoring one style of philosophy over others—Anglo-American over Continental. I see clear links between Sartre's work and that of more "orthodox" philosophers of mind, especially with regard to "externalism" and "direct reference."

resulting amendments.[10] Knowledge had already been defined as "true justified belief" using the same basic method. Analysis seemed to be thriving. The procedure initiated by Plato and Aristotle, with reinforcements from Euclid and the pre-Socratics, followed by the Schoolmen, reinvigorated by the moderns, given a solid logical foundation by the early "analytic philosophers," refined by the later "ordinary language" school, had been followed throughout the history of the subject and had achieved notable successes—why should it be questioned? As philosophers refined their analytic techniques and perfected their skills, they should be able to achieve their central goal—to discover and formulate a complete analysis of reality, as reality is reflected in our conceptual scheme. This would supply us with a definitive metaphysics, to be adjoined to the empirical results of the natural sciences. Philosophy gives the general picture of reality, and then the sciences fill in the detail. So it was commonly assumed.

But this optimistic picture began to be threatened by a number of developments in twentieth-century philosophy, coming from different directions. By the century's end, it is fair to record, the consensus seemed to be that analysis was bankrupt, misguided, impossible, confused, disreputable—not something a self-respecting person should be caught doing. The causes here are many, and often unrelated—but they seemed to point in only one direction: analysis is dead, finished. Let me rapidly list the familiar deathblows that were held to bring about the demise of analysis. Logical atomism ran into difficulties about the alleged isomorphism between propositions and facts, with general facts and negative facts provoking disquiet in the ranks; nor was it made clear what the simples might be, or whether facts were really separate from (true) propositions. Positivism ran into the ground from its own overreaching, its lack of a convincing account of what an analysis might be (consistent with its own outlook), and its empiricist reductionism. Phenomenalism and behaviorism, as reductive analyses, soon showed glaring defects. Wittgenstein dropped the thoroughgoing logical analysis of the *Tractatus*. Frege's logicism led to paradox and needed shoring up in other ways as well. Russell's empiricism led him in the direction of implausible analyses of statements about the external world. The later Wittgenstein, generally anti-analytic, introduced the idea of the family resemblance concept, in which not even necessary conditions could be devised. Quine launched his attack on meaning, synonymy, and the entire analytic-synthetic distinction—with analysis apparently resting on shaky foundations. Gettier shocked the world by showing that the prized example of the analysis of knowledge as true justified belief didn't work after all. This was soon followed by counterexamples to Gricean analyses of perception and meaning ("deviant causal chains," problems of sufficiency). Davidson showed that intentional action could not be analyzed as the causation of action by intention. He also argued that a proper theory of meaning should specify logical forms for sentences but not analyze

---

[10] A classic example is Grice's 1957 paper "Meaning," which well illustrates the power of analysis to produce surprising and substantive results, mainly by producing counterexamples to sufficiency and then working to fix the analysis. Anyone who cannot appreciate such work does not, in my view, deserve to be a philosopher; he or she belongs in another field.

the semantic primitives. Kripke, Putnam, Donnellan, Kaplan, and others questioned the description analysis of names and natural kind terms, suggesting that such terms have no analysis, being merely primitive labels. Ordinary language analysis by means of "what we would say" was shown to be methodologically flawed, because what we say is no sure guide to what is true (here Grice's work on conversational implicature played a major role). Latterly, cognitive science has seemed to many people to undermine conceptual analysis as traditionally conceived: there is no room for an armchair investigation of our concepts—the proper procedure is an empirical investigation of concepts. Thus we have the recent enthusiasm in some quarters for "experimental philosophy"—doing philosophy by means of empirical psychology, eschewing any a priori methods. A priori investigations are deemed irrelevant at best and pernicious at worst, in the project of understanding our concepts. Nowadays a series of pointed (not to say jabbing) questions will be put to the would-be conceptual analyst: Isn't that just old-fashioned logical atomism? Didn't Wittgenstein refute analysis in the *Investigations*? What about Gettier cases? Can you name one successful analysis of a concept? How could analysis of a psychological thing (a concept) ever yield knowledge of a non-psychological thing (an entity in the world)? Aren't all putative analyses circular in the end? What about the paradox of analysis? You don't still believe in ordinary language philosophy, do you? Don't you think the best way to study concepts is to look at the science of concepts? Isn't conceptual analysis inevitably trivial? Isn't it a category mistake to think that concepts have parts? What *is* a concept anyway? Didn't Quine prove that the analytic-synthetic distinction is a dogma of empiricism? Apart from all that, isn't conceptual analysis just plain boring? What is the *point* of it?

And so it has come to pass that a once fresh and vigorous method of doing philosophy has fallen drastically out of favor, done in by a succession of problems, large and small. Philosophy must then struggle to redefine itself, to gain a new self-conception—and what will that be? No consensus has emerged, and the discipline seems to have reached a rocky point in its long history. What *are* we up to? What kind of job does a professional philosopher have? Scientism offers itself as a model, but that seems to leave a lot of traditional philosophy high and dry.[11] There are sporadic attempts to defend conceptual analysis, at least as one type of philosophical endeavor, among contemporary analytical philosophers, such as Frank Jackson in his *From Metaphysics to Ethics: A Defense of Conceptual Analysis*;[12] but they lack the

[11] Quine happily endorsed that result in his influential paper "Epistemology Naturalized," consigning traditional epistemology to the flames (or appearing to). Since then, many authors have campaigned on the same platform: I might mention the work of Paul and Patricia Churchland, Stephen Stich, Jerry Fodor in some of his moods, and recently Penelope Maddy and Don Ross and James Ladyman. Needless to say, I am deeply opposed to this viewpoint (that is putting it mildly).

[12] I read Jackson's book with high expectations, given its affinity with my own position, but I find it far too concessive to the prevailing "naturalistic" mood in philosophy. I would like to have seen something more forthright and uncompromising. Still, his heart is definitely in the right place, and there is a good deal of careful analysis there. Other than that, I can't think of another contemporary defense of conceptual analysis as a philosophical method—hence the book before you.

unabashed self-confidence and scope to put conceptual analysis back at the center of philosophy again. Jackson's book defends analysis only as an adjunct to what he calls "serious metaphysics," in his case the defense of physicalism; there is no defense of the traditional ambitions of conceptual analysis, or of types of analysis not connected to "serious metaphysics" (I myself think that analysis *is* serious metaphysics). There is no attempt to defend a division of concepts into the complex and the simple, with a mereological conception of complexity. In fact, Jackson considers only a very narrow range of concepts in his book—chiefly, natural kind concepts (as well as color and ethical concepts, which he treats according to the natural kinds model). Nor, I think, is he really considering conceptual analysis in the classic sense; instead, he focuses on the "folk theory" we hold of various things, consisting of various "platitudes" concerning those things. But among these platitudes, some may hold analytically and some may hold synthetically: it may be a folk platitude that bachelors often resent their status, but it is not analytic that they do. So a robust distinction between what belongs to a concept and what is extrinsic to that concept has no role to play in Jackson's official story. In any case, Jackson does not attempt the kind of systematic overall defense of conceptual analysis that I aim to provide in this book, and I doubt that he would agree with much of it, because it is so uncompromising and lacking in concession to recent trends. This is not to say that no one is doing conceptual analysis any more; in fact, it is regularly practiced under the table by other names (Quine himself indulges in quite a bit of it, in my view: see Chapter 6). Since philosophy, correctly conceived, simply *is* conceptual analysis, it is highly likely that philosophers will be found engaging in it, even if it is against their principles and official meta-philosophy. My aim is to release them from the closet, loosen their inhibitions, and improve their self-esteem. Being a conceptual analyst, I contend, is a perfectly good and worthy thing to be. It is a serious occupation for a grown woman.[13]

It will be helpful if I make two anticipatory points at this stage. The first is that analysis, as I understand it, is not confined to predicate expressions. I include expressions of all logical and grammatical categories: proper names and definite descriptions, quantifier words both standard and nonstandard, sentence operators extensional and intensional, adverbs and prepositions, indexical words and demonstratives. Thus Russell's theory of "the" counts as conceptual analysis for me, as does Frege's construal of "something" and "everything," as does Davidson's theory of adverbial modification, or quantificational treatments of modal expressions. I am including translations into logical form under the heading of conceptual analysis—that is, propositional analysis generally. The form of an analysis is not

---

[13] There are market analysts, psychoanalysts, chemical analysts, literary analysts—and conceptual analysts. Analyzing things is a well-established intellectual practice. Concepts should not be regarded as an exception (I discuss this further in Chapter 6). Note that my policy in the matter of pronoun gender decisions is to reserve the more prestigious occupations for the female gender; otherwise, I just try to keep a balance between male and female, without spoiling the grammar.

then invariably: x is F iff x is G & x is H & .... The analysis might be "contextual," as with Russell's theory: what matters is giving necessary and sufficient conditions for the truth of a proposition in non-circular terms. I thus do not *oppose* conceptual analysis to the specification of logical form: the latter is a special case of the former. In fact, the whole distinction rests upon the idea that we have a good criterion for being a logical constant, which I think we do not.[14] In any case, saying what "the" means is the same kind of thing as saying what "know" means—spelling out the content in non-circular terms.

The second point is that I am not supposing that *every* predicate has non-trivial necessary and sufficient conditions. There are three exceptions to such a claim. First, and most obviously, some predicate meanings are likely to be primitive or simple, that is, not made up of other predicate meanings; for these, the analysis just consists of repeating the predicate ("red" might be an example). Second, some predicates are ambiguous, such as "bank" or "table": here we do not expect to find univocal analysis. We will need to disambiguate the predicate before analysis can be performed on it. Third, there may well exist nonsense predicates that have no meaningful analysis—such as "slithy" and "tove"—and there may be interesting cases in which the nonsense lies hidden—in which the predicate expresses a pseudo-concept of some sort (I explore this most fully in Chapter 11). It is only complex concepts expressed by unambiguous, meaningful predicates that have interesting analyses. And it can be a substantive question whether a given predicate falls into one or other of these categories—a question to be answered by trying to give an analysis of the (putative) concept.

The consequences of the viability of conceptual analysis for philosophy at large are considerable. First and foremost for metaphysics: if concepts have analyses, and we can produce them, then we can provide informative accounts of the nature of various kinds of being—of objects, causality, selves, laws, events, necessity, and so on. Not that all such general concepts will necessarily have a decompositional analysis—some will no doubt be primitive (then their analysis will simply be themselves functioning as necessary and sufficient conditions: I discuss one such in Chapter 12). But some concepts will surely be complex, and so we will be able to reveal their constituent concepts. We will be able, that is, to disclose the "essence of things": the what-it-is-to-be of things. Second, episte-mology: if a concept C has an analysis A, then in knowing that C is instantiated we know that A is instantiated—what it is for attributions of C to be known is what it is for attributions of A to be known, for propositions involving C neces-sarily involve A. Third, philosophy of mind: to possess a concept will be to know

---

[14] This is why there is now a proliferation of logical systems going beyond dear old classic predicate calculus: modal, deontic, epistemic, free, vague, etc. There is a logical system to be con-structed wherever there are systematic patterns of inference—we need not restrict ourselves to the classic logical constants. Basically, there is logic wherever there is entailment, in my view. Accordingly, the notion of logical form has many varieties.

(in some sense to be explained: see Chapter 4) its analysis—so thoughts involving *C* will incorporate *A*. Fourth, theory of meaning: for a word *W* to express *C* will be for *W* to express *A*—so a specification of the meaning of *W* will involve citing *A*. Fifth, meta-philosophy: the proper method of philosophy (the sole method, as I argue in Chapter 7) is conceptual analysis, neither more nor less. Thus, quite a bit hangs on whether the credentials of conceptual analysis can be made good. I must now proceed with that task.

2 Definition and Family Resemblance

To define a concept—to provide an analysis—is to specify a set of conditions that are individually necessary and jointly sufficient for the concept to apply. For instance, we can define a husband as someone who is both married and a man: both conditions are necessary, but neither alone is sufficient, for the concept to apply—as can be seen from the definition of a wife as someone both married and a woman. In a way, necessary conditions are more basic than sufficient conditions, because it is the conjunction of them that gives a sufficient condition; the sufficient condition is not a *new* condition, added to the necessary conditions, but simply the necessary conditions taken together. If a concept has no (non-trivial) necessary conditions, then it has no analysis: it is indefinable in the present sense, that is, not resolvable into parts. Necessary conditions are the building blocks of analysis; without them no analysis is possible. The analyst knows that such unanalyzable concepts must exist, because some concepts must be primitive—but primitiveness is the *only* way that analysis may be thwarted. If it could be shown that some concepts are both non-primitive and yet lacking in necessary conditions, then analysis would not apply to such concepts—and the whole project would be brought into doubt.

Wittgenstein famously claimed that just such concepts exist. In *The Blue and Brown Books*, speaking of the philosopher's "craving for generality," he writes:

This craving for generality is the resultant of a number of tendencies connected with particular philosophical confusions. There is—(a) The tendency to look for something in common to all the entities that we commonly subsume under a general term.—We are inclined to think that there must be something in common to all games, say, and that this common property is the justification for applying the term "game" to the various games; whereas games form a *family* the members of which have family likenesses. Some of them have the same nose, others the same eyebrows and others again the same way of walking; and these likenesses overlap. The idea of a general concept being a common property of its particular instances connects up with other primitive, too simple, ideas of the structure of language.[1]

In *Philosophical Investigations*, Wittgenstein imagines his interlocutor objecting that he has "nowhere said what the essence of a language-game, and hence language, is: what is common to all these activities, and what makes them into language or parts of language." He replies:

And this is true.—Instead of producing something common to all that we call language, I am saying that these phenomena have no one thing in common which makes us use the same word for all,—but that they are *related* to one another in many different ways. And it is because of this relationship, or these relationships, that we call them all "language." I will try to explain this. (65)[2]

Wittgenstein thus denies that the concept *language* has necessary conditions that jointly determine its extension—there is nothing "common" to all instances of language. There then follows the famous section about games and family resemblance, which it is necessary to quote in full:

Consider for example the proceedings that we call "games." I mean board-games, card-games, ball-games, Olympic games, and so on. What is common to them all?— Don't say: "There *must* be something in common, or they would not be called 'games'"— but *look and see* whether there is anything in common to all.—For if you look at them you will not see something that is common to *all*, but similarities, relationships, and a whole series of them at that. To repeat: don't think, but look!—Look for example at board-games, with their multifarious relationships. Now pass to card-games; here you find many correspondences with the first group, but many common features drop out, and others appear. When we pass next to ball-games, much that is common is retained, but much is lost.—Are they all "amusing"? Compare chess with noughts and crosses. Or is there always winning and losing, or competition between players? Think of patience. In ball games there is winning and losing; but when a child throws his ball at the wall and catches it again, this feature has disappeared. Look at the parts played by skill and luck; and at the difference between skill in chess and skill in tennis. Think now of games like ring-a-ring-a-roses; here is the element of amusement, but how

---

[1] *Blue Book*, p. 17
[2] I will cite section references to *Philosophical Investigations* in the text.

many other characteristic features have disappeared! And we can go through the many, many other groups of games in the same way; can see how similarities crop up and disappear. And the result of this examination is: we see a complicated network of similarities overlapping and criss-crossing: sometimes overall similarities, sometimes similarities of detail. (66)

Having satisfied himself that games are not united by any common feature or features, Wittgenstein goes on to characterize the conception of concepts suggested by his case-study: "I can think of no better expression to characterize these similarities than 'family resemblance'; for the various resemblances between members of a family: build, features, colour of eyes, gait, temperament, etc. etc. overlap and criss-cross in the same way.—And I shall say: 'games' form a family" (67). The section then proceeds to assert that numbers form a family in the same way—with nothing in common to all numbers.

These passages have struck readers as powerful and cogent: games, language-games, and numbers are very various, with important differences between the sub-groups; and we do seem prone to overlook the differences that exist in our "craving for generality." Certainly, in the case of games, it is not at all clear what the necessary and sufficient conditions for being a game would look like—no analysis springs immediately to mind. Observation of games fails to disclose any feature that might serve to define all games, though individual games seem to have defining perceptible features—such as a ball, racquets, and a net in tennis.[3] If Wittgenstein is right, then, meanings and concepts don't necessarily work by decomposing into parts that give necessary and sufficient conditions, but by a much looser kind of structure—family resemblance. The question becomes: How far does this idea of family resemblance extend—to how many concepts does it apply? Wittgenstein does not say, confining himself in these passages to three examples, but other philosophers have conjectured that his picture might apply very generally. For his fundamental observation—the great heterogeneity in the class of things falling under a given concept—seems to apply to many cases, such as: *work, art, science, name, predicate, sentence, funny, reason, life, truth, psychological, physical, necessary, law, furniture, clothes, particle, plant.* That is, all these concepts are such that their extensions come in an enormous variety, with nothing perceptibly in common between them. And if Wittgenstein's family resemblance model works for *game, language,* and *number,* then it should work for many other concepts, too—those that are similar to these three examples. In all these cases,

---

[3] It is worth noting that Wittgenstein does not claim that concepts for specific games are family resemblance concepts, e.g., the concept *tennis.* These might well have necessary and sufficient conditions, so far as his point about games in general is concerned; and that seems plausible, given that games are defined according to their constitutive rules. Activities don't count as tennis by dint of family resemblance, but tennis counts as a game by family resemblance. There is no contradiction here, but it does raise the awkward question of why "game of tennis" is not a family resemblance term but "game" is.

the project of conceptual analysis will be undermined: concepts just don't work in the way that project assumes. Concepts are more fluid, looser, more open-ended than the analytical model assumes, with its precise boundaries, clear-cut definitions, and conceptual mereology. Concepts have unity, to be sure, but it is built around a different kind of principle—the overlapping of threads, not the overarching steel girder. The *use* determines the unity, not the internal architecture of the concept. The analytical conception forces a logical model onto concepts that they simply do not possess—the model of the definitive essence. Maybe geometrical concepts have precise definitions, but they are a special case; our ordinary concepts have no such desiccated structure, but are living things woven into our various "forms of life." So, at least, many post-Wittgensteinian philosophers have been quick to infer: the early analysts were fixated on logic and mathematics, failing to appreciate the actual workings of our ordinary concepts, with their vagueness and flexibility. If we just reflect for a moment on the humdrum word "game"—hardly the rigorous analytical philosopher's favorite word—we will see that the whole idea (and ideal) of conceptual analysis is (in Wittgenstein's phrase) "a house of cards" (118).[4]

But is that the right conclusion to draw? And does Wittgenstein really demonstrate that there are family resemblance concepts in his sense? Is it true that there is nothing in common to all games? Let us begin by distinguishing the concept *family* from the concept *family resemblance*—that is, being a member of a particular family and resembling those who are members of that family. Wittgenstein himself slides between these two concepts: he begins by introducing the notion of "family resemblance" and then quickly moves to announcing that games form a "family" (he says the same of numbers). But the concepts are quite distinct, despite an orthographic similarity (ironic, this, in view of his general account of philosophical error): it is neither necessary nor sufficient to be a member of a particular family that an individual bears a family resemblance to members of that family. It is possible for someone to be born into a family and not superficially resemble members of that family—to "look nothing like" his brothers and sisters, say. And it is also possible for someone not to be a member of a family and yet to resemble members of that family in various ways—people often have "look-alikes" not related to them. The reason for this lack of entailment either way is well-known: genetic heritage is not necessarily correlated with physical appearance. You can get your genes from your mother and father and yet the vagaries of development result in a lack of physical similarity; and someone else might superficially resemble you and yet not share your specific genetic

---

[4] See Griffin, "Wittgenstein, Universals and Family Resemblances" for a useful general discussion. His footnote 3 contains the surprising information that the notion was not original to Wittgenstein but was anticipated by the Scholastics, William James, J. S. Mill, and J. F. Moulton (who coined the term "family likeness"). It is quite clear to me that Wittgenstein did not intend to claim that *all* concepts are family resemblance concepts (as Renford Bambrough went on to do); indeed, his point is to draw a *contrast* between certain terms, notably "language," and other terms that do have precise definitions, as perhaps "equation" or "circle." Still, he is far less clear about this than one might wish.

inheritance. The concept of a family relates to genetic derivation and/or actual generation (who you were actually born to), but the concept of family resemblance relates to observable physical traits—and these are not overlapping facts. It is much the same with other concepts: the concept *gold* is not the same as the concept *resembles gold,* and the concept *husband* is not the same as the concept *resembles husbands.* In both cases, the latter concept is neither necessary nor sufficient for the former: some gold doesn't look like gold and some things that look like gold aren't gold, and some husbands don't look like (typical) husbands and not all people who look like husbands are husbands. Nor am I being unfairly pedantic in chiding Wittgenstein for conflating the two concepts: for the concept of a family clearly possesses a much greater natural unity than the concept of a family resemblance, which can hold between things quite disparate in nature (see below for why this matters). It is a very different thing for different games to form a "family" than for them to fall into a class of things that have "family resemblance": the former corresponds to a natural classification, but the latter stitches together (to follow Wittgenstein's metaphor) fabrics of many kinds. And it is a real question, as we shall see, whether mere family resemblance can suffice to determine *any* workable concept.

The heart of Wittgenstein's case against the analysis of "game" is the contention that games have nothing in common. Is that true? Is it even true by Wittgenstein's own lights? I think not. In the first place, surely this is a necessary condition for being a game: *having a family resemblance to things called "games."* According to Wittgenstein, nothing can count as a game unless it has such a resemblance to activities already classified as games (presumably to certain paradigms): this is a nonnegotiable necessary condition for being a game. He also takes this to be a sufficient condition—so there *is* something common to everything we call a game that justifies us in describing those things as games, namely, family-resembling (paradigm) games. Moreover, this analysis in terms of necessary and sufficient conditions is not viciously circular, since it explains "game" by way of the different batch of words "family resembles games"—and we could even eliminate the word "game" from the *definiens* by listing a few paradigm games. *Every* game has *this* property, according to Wittgenstein. Compare the concept *look-alike*: everything that falls under this concept resembles another thing, so that it is a necessary (and sufficient) condition for being a look-alike that an object looks like some other object. Wittgenstein's position on games is the exact analogue: to be a game is to resemble other games along some dimension or other—this is a necessary (and sufficient) condition for being a game.[5] He is not rejecting classical analysis, then, but simply favoring a particular

---

[5] This would appear to have the consequence that there could not have been just one game, because that would imply the existence of a game that had no family resemblance to *other* games. That seems plainly false: What about the existence of the *first* game? This point by itself strikes me as a definitive refutation of Wittgenstein's position, though I pursue different lines of objection in the text. In fact, it is hard to see how his position is consistent with the existence of just two or three games, since that is scarcely enough to ground a notion of family resemblance: the family needs to be bigger than that.

form of it—one in which the analysis takes the form "family-resembles paradigm games (such as chess, tennis, etc.)."

If this point is thought to be a cheat, perhaps on the ground that family resemblance is not a genuine property (but why not?), or to be merely *ad hominem*, then consider the following: Isn't it true that every game is *played* (or at least is *playable*)? Can't we analyze *game* by *play activity*? Wittgenstein never considers this kind of natural response to his thesis—why not? He might reply that *play* is itself a family resemblance concept, so that we have not made good the ideal of classical analysis. But, even if that were true, how does it show that *game* has no noncircular necessary conditions? We have explained a concept for certain entities (games) by means of a concept that relates to human action and intention (play), and that explanation makes conceptual progress. We might even add that a game is a *rule-governed* play activity, on the assumption that all games involve rules (and it is notable that Wittgenstein never denies that all games involve rules—though not necessarily rules that define winning and losing). This is now beginning to look like a straightforward conceptual analysis, though not a particularly profound one. And is the concept of play itself a family resemblance concept? That seems far from clear, and certainly not argued for by Wittgenstein: play seems to require a certain kind of attitude or intention that contrasts with the attitudes and intentions characteristic of *work* or *labor* (see Chapter 10). The idea of *leisure* seems built into it—of pastimes, hobbies, and fun. (Of course, there are professional players of games: but that doesn't show that games are not in their nature leisure activities—it is perfectly possible for a leisure activity to be performed for money, say.) At any rate, it would need to be shown that *play* is a family resemblance concept, and that has not been shown. Wittgenstein has simply been looking in the wrong place for what is common to all games—at particular features of specific classes of games, not at the general concept.[6]

It should be noted that we do not strictly need to provide a full analysis of *game* in order to refute Wittgenstein; we need merely to specify some necessary conditions that all games satisfy. That does not seem hard: all games are surely activities (not substances), and presumably they are all intentional activities, and as such goal-directed (even if the goal is just to have some fun). If so, all games involve intention and will, which themselves involve belief and desire, which involve the idea of a rational agent: these are all necessary conditions of playing a game. Merely inanimate objects cannot play games, or plants, or bacteria. I just observed, also, that games are essentially leisure activities, in contrast to work activities. This concept

---

[6] Compare examining all the different kinds of eyes there are in organisms of different species, finding tremendous anatomical variation, and concluding that *eye* is a family resemblance concept. That would be to ignore the identical *function* that every eye has, despite its anatomical individuality, namely to enable the organism to *see* ("the eye is the organ of vision"). Wittgenstein focuses on the "anatomy" of particular games and ignores their generally rule-governed intentional character and their common playfulness. In fact, the whole idea of trying to discover definitions by "looking and seeing" is misguided, if taken literally, since not everything about games (and other things) is revealed to the senses: what is in common may not be something you can *see*.

itself requires work to unpack its content, but it is plausibly a necessary condition for being a game—a game is characteristically something engaged in for the purposes of leisure (perhaps enjoyment will come into the analysis of that concept). It might be objected here that these necessary conditions are far from sufficient: many goal-directed intentional activities, even those undertaken for leisure, are not cases of playing a game—for example, bird watching or sightseeing or listening to music. Wittgenstein was claiming, it may be said, that no such necessary condition is also a sufficient condition (hence his talk of "one thing in common that makes us use the same word for all" (65). But two points need to be made as against this. First, his official doctrine is that there is nothing in common between all games, that is, there are no necessary conditions—not that there are no necessary *and* sufficient conditions. But, second, if we insist that any necessary condition must also be a sufficient condition, we issue a preposterously strong demand on the conceptual analyst, namely that the analysis must contain only a *single* necessary condition—since that condition must also be sufficient. Typically, however, the analyst provides a plurality of necessary conditions that together are sufficient. There is nothing wrong with saying that all games are necessarily rule-governed intentional activities without thereby claiming that this condition is *sufficient* for being a game. And clearly the entire spirit of the relevant sections from Wittgenstein is to contest the belief that all concepts have necessary conditions (whether or not they have nontrivial sufficient conditions). So the counterexamples I have cited are genuine counterexamples to his position, and curiously are not considered by him.[7]

Nor is that the end of Wittgenstein's troubles. For it is not difficult to convert Wittgenstein's own account of the concept *game* into a classical analysis by using the concept of probability. His position is that certain features—such as winning and losing or amusement or competition or the mixed role of skill and luck—are *characteristic* of games without being necessarily found in all games. That is, these features are typical of games while *not* being typical of non-games (such as writing a book, or digging a ditch, or adding up some numbers while doing one's taxes). In other words, it is more *likely* that you will find such features manifest in games than in non-games. And Wittgenstein had better be saying something like that, or else he will have no account of the content of "game" at all—nothing that distinguishes games from non-games. But now we can build this concept of probability directly into the account of what makes something a game: *x* is a game iff *x* is more likely to have such features as competition, amusement, and winning and losing, than other types of human activity. If we come across a new activity and wonder whether it is a game, we will not be able to say that it *must* possess one of a number of characteristic features; but we will be able to say that it is more *likely* to possess such a feature if it

---

[7] One cannot help thinking that Wittgenstein did not even *try* very hard to find necessary conditions for *game*, because he was convinced in advance that there were none—thus the paucity of candidates he considers. Was he simply not aware of the kinds of common properties I have cited? That seems hard to believe. The passage starts to feel like a clever sleight of hand.

is a game than if it is not. This notion of probability will merely give expression to the accepted point that the features in question are found more frequently in the class of games than in other classes—since they are "characteristic" of games. Statistically, a game is more likely to involve winning and losing than, say, performing physical labor in the line of manual work—so it is a necessary condition for being a game that this statistical fact holds. If we don't allow for such statistical facts, then we will have *nothing* to say about what a game is—if we follow Wittgenstein's general line. The case is rather like the concept of a *high-risk driver*: such a driver need not necessarily be involved in a crash, but he must be more likely to do so than a low-risk driver. Similarly, being a game need not entail winning and losing, but being classified as a game must raise the probability that an activity involves winning and losing. The connection is looser than entailment, but it exists anyway (even according to Wittgenstein), so it can be readily converted into a *probabilistic* necessary condition (which is also sufficient). It is harder to avoid necessary conditions than Wittgenstein appears to recognize.[8]

It may be felt that Wittgenstein must have been onto something in the passages cited, because it is very hard to produce an analysis of "game": the *essence* of being a game does not stand forth to the serious conceptual analyst, even if some (rather mundane) necessary conditions can be identified. What is the *nature* of games? What is to *be* a game? If the analyst has no reply, then he or she is simply declaring an article of faith—that there must *be* an analysis, even if hitherto undiscovered. This is a very reasonable protest, and it must be answered. Fortunately, we have at hand the very analysis being demanded: the analysis worked out by Bernard Suits in his brilliant (and neglected) small masterpiece *The Grasshopper: Games, Life and Utopia*.[9] In this remarkable book, Suits gives noncircular necessary and sufficient conditions for being a game, patiently defends the analysis against a variety of putative counterexamples, and draws the necessary methodological lessons. We cannot do better here than to follow his example. Since Suits's work is not generally known

---

[8] And it is harder to avoid than the vast majority of his readers have recognized (I include my earlier benighted self). The sections on family resemblance seem easy to accept at first glance, a clear island in a somewhat murky surrounding sea—the one area in which Wittgenstein was quite clearly correct! I myself have repeatedly and uncritically invoked the notion of family resemblance in my earlier writings, evidently seduced by Wittgenstein's presentation. I now wonder why I was so ready to accept his position: Was it my suspicion of my own "craving for generality," or the cunning way the notion is introduced, or the widespread uncritical acceptance of the idea? I am now somewhat shocked and chastened by my own earlier credulity.

[9] The book was first published by Toronto University Press in 1977 in an exceptionally fine edition, with beautiful illustrations by Frank Newfeld (I now proudly own a first edition); the later paperback by Broadview lacks the aesthetic quality of the original and does not include Newfeld's illustrations. This is a pity. When I first read the book I was strongly resistant to its main thesis—that the concept of a game could be defined—having been long persuaded of Wittgenstein's position. It wasn't until a third reading of it that I was finally brought to abandon my earlier opinion, with much self-recrimination at my earlier obtuseness and conformity (that was the worst). Since that time I have become a keen Suits proselytizer. (Page references to the book appear in the text.)

nor its importance appreciated (except by a growing minority), I shall take some time to lay out his analysis, but I cannot claim to provide an adequate substitute for the original text, with its patience, subtlety, and ingenuity; I urge the reader to study the book for himself or herself. In the Preface to *The Grasshopper,* Suits writes as follows:

The orientation of the book is philosophical in one traditional sense of that word. It is the attempt to discover and formulate a definition, and to follow the implications of that discovery even when they lead in surprising, and sometimes disconcerting, directions. I am aware, of course, of the fairly widespread disenchantment with the search for definitions that currently prevails in the philosophical community [he is writing *circa* 1976], and indeed in the intellectual community generally. And Wittgenstein, one of the most forceful spokesmen (and certainly the most exotic) for the anti-definitional attitude, is famous for having singled out the attempt to define games as illustrating par excellence the futility of attempting to define anything whatever. "'Don't say,' Wittgenstein admonishes us, 'there must be something common or they would not be called 'games'—but *look and see* whether there is anything common to all." This is unexceptionable advice. Unfortunately, Wittgenstein himself did not follow it. He looked, to be sure, but because he had decided beforehand that games are indefinable, his look was fleeting, and he saw very little. So I invite the reader to join me in a longer and more penetrating look at games, and to defer judgment as to whether all games have something in common pending completion of such an inspection. (21)

Three main points emerge from this measured passage: that definitions may be hard to discover and lead us in surprising directions; that there is a general distrust of the enterprise of definitional analysis; and that the nature of philosophy turns on the question of whether illuminating definition is attainable. It is therefore no small matter to be able to deliver an adequate analysis of the concept of a game—which is precisely what Suits succeeds so impressively in doing. I shall now summarize his contribution.

He begins by suggesting that the concept of a game might best be understood by contrast with the concept of work, its natural antithesis. Work is a "technical activity," in which "an agent seeks to employ the most efficient available means for achieving the desired goal" (37). If our goal in working is to bring about a given state of affairs, such as the construction of a road or writing an article, we will naturally choose the most efficient way available to us to achieve that goal—the best equipment, the most economic sequence of actions, the quickest route. The point is to achieve the final goal and the means are just that—necessary steps to achieving it. This is why we constantly strive to invent better ways to get work done—so that we can get more done in less time and with less effort. If playing a game contrasts with working, then, we might expect that it is *not* a matter of selecting the most efficient means to achieve a specific goal. Playing games is goal-directed activity, and means are employed, but we do not seek to maximize efficiency in bringing about those goals—that is the hypothesis to be considered. For instance, the goal in a foot race is to reach the finish line, but the runners do not maximize efficiency by cutting across the infield so that they can breast the tape with as little effort as possible—they take the long route. That is the rule of the game. In the same way, the goal of a golfer is to place small balls in widely dispersed holes. What is the most efficient way to achieve this end? Presumably it is to travel to each hole and drop the ball in by hand. This is what you would do if you had been assigned the *job* of putting the balls in the holes: you would get it done efficiently, so that you can move on to other tasks. But a golf player does no such thing: he adopts an extremely *in*efficient way to get ball to hole—he positions himself hundreds of yards away from the hole and endeavors to get the ball into the hole by striking it with an elongated club. This is a *very* difficult way to get a ball into a hole. But the golfer is not *working* to fill holes with balls, as a gardener might work to distribute seeds into holes; he is *playing a game*—and this consists precisely in intentionally choosing inefficient means of achieving goals. In fact, the rules of the game *proscribe* the use of maximally efficient means—that is called *cheating*. The rules tell the players that they must employ only methods and tactics that limit the means at their disposal.

It is, however, quite true that the runner and the golfer use the most efficient means *within* the rules of the game: the runner doesn't run backward or on her knees, and the golfer doesn't shut his eyes or lie on the ground. He or she is trying to *win*, after all, as the rules describe winning, and there is no cheating in trying to do this as efficiently as possible within the rules—pumping the legs, hitting the ball hard. So we need to distinguish two goals that the player has in such cases, which Suits calls the "prelusory goal" and the "lusory goal." The prelusory goal is to achieve a state of affairs that can obtain independently of the rules of a game, such as breasting a tape or putting a ball in a hole. The lusory goal is to bring about a state of affairs in which the game is won (or completed) only if the rules of the game are obeyed: getting to the tape first while running around the track, not elbowing one's competitors, and so on; and putting the balls in the holes only by use of a club, from a prescribed distance, without ever handling the ball. In football (soccer) this duality of goals is particularly conspicuous and the restriction of means apparent: the prelusory goal is to get the ball in the net, and the lusory goal is to do so according to rules that proscribe the use of the hands, or cudgeling the opponent, or the employment of a cannon. Clearly, football drastically curtails the employment of efficient means, simply by ruling out use of the hands: it is far harder to propel a ball into a net with the feet or head alone. But that is the nature of the game—what *makes* it a game. Propelling balls into nets, as a technical activity, would simply be accomplished by whatever means was judged most effective—such as throwing. Suits sums up these reflections in a preliminary definition of "game": "We may therefore say that games require obedience to rules which limit the permissible means to a sought end, and where such rules are obeyed just so that such activity can occur" (47).

That last clause is important, because it is possible to engage in an activity in which one intentionally chooses inefficient means for reasons quite other than playing a game—for prudential or moral reasons. For example, in driving to a particular destination I don't just take the shortest route, which might involve going the wrong way down a one-way street or hopping the meridian. I obey the rules of the road and these prohibit taking the shortest route in many cases. Am I then playing a driving game as opposed to engaging in a technical activity? I *might* play a driving game, say by deciding to use only the right-most lane or varying my speed every ten seconds or taking a left turn whenever the road has a name beginning with "p"—but in the normal case I am not playing such a game. Why not? Because my reason for obeying the rules of the road is not to engage in an activity I value for its own sake—driving legally—but rather to avoid being arrested or causing an accident or perhaps because I respect the law in all its forms.[10] But when I play tennis, say, I obey the rules *because I want to be playing tennis*, and obeying the rules of tennis is the only way to do that; I don't do it to avoid being arrested, and so on. Indeed, I strive to achieve the prelusory goals of tennis precisely in order to achieve the lusory goal of tennis, namely, winning by the rules. So we need to add the provision that the player accepts the rules *so that* he or she can be playing the game, and not for some extraneous reason, such as morality or prudence. Suits describes this provision as the necessity for the player to have a "lusory attitude" toward the rules. With these concepts and considerations in place, Suits now offers his official definition of a game:

To play a game is to attempt to achieve a specific state of affairs [prelusory goal], using only means permitted by rules [lusory means], where the rules prohibit use of more efficient in favor of less efficient means [constitutive rules], and where the rules are accepted just because they make possible such activity [lusory attitude]. I also offer the following simpler and, so to speak, more portable version of the above: playing a game is the voluntary attempt to overcome unnecessary obstacles. (54–55; square brackets his)

Having proposed his definition, Suits now spends the ensuing chapters responding to potential counterexamples. I shall briefly summarize the most important of these, recommending the original text for a full treatment (and a charming series of stories). Some games lack a prelusory goal as originally characterized: the goal of chess is to move the pieces into a position in which one checkmates one's opponent, but this position must be characterized in terms of the rules of chess, not merely physically. Doesn't one try to achieve this position as efficiently as possible, since it is a lusory goal? Just as I try to win at tennis in as few strokes as possible, so in chess I try to checkmate my opponent in as few moves as possible—so how does Suits's analysis fit chess? The answer is that some prelusory goals are indeed rule-defined,

---

[10] Suits makes the point by way of his Professor Snooze example in Chapter 3. The case is a little complicated to state, and I think my example of driving is more immediately graspable; but I recommend working through Suits's discussion of saving Snooze.

but it is still possible to achieve them in ways that are not rule-governed. We must distinguish the *descriptive* use of rules to define what winning is from the *prescriptive* use of rules to govern the procedures used in winning. As Suits observes, there is *playing the game* of chess and there is the *institution* of chess (58): the latter is what defines the goal of chess, but the former is what engaging in the activity of chess playing consists in. Thus it is entirely possible to bring about a position defined as checkmate without playing the game: you can do this by sly cheating or simply by holding your opponent at bay with a knife while you arrange the board so that you are in a winning position. These are much more efficient ways of achieving the goal of chess than playing by the rules—following legal chess procedures. So the definition *can* be made to apply to this class of games. Again, we must note that players can be as efficient as they like in playing *by* the rules; the point is that the rules *themselves* prohibit the use of maximally efficient means that flout the rules. People learning games often fail to see what moves or procedures are legal in the game, going for actions that will quickly achieve their lusory goal; then the teacher will have to point out, perhaps testily, "No, you can't do it *that* way—you have to do it *this* way," thus proscribing certain possible means (e.g., serving in tennis from any position other than behind the baseline).

What about games without rules? They cannot have rules that restrict the means to achieving a goal. Suits tells us the story of Ivan and Abdul, military men with no patience for rules. They enjoy contest but they can't abide namby-pamby rule adherence. Their idea of a good chess game is a rule-free attempt to achieve checkmate position, by fair means or foul. Knocking over the board is an acceptable tactic, as is gluing your opponent's pieces down, or using solvent on the glue. They finally reach the conclusion that only a fight to the finish will satisfy them, because otherwise a win at chess today might be overturned tomorrow by some sort of surprise attack by the opponent (just as a military victory is always hostage to future depredations). True to their military creed, there will be no restrictions on weapons or tactics—this will be a no-holds-barred fight to the finish. They agree to meet the next day at dawn ready to kill each other. As they see it, this is the ultimate competitive game, with no rules to spoil the action. But during the night both are visited by the Voice of Logic, who points out that the game they plan is actually not free of all constraining rules— for the agreement is to meet *at dawn* and have it out man to man. To steal into the other man's bedroom during the night and garrotte him sleeping then and there would be to *break* the implicit rule; and, as Ivan points out, he doesn't hate Abdul at all—he just wants to play vigorous games with him. Merely slaughtering him as he slept would not be any kind of game, just a pointless murder. The upshot is that, despite their best efforts, the two men have not devised a rule-free game. And I would add that even the most unstructured of childish games have their implicit rules: playing catch requires standing a reasonable distance apart, so that there is some challenge to the activity—it would not do simply to hand the ball to each other. Simple long-jumping games involve getting to a particular place in one bound and not in a succession of steps (and without use of shoes equipped with rockets, etc.) There is always a goal with respect to the achievement of which certain means are ruled out.[11]

In a series of ingenious chapters, Suits extends his analysis to games of make-believe, such as "cowboys and Indians" or "cops and robbers." Interestingly, Wittgenstein does not cite such games, though they seem *prima facie* to confirm his position, since they differ markedly from ordinary competitive games and others that have clear end-points. The challenge for Suits is to explain what their goal is in such a way as to show that they try to achieve it by inefficient means. What is the goal of "cowboys and Indians," and what means are used to achieve that goal? Suits first invites us to consider a game of ping-pong in which the aim is not to beat the opponent by ending each rally as quickly as possible in your favor, but rather to keep the ball in play for as long as possible. This is a cooperative game (though two such players might compete in a contest with other pairs of players, each pair trying to produce the longest rally) and it looks to have a very different structure from that of games that seek to bring things to a satisfactory conclusion. Suits refers to such games as "open games" in contrast to the usual "closed games." His suggestion, persuasively presented, is that the goal of an open game is precisely the *prolongation* of the activity, not its termination; and the means of prolongation involve, say, the use of ping-pong bats and a table of a certain size. In the same way, games of make-believe aim to keep the action going for as long as possible (making allowance for fatigue, boredom, or hunger), and the means involve certain theatrical performances on the part of the players—shooting, falling, moaning, and so on. But why are these means *restrictive*? Aren't the players trying to do everything they can to keep the game going—to keep the ball flying and the ambushes ceaseless? No, because (a) the ball must be kept in play by two people with ping-pong bats and not by an elaborate machine for whacking balls back and forth, and (b) because it would be more efficient in prolonging the make-believe to employ a *script*, so that the players would never be at a loss for what to do next. But if the players used a script they would be like actors in a play, and acting in a play is not a *game*—it is species of *work*. The children, by contrast, intentionally make it difficult to keep up the pretense by requiring themselves to extemporize. As Suits has his Grasshopper explain to the doubting Skepticus, who asks whether the children abjure the use of a machine to keep the action going, as in the ping-pong case: "Yes, Skepticus, if a script is a kind of machine. For like a ping-pong machine, use of a script by players of make-believe

---

[11] Exercising is not a game, but a technical activity, since its goal is to improve one's health and fitness—and so there are no restrictive rules governing how one should exercise. Weight lifting, say, has no rules; you can do it any way you like so long as it works to make you fitter and stronger. If we could get the same results without the exercise, we surely would—thus avoiding the pain of the gain. The confirmed workaholic can therefore happily exercise, but game playing will always carry an element of the frivolous and unjustified for the work-addicted. I note that academics tend to exercise rather than play strenuous games (and they assume that I play a lot of tennis for the payoff in fitness).

games would be a more efficient—less risky—means for keeping a dramatic action going than is the invention of dramatic responses on the spot, which is what the game requires" (125). The essence of a game is the overcoming of self-imposed challenges in the achievement of a given end, and in make-believe games the challenge is to one's ingenuity and energy in acting a part. Thus we have the usual structure of prelusory goal, lusory means, and rules that restrict efficiency, along with the intention to obey the rules so as to be playing the game (lusory attitude).[12]

We must now return to Wittgenstein (with his language "games," chess analogies, and rule-obsessions). What has Suits taught us? He has taught us that the concept *game* can be defined in terms of necessary and sufficient conditions, without circularity. So Wittgenstein was quite wrong to declare games indefinable and to deny that they had necessary conditions. He looked at games, but he looked in the wrong place. Instead of searching for abstract structural features, he focused on the easily perceptible features that games display. He didn't dig down into the underlying essence, but stayed at the surface. If he had tried to define "work," he would probably have noted the many different kinds of work that exist and declared family resemblance—instead of seeing work as a goal-directed activity employing efficient means.[13] Yes, we must look and see, but we must employ the right lens—and we must look *into* and not merely *at*. After all, family resemblance, taken literally, is a similarity in how people *look* (appear, present themselves), and there is no guarantee that what unifies games belongs at the level of sensory appearance or anything close to it—we should not be *empiricists* about the concept of a game. It appears that Wittgenstein was thinking in just such terms—at what you would notice if you cast a cursory eye over all the things that we call games. Instead, he needed to think more structurally, thematically, and analytically. In fact, it is not even clear that Wittgenstein has supplied necessary conditions for being a game in terms of family resemblance, as Suits's treatment of make-believe games suggests. The activity of "cops and robbers," say, doesn't *look* much like paradigm games such as chess or tennis—there is not much in the way of *resemblance*. It is only at a highly abstract level that the

---

[12] Here we see how an analysis can be surprising and hard to obtain, as well as highly illuminating. The puzzle of why chess and children's make-believe are both games is resolved by a uniting general principle specialized to specific cases. We come to see *why* one thing counts as a game and another does not—the analysis is explanatory. There is nothing trivial or obvious about Suits's analysis.

[13] The concept *work* seems to have exactly the same degree of appeal as the concept *game* to be declared a family resemblance concept: it too has a highly heterogeneous extension, without anything standing out as a common property, and it is the logical complement to *game*. But actually it is quite easy to define as a technical activity: work is a goal-directed activity employing maximally efficient means. Try substituting "work" for "game" throughout Wittgenstein's sections on family resemblance, *mutatis mutandis*—plausibility does not alter. The problem, evidently, is that we are not looking in the right place for the definition of "work"—we need to look at its goal-directed structure and motivation, not the perceptible details of this or that work activity. It is very strange, I think, that Wittgenstein does not offer more examples of family resemblance concepts in these sections than he does, as if he doubts that they will be as convincing as "game"—not even "work."

commonality begins to emerge; at the level on which Wittgenstein is operating, make-believe games no more resemble other ("closed") types of games than work activities do—yet they are games nonetheless. Of course, there is "resemblance" at the level of analysis developed by Suits, but that is not the level at which Wittgenstein chooses to characterize games—by reference to balls, boards, racquets, cards, tracks, winning and losing, and amusement.

But it is with respect to sufficiency that Wittgenstein's most serious theoretical problems arise. Since the concept of family resemblance is extremely loose and elastic, he can always find a way to declare that one thing resembles another; but for that very reason there is a threat that the account will be too permissive—that it will count as games things that palpably are not games. Here is where Suits does some of his most trenchant work, speaking now in his own voice and not that of his philosophical Grasshopper (in "Appendix I, The Fool on the Hill"). He begins by noting that Wittgenstein gets off to a bad start by speaking of the things "called" games, instead of simply the things that *are* games. For the fact that we *call* something a game is neither necessary nor sufficient for it to be a game—and so with almost any other predicate. The reasons we have to call something a game can be very various and may not include the requirement that such a labeling be *true*: we may be speaking metaphorically or erroneously or loosely (as with saying "the sun rises in the East"). This is a Gricean observation, about the difference between conversational point and strict truth. It is even logically possible to envisage a case in which a linguistic community *never* calls games "games" (no one ever says "that's a game," or any translation of it), perhaps because games are regarded as sacred and it is impious to utter their name or there is a law against it. If Wittgenstein's use of "called" is simply another way of saying "are," then there is no objection, but it invites a misguided response which Suits is at pains to rebut: namely, that one of his paradigm examples is foot races and these are not commonly called "games"; and something that is called a "game," ring-a-ring-a-roses, does not fit his definition. But, as Suits explains, definitions are not attempts to capture common usage, but the essence of the thing—in this case, the essence of games. Foot races are games because they are best classified along with central cases of games, and ring-a-ring-a-roses is best seen as a kind of theatrical performance, not a game. Thus his analytical procedure is not methodologically flawed in the way that the objection from what we "call" games suggests.[14] But Suits goes on to make the devastating point that Wittgenstein's own positive account has trouble excluding certain non-game activities from the class of games. He considers the case of a policeman chasing a suspect: the policeman, let us say, is out of uniform and both men are wearing running

---

[14] Compare how misguided it would be to make an analysis of *seeing* responsible to all the things we *call* "seeing," with all their looseness, metaphor, analogy, error. Or, to take Grice's example, analyzing *seeming to see* by reference to when we *say* "seem to see": we don't say it when a person is really seeing, because of the conversational implicatures, but clearly you can see and seem to see at the same time, as a matter of simple truth.

clothes, and you observe one man running close behind the other, panting and sweating. You naturally form the belief that they are engaged in a race—and indeed you also observe what seems to be tape across the road some way down. Perhaps there are even some clapping spectators. In fact, the scene looks *exactly* like a hundred-meter race. If anything ever bore a family resemblance to anything, then this bears a family resemblance to the race you saw a few weeks ago at your local athletic stadium. But it is not a race and not a game: it is a policeman chasing down a thief in deadly earnest, doing his job, working (if he could catch the thief without running so hard, he would). *Therefore*, it is not sufficient for being a game that an activity has a family resemblance to standard games. Nowhere near—not even close. Suits's analysis captures the distinction perfectly, but Wittgenstein's proposal gets it completely wrong. But now, isn't it easy to generate further counterexamples *ad libitum*? For surely almost *any* activity will bear *some* resemblance to standard games in *some* respect: running for buses, swimming to save a life, working at a computer (versus playing computer games), exercising to stay fit, acting in a play, psychic card readings, throwing spears at buffalo, jumping across brooks, planning a battle on a board, reading a map, gambling, walking. All these activities bear a striking resemblance to activities that can constitute playing a game, yet they are not as such instances of game playing. The simple point is that the *behavior* characteristic of playing a game can occur outside games. Chases look a lot like races, but races are games and chases are not.

It is a consequence of the foregoing that Wittgenstein will have trouble accounting for the possibility of *mistakes* in the attribution of "game." He wanted to account for the vagueness and open-endedness of the concept (as he saw it), so he kept the conditions for membership loose; but the danger is that the conditions are *so* loose that virtually anything will end up counting as a game—including things that are palpably not games. That is, he cannot capture the *normative* dimension of the concept—anything that *seems* right is going to *be* right (to quote his own words against him). If it looks like a game (bears a family resemblance to paradigm games), then it will be a game—but, as we have seen, that lets in far too many things. Chases are not races, no matter how much they may superficially resemble each other. And this raises the further prospect that the very notion of a family resemblance concept is *incoherent*. It is incoherent because the conditions for falling under the concept are hopelessly weak as a means of securing the unity and integrity of a typical concept. Only for cases in which superficial resemblance is sufficient for falling under a concept will such an account work. It clearly won't work for natural kind concepts, like *gold* or *man*, and it won't work for concepts of intentional activity (e.g., playing versus working), and it won't work for functional concepts (something can resemble a heart perceptually and not be a heart), and it won't work for social concepts (someone can be dressed up as a judge and not be a judge), and so on and so forth. In general, it is not sufficient for being an *F* that an object *looks like* an *F*. As I noted earlier, it is not even sufficient for being in the same family that two people bear a family resemblance to each other—someone can have my nose and gait and not be genetically related to me. Having a family resemblance to paradigms is hardly ever sufficient for falling under a given concept (except the concept of family resemblance itself). There is a distinct danger that on Wittgenstein's picture there will turn out to be only one concept and everything falls under it—because everything bears *some* sort of resemblance to everything else, especially if we allow (as Wittgenstein does) intermediate links in the chain of resemblance. Concepts need discontinuities, and family resemblance is all continuity. Contrast the way in which Suits's definition provides a clear principled line.[15]

Wittgenstein, unlike Suits, is not interested in the notion of a game for its own sake, but rather for its use in weakening the hold of certain philosophical assumptions about language and its analysis. The sections of the *Investigations* that deal with games occur in the context of his general discussion of whether language has an essence. In the *Tractatus* he had maintained that the essence of language is the assertion: *this is how things are.*[16] Thus a sentence is defined as what can be true or false. In the *Investigations* he stresses the multifarious (his word) forms of language, the unlimited variety of speech acts, of words, of linguistic purposes. There is no essence common to all types of "language game," as there is no essence common to all games themselves. He is surely right that his earlier account was far too narrow and dogmatic—not every speech act is an assertion, and truth and falsity are not the marks of everything linguistic. The following is *not* a good analysis of language: *x* is a sentence iff *x* is true or false. But in the later work he veers to the opposite extreme, rejecting all attempts to render what is in common to the different areas of language. He thus fails to consider some obvious proposals that would be neither too narrow nor too wide, such as: a language is a system of elements (words) that combine according to syntactic and semantic rules and which may be used in communication and thought.[17] That sounds to me like a pretty decent definition—certainly much better than the procrustean definition of the *Tractatus*. From the fact that he had earlier given a *bad* definition of language it by no means follows that *no* general definition can be given. Perhaps my thumbnail definition needs some refinement and

---

[15] This is not to rule out vagueness and borderline cases in the case of games, since a distinction can be both principled and vague. Maybe there are cases in which the restriction of means is half-hearted or variable over time—so that it becomes unclear whether the person is really playing a game (some types of fighting play are like this). But the principle to be used is clear and unequivocal, if sometimes difficult to apply to a concrete case (to what extent does the agent have a genuinely lusory attitude in engaging in the activity?). Nothing here amounts to an objection to Suits's analysis. In fact, I think Wittgenstein and his followers have greatly exaggerated the vagueness of "game," no doubt because they have focused too much on when the word "game" is (de facto) *used.*

[16] At *Tractatus* 4.5 Wittgenstein says: "The general form of a proposition is: This is how things stand."

[17] The *Oxford English Dictionary* has: "the method of human communication, either spoken or written, consisting of the use of words in a structured or conventional way." This definition doesn't appear to exclude any of the things Wittgenstein would have wanted to call language; and it sounds just like the essence of language to me (though we might want to strike out the word "human").

supplementation, but it is hard to believe that it is simply way off track—isn't that simply what language *is*? Wittgenstein is far too quick to dismiss the very idea of definition without canvassing some plausible candidates—he is too fixated on his former *Tractatus* self.

It is the same story with the definition of "number." It is somewhat startling to find Wittgenstein declaring *this* concept a family resemblance concept: Isn't mathematics an area of precision and clear definition, whatever the case may be with the informal vernacular word "game"? True enough, the concept of *number* is applied very broadly to encompass many different kinds of number (he mentions cardinal numbers, rational numbers, and real numbers), but that might equally be said of the concept *animal* or even *chemical element*—and Wittgenstein does not declare *these* family resemblance concepts. There is no need to deny the variety subsumed by these general concepts, but it doesn't follow that no all-encompassing definition is possible. And again, Wittgenstein fails to consider any plausible candidates, such as: a number is a mathematical entity, subject to operations such as addition and subtraction, and which can be used in counting and measuring. That again sounds pretty accurate to me, and it doesn't bias the definition of number toward any particular sub-class of numbers (say, positive whole numbers). Why rush to embrace the family resemblance model when we have a definition like that available? Consider also: there are many kinds of triangle—equilateral, scalene, isosceles—but is it right to think that *triangle* is a family resemblance concept? Do we "extend our concept of number [triangle] as in spinning a thread we twist fibre on fibre" (67)? I would have thought not: we don't start with the equilateral case and then gingerly extend out to the other cases, with nothing to say to unify the cases. We just say: a triangle is a three-sided plane figure. We give a definition in terms of necessary and sufficient conditions. Why should it be different with the concept *number*?[18]

Philosophers inspired by Wittgenstein have suggested family resemblance accounts of concepts of philosophical interest: the concept *art* and the concept *sport* are two examples. Impressed by the heterogeneity within the extensions of these concepts, such philosophers have despaired of a neat conceptual analysis and have followed the model of Wittgenstein's treatment of "game." But now that we have abandoned

---

[18] It is not clear to me whether Wittgenstein means his claim about numbers to refute classical logicist definitions of number in terms of classes. But if so, the objection is weak, since such analyses have in fact been given—so isn't the concept of class common to all numbers, assuming logicism to be correct? I am not saying that it is correct; I am only saying that Wittgenstein's remarks about number do not refute that kind of position. It might equally be said, by an intuitionist, that all numbers are mental constructions; or maintained by a Platonist that they are all "abstract." These claims imply common properties, i.e., necessary conditions. Also, where does the family resemblance concept stop in the area of mathematics for Wittgenstein? It doesn't apply to Euclidian geometry, as I point out in the text; but what about topology or set theory or calculus? Are the concepts of integration and differentiation family resemblance concepts? What about whole numbers, which include the very different odds and evens? Is there only family resemblance between odd and even numbers? None of that sounds remotely plausible. How can Wittgenstein make his claim about numbers in general and yet not consider these questions? What exactly is he up to?

that approach, braced and emboldened by Suits's analysis, we might wish to think again about art and sport. Can these concepts be defined after all? I think Suits's model can help us here. He nowhere offers an analysis of sport as such in his book, and I think it is clear that his analysis of games will not carry over unchanged (the restricted means condition does not apply to such sports as kayaking and swimming when these are engaged in non-competitively). Some sports are solitary and are subject to no rules (rules come in only when the sport is competitive). However, the notion of contest or challenge always seems present: not necessarily contest with another person, but with *nature*. You pit yourself against the forces of nature, using skill, fitness, and determination. But not all contests, or all contests with nature, count as sport: wars and elections are contests but not sports, and fighting a chill wind on the way home isn't a sport either. I think we need to add two further ingredients. First, the contest must not occur in the ordinary course of life, as part of achieving some non-sporting end (e.g., getting home); so let us add that the contest must be *staged*, intentionally set up, planned. Second, the activity must be engaged in for its own sake, not to further some other end (compare Suits on the lusory attitude): one is kayaking as a sport if one does it for its own sake and not (say) to escape from an enemy or to catch fish for dinner (so Eskimos who are hunting are not kayaking for sport). So: x is a sport iff x is (or involves) a staged contest with man or nature undertaken for its own sake—that is, it is a staged contest in which the attitude is one in which the activity is valued for itself. Put simply, if possibly misleadingly, it is a staged contest in which the contest is enjoyed intrinsically and not as a means to anything else. Thus sport fishing differs from food fishing and sport swimming differs from shark fleeing.[19]

I hesitate to enter the murky (shark-infested) waters of art, but again Suits provides a fresh angle on the question. What is the goal of artistic activity? Let us say that it is the production of an aesthetic response in an audience, leaving this notion fairly vague (we can suppose, to fix ideas, that it is a response of finding the art object beautiful). Is that sufficient for art (it sounds necessary, if in need of clarification)? No, because I might produce such a response in you by sending you out into nature to view the beautiful natural sights—no *art* would have been thereby created. The amendment is obvious: I must produce an *artifact* that generates the aesthetic response I seek—a painting, a poem, or a piece of music. To be an art object, then, is to be an artifact produced with the intention of securing an aesthetic response (perhaps with the addition that the intention is at least partially fulfilled). Thus there are two necessary conditions: being an artifact, and securing an aesthetic response (intentionally so), which are separately insufficient, but together sufficient to qualify an object as an art object. The intuitive idea is plain: art involves artifice (intentional creation, making), and art involves an aesthetic response (at least the possibility of it

---

[19] In my book *Sport* I adopted the family resemblance account of that concept, not having yet read Suits. I must now humbly retract that position, and the suggestion in the text is my attempt at providing a proper definition (no doubt it needs further work).

or the intention to produce it). There is a goal that is "pre-artistic" (cf. prelusory), the production of an aesthetic response; and there is a means for producing that goal that occurs within the practice of art, that is, the making of a suitable object: together these constitute the essence of art. You can point at a beautiful bird and produce an aesthetic response in someone, and you can construct a technical drawing of an engine: in neither case are you engaging in art. But if you produce a drawing of a bird and thereby elicit an aesthetic response, then you have done something artistic. This elementary formula unifies the various arts under a common rubric, and enables us to offer an alternative to the family resemblance theory of the concept of art. No doubt it is crude and defective as it stands, but it is the *kind* of thing that the conceptual analyst is seeking.[20] And there seems to be no reason (deriving from Wittgenstein) that he should not achieve it. What the philosopher of art certainly cannot do is cry off the obligation to produce an analysis by pleading family resemblance.

[20] The main weakness of this analysis sketch is that it does not require the aesthetic response to be *to* the artifact; it merely stipulates that the artifact produces the response. But it is a nontrivial question what it is for such a response to be *to* an object, as opposed to simply being caused *by* that object. The artifact must somehow be represented in the *content* of the response, so that it takes that object *as* object. Thus we really need a three-part analysis: artifact, aesthetic response caused by the artifact, and the response being *to* the artifact. Now all we need to do is analyze the *to* relation.

3 Sufficiency and Circularity

In the last chapter I rejected an influential argument from Wittgenstein purporting to show that some concepts lack necessary conditions. I also endorsed an analysis of the concept *game* that supplies both necessary and sufficient conditions. In this chapter I shall address the question of whether some concepts lack sufficient conditions. Of course, in a trivial sense every concept has a sufficient condition (constructed from its necessary conditions), since every concept is sufficient for itself: every concept *C* is such that if *C* applies then *C* applies. The sufficiency of every concept for itself indeed follows from the law of non-contradiction, since it is not possible for *C* to apply and yet not apply. We have here a kind of tautology. But the question is whether *C* has an analysis in which *C* does not occur as a necessary condition: that is, does *C* have a *non-trivial* sufficient condition? Can we, in other words, give a noncircular sufficient condition for *C*? The concept *husband* has a noncircular sufficient condition because none of its necessary conditions includes itself: neither the concept *married* nor the concept *male* is the same as the concept *husband*, but only the conjunction of the two. No compositional *part* of the concept *husband* is identical to the concept *husband*. Sufficiency arises from the combination of the parts, so that the analysis is non-trivial and non-circular. If the concept must occur as its own sufficient condition, then that tells us that the concept is unanalyzable. There will be such concepts, according to even the staunchest conceptual analyst, because not all concepts are complex: the elementary parts of a concept—the concepts that cannot be further analyzed—will be precisely concepts that form their own necessary and sufficient conditions. But for a complex concept—one that has parts—the analyst believes that noncircular sufficient conditions exist, however difficult it may be to identify them. No complex concept is such that it is itself one of its (proper) parts. The picture is that the concept has a cluster of necessary conditions, none of which severally is the concept being analyzed, that jointly suffice for the concept to apply. Thus every complex concept has noncircular sufficient conditions, according to this picture.

But the picture, traditional and appealing as it is, has been thought to encounter insurmountable obstacles. It has been thought that there are a number of concepts that resist conceptual analysis, precisely because they lack non-trivial sufficient conditions. Any "analysis" that we give of them will be inevitably circular. Thus the concepts in question have been declared indefinable. Now I am not so much concerned with the detail of particular proposed analyses (and their problems) as I am with more general questions, but let me give a couple of examples to illustrate the point— examples that I trust will be familiar, if not uncontroversial. They are certainly examples that convinced me in earlier days that the project of analysis is not feasible, because of the problem of noncircular sufficiency. Consider first perception—say, seeing an object. Two necessary conditions immediately suggest themselves: (1) the subject must have a visual sense experience of a certain kind (e.g., as of seeing a striped cat in front of him); and (2) there must be an object of a certain kind there (e.g., a striped cat in front of him). That is, the content of the sense experience must be veridical and there must *be* such an experience: no one can be seeing an object unless he has a visual experience with a certain content and there is an object out there that fits the content of the experience. As we might say, the *fact* of seeing breaks down into these two components, and so does the *concept* of seeing. This seems evident and undeniable: seeing something is not "simple" but is built of (at least) these two elements. The *property* of seeing an object is a compound of a subjective property (having a visual experience) and an objective property (the presence in the environment of a suitable object).[1] It might naively be supposed that these two necessary conditions jointly suffice for seeing an object, since they rule out both blindness (lack of visual experience) and hallucination (lack of object). But, as Grice originally pointed out, that is not right: for there are possible cases of *veridical hallucination*— that is, cases in which we have both the sense experience and the object, and a fit between them, but no *seeing* of the object.[2] Such a case would be one in which there

---

[1] I suppose that the "disjunctivist" view of perception is incompatible with the conjunctive view here presupposed, but it is difficult to be sure, given the obscurity of the usual presentations of the disjunctivist view. I would have thought the conjunctive view that I sketch in the text comes as near to self-evidence as one could wish, but apparently some people wish to deny it. For what looks to me like a decisive refutation of disjunctivism, see Burge's "Disjunctivism and Perceptual Psychology." One question for disjunctivists: Is veridical hallucination a conjunctive fact or not? The subject is having a hallucination and there is a state of affairs in his environment that fits it, though he is not perceiving that state of affairs: Isn't *that* undeniably conjunctive? Now add the condition that the experience is a case of perceiving the state of affairs: Has the conjunction now been eliminated?

[2] See Grice, "The Causal Theory of Perception."

is an opaque barrier between subject and object, and the experience has its origin in something quite other than the object in question (for example, a scientist stimulating the subject's brain). This counterexample led Grice (and others) to add a further necessary condition: that the object *causes* the sense experience—it is not causally isolated from the subject's visual response. Now, is that threefold necessary condition itself sufficient? It might well appear to be, but it turns out that we can make trouble for it by imagining "deviant causal chains" that run from the object to the experience but that do so in a way that seems incompatible with an attribution of genuine seeing. What if the scientist himself sees the object behind the screen and intentionally causes in the subject a sense experience that matches that object? Then it seems that the object has ("indirectly") caused the subject's sense experience, via the scientist, and yet we still don't think that the subject is seeing the object. So we need a further necessary condition to restrict the type of causal chain that is operative; and what is that condition to be? Some variant on the idea of directness might be invoked, but many philosophers began to worry that no specification of the type of causal chain needed could avoid circularity—it is the type of causal chain that *produces genuine seeing.* Thus in trying to define *seeing* we end up stipulating that the necessary causal connection must be such as to ensure *seeing*; among all the possible types of causal connection, the one that underpins seeing is just the one that underpins seeing. Circularity!

Davidson describes an analogous case in relation to intentional action. Two necessary conditions suggest themselves: (1) the agent must have an intention, and (2) his body must move appropriately (it must "fit" the intention). But these two conditions do not suffice, because the movement might be caused independently of the intention (that interfering scientist again). So let us say that the intention has to cause the movement: Is that sufficient for having performed an intentional action? It might well seem so, but again there is a problem from weird causal chains. What if a mountaineer is holding onto his partner who has just slipped and may cause both of them to fall, and he forms the intention to let go; but this intention so unnerves him that he begins to shake, thus inadvertently losing his grip on the rope and dropping his partner?[3] Then the intention caused the movement, but only via the nervousness and shaking, and so we are reluctant to say that the mountaineer performed the action of intentionally dropping his partner. The intention must cause the action "in the right way": But what way is that? Again, many philosophers were inclined to conclude that no specification of the "right way" could be given that avoided circularity: the "right way" is simply that way that produces genuine intentional action. Thus a causal analysis of intentional action, like a causal analysis of perception, runs into sufficiency problems, and the tempting conclusion is that the circularity is unavoidable and vicious—the concepts cannot be analyzed after all. True, we can give some interesting necessary conditions, which *almost* get us to sufficiency, but in

[3] See Davidson, "Freedom to Act," p. 79.

the end we have to invoke the very concept being defined as one of its own necessary conditions—and that brings circularity. The concept is therefore indefinable and unanalyzable.

My final case is even more familiar: the analysis of knowledge. Here I shall be very brief: Gettier cases persuaded many philosophers (though not all) that the concept of knowledge is indefinable. Knowledge must be understood as true justified belief arrived at by means that *produce knowledge*. Since not all true justified beliefs count as knowledge, we need a further necessary condition: but identifying that extra condition proved analytically challenging, and so it was tempting to infer that knowledge has no noncircular analysis. The class of counterexamples just consists of those situations that are not *knowledge* inducing. The problem is not that no non-trivial necessary conditions can be identified (as with Wittgenstein's contention about games)—indeed, we seem to have an abundance of *those*; the problem is that we cannot convert our list of necessary conditions into a sufficient condition, except by adding the concept of knowledge explicitly. Thus the purported "analysis" ends up looking like this: knowledge is true justified belief that supports an attribution of *knowledge*. The concept of knowledge here occurs as one of its own necessary conditions, as infuriatingly primitive as ever. And if we try to analyze it in turn, supplying necessary conditions, we inevitably find it recurring, thus generating an infinite regress. Circularity, regress, and primitiveness—the very opposite of successful analysis; so many were inclined to conclude (though not all). Taken together with the previous two apparent failures, a pattern seemed to be emerging: the analysis of a concept could be begun, and could even progress quite nicely, but then it would inevitably run into sufficiency problems that thwart completion. So perhaps analysis is a misguided enterprise, despite its initial promise. A concept could be partially dismantled, its underlying structure partially revealed, but it could not be completely broken down—there was always an indefinable residue. The concept itself always had to be wheeled in as a primitive in the end.

The situation is certainly problematic: the desired analysis is elusive. But does it really spell the demise of conceptual analysis? I think not. First, the mere fact of failure so far does not prove that further efforts will inevitably fail—obviously. The pessimism may be premature. Maybe we just haven't been ingenious enough to find the extra condition needed. Or maybe we have but it is not generally recognized as such (either from obduracy or lack of persuasive statement). Here Suits stands as an exemplar: people generally doubted that the concept of a game could be analyzed, and some even erected an entire meta-philosophy around that skepticism, but along comes Bernard Suits, who provides the elusive definition! (I don't know if he ever devoted his analytical powers to perception, action, and knowledge; but his was evidently the kind of talent that could snatch victory from the jaws of defeat.) Causal analyses were a notable step forward, and quite new at the time—maybe some other style of analysis will be invented in the future and will lay the problematic cases to rest. So: we should keep trying.

Second, from the fact that we have been unable to produce an analysis of a concept, and have no prospect of remedying this lack, and will never in point of fact ever produce such an analysis, it does not follow that the concept *has* no analysis. It may just be that the correct analysis is beyond us—that our powers of conceptual analysis are too feeble and myopic. Maybe this is just another of those areas in which the limitations of human knowledge must be acknowledged. Insight into our own concepts is denied us. However, though I have nothing against claims of cognitive limitation in general, in the present case this diagnosis seems unlikely, for an analysis of a concept is precisely an analysis of what we already grasp; it is the attempt to make explicit what is implicit—and implicit knowledge is still knowledge. Moreover, there is no universal failure of analysis: for many concepts we do know the analysis perfectly well already, even in difficult cases. And we do know *some* of the necessary conditions of even our most analytically recalcitrant concepts—so it is hard to believe that the remaining necessary conditions are beyond the scope of human knowledge. Cognitive closure with respect to the difficulties of conceptual analysis seems like an overreaction—though it is a salutary reaction, because it forces us to separate the question of whether a concept *has* an analysis from the question of whether we can *provide* such an analysis. The conceptual analyst, as I interpret her, claims only that every (complex) concept has an analysis, not that we are guaranteed to discover the analysis—though the fact that the concept has an analysis certainly gives us reason for trying to find out what it might be.[4] The existence of the analysis is an investigation-independent fact, but the investigation is premised on the assumed existence. In fact, the correct analysis often strikes us as lying close to the surface, grinning up at us, and it is distressing and puzzling that we can't unearth it completely: we feel that it is only inches away and yet we can't quite put our finger on it. We are *surprised* that we can't complete the analysis, not antecedently resigned to it.

Third, it would be very odd if the class of concepts mentioned above resisted analysis altogether, in view of the availability of analysis elsewhere. Unless a concept stands for a simple quality, it tends to have an analysis, either obvious or unobvious. The concept *husband* has an obvious analysis; the concept *game* has an unobvious analysis. You would think that other concepts, assuming they are not simple, would follow suit (or Suits!): Why should some complex concepts have analyses and some not? Shouldn't there be a general rule—a kind of law of analysis? Every complex concept has a noncircular analysis—something along those lines. Induction, if

---

[4] We can imagine creatures that possess complex concepts with associated analyses but that are quite inept at conceptual analysis, perhaps because of some kind of modal blindness—they are terrible at thinking about possibilities. They are quite unable to arrive at statements of necessary and sufficient conditions for their concepts, even though the concepts *have* such conditions. For them, there could be cognitive closure about conceptual analysis. God, of course, knows the composition of his concepts instantly, right down to their most elementary parts. We seem intermediate between these extremes—neither blind nor all-seeing.

nothing else, suggests that concepts like *seeing, knowledge,* and *intentional action*—which are hardly conceptually simple—should have analyses, given that other allied concepts do (consider *seeing-as, knowing* a priori, and *acting freely*). Of course, they *may* be exceptions to the general rule—anomalies, strange cases—but it is odd if they are; and we would like to know why they should be thus exceptional. Isn't it more likely that we haven't stumbled on the correct analysis yet, or have failed to see that an extant analysis is actually correct when properly understood? Russell showed that the word "the" can be analyzed in terms of existential quantification and identity; it would be very odd indeed if the word "a" (the indefinite article) turned out to be resistant to analysis—and, of course, Russell's analysis applies equally to "the" and "a" ("a" being equivalent to existential quantification without a uniqueness condition). Analyses cluster.

Fourth, an ascription of simplicity or primitiveness to the problematic concepts appears implausible. It is quite true that some concepts have to be primitive and indefinable, in order that the whole conceptual hierarchy should have a foundation; but it is implausible that the foundation consists of concepts like *knowledge* and *perception*. The concepts expressed by the following words are arguably primitive: "red," "pain," "not," "exists," "is," "necessary," "true," "point," "law," "good," "add," "think."[5] But "know" and "see" surely don't belong on this list. The reason is obvious: the corresponding concepts have non-trivial necessary conditions, and these conditions can be combined to produce what looks like an *approximation* to the concept. That is, the fact of knowing involves certain other more basic facts, such as truth, belief, and justification; and the fact of seeing involves more basic facts, such as sense experience, material object, and causation.[6] There is a palpable complexity to the property

---

[5] I discuss the primitiveness of logical concepts like *existence* and *identity* in *Logical Properties*. Just as it is important to recognize when a concept is complex, so it is important to recognize when it is simple.

[6] In my 1984 paper "The Concept of Knowledge" I suggest that knowledge is more basic than belief in one important way: it is possible to have knowledge without belief, as with certain kinds of animal knowledge or our knowledge of the grammar of our language. However, this does not substantially affect the point I am making in the text, since *some* sort of cognitive or informational state is still required for such "sub-doxastic" knowledge. The essential consideration is that knowledge is a compound of a belief-like state and certain other conditions. Williamson in *Knowledge and Its Limits* also suggests that knowledge might be conceptually more basic than belief (he makes no reference to my paper). Does his position conflict with the compound conception sketched in the text? Not that I can see, but if it does, I think it has to be wrong. There are different notions of conceptual priority, and knowledge may be prior to belief according to some but not according to others. For instance, belief can be naturally understood as what the believer *takes* to be knowledge, and belief is essentially something that *aspires* to the condition of knowledge. But neither of these priority claims is incompatible with supposing that someone who knows is necessarily in a belief state (or a belief-like state) that is by itself logically insufficient for knowledge. The concept of knowledge can be basic in a variety of respects and for different reasons, but it would be quite wrong to suppose that this shows that knowledge does not have necessary conditions that include belief (or truth). That is, it would be wrong to think that the concept of knowledge has no analysis in the sense intended here (and by those in the past who set out to analyze it). Similarly, if the concept of truth could be shown to presuppose the concept of knowledge in some way, that would *not* show that truth fails to be a necessary condition for knowledge.

or relation being referred to; these are not simple qualities that resist any kind of breakdown into sub-qualities. The concepts thus have *analytical depth*. When the necessary conditions are identified for us we *feel* the underlying complexity; the concept strikes us as a *synthesis* of more elementary components. The combinatorial character of the concept is quite evident and undeniable. Thus we naturally report that there is a subjective and an objective component to knowledge and perception: a psychological state of the subject and a worldly success condition—truth or the existence of the perceptual object. This sense of complexity coexists with an inability to supply noncircular sufficient conditions. It is not undermined by that inability. The concept of knowledge brings together elements that are not themselves instances of knowledge—truth, justification, and belief—and so it cannot be simply primitive or without inner division (similarly for perception). This is precisely why my third point above has force: since the concepts of knowledge, perception, and intentional action have an undeniable complexity, an internal structure, they belong with other concepts that are likewise complex and structured—and which *can* be provided with sufficient (as well as necessary) conditions. They are not like those much simpler concepts that I recently listed. They are more like *husband* or *vixen* or *hope* or *regret* or *person* or *death* or *democracy* or *epistemology*—concepts with definitions. Thus, the problem of circularity of definition does not arise from their inherent irreducible simplicity, their indivisible constitution, but has some other source.

Fifth, there is actual *incoherence* in the idea that a concept can have non-trivial necessary conditions and yet no non-trivial sufficient conditions. I regard this point as particularly important, so I want to state it as clearly as I can. As we saw in the case of knowledge and perception, we cannot seem to complete the list of necessary conditions so as to achieve a sufficient condition; we seem to need to tack on the very concept that we are analyzing at the end. *That* concept is needed as a further necessary condition. But we did have a list of non-trivial necessary conditions at hand before we reached the point of having to reintroduce the concept being defined. Schematically, the situation looks like this: x satisfies C iff x satisfies F & x satisfies G & x satisfies C. That is: the concept C is satisfied by an object just when that object satisfies two non-trivial necessary conditions F and G and when it *also* satisfies C itself. This is not at all comparable to the case in which all we can say is that an object satisfies C just when it satisfies C (i.e., when the concept is simple and primitive). In the former case, the concept is satisfied just when certain other concepts are satisfied *and* when that concept itself is satisfied—as it might be, truth and belief combined with knowledge itself. The concept of knowledge thus has (simplifying) three components: truth, belief, and knowledge (think of it as an ordered triple of these). So we can say that x knows that p iff x believes that p & it is true that p & x knows that p. The last conjunct tells us that x's believing that p must be a case of his knowing that p, or else the analysis is insufficient—in which case it is circular. So, according to this picture, the concept of knowledge has a combinatorial structure—it embeds non-trivial necessary conditions—but it also embeds itself as a necessary condition (thus ensuring sufficiency). But now isn't the problem with this whole picture becoming painfully clear? The problem is that *the last conjunct renders the previous two redundant.* For that conjunct is itself the concept of knowledge and so it entails the previous two conditions. It is therefore unnecessary to mention those conditions. But those two conditions *are* non-trivial necessary conditions for knowledge—they are separable components of the concept. So how can the concept of knowledge contain those conditions twice over? In fact, it contains them over infinitely many times: for we can unpack the third conjunct into the same necessary and sufficient conditions again, and so on ad infinitum. Either the concept consists simply of itself (no non-trivial necessary conditions) or it has non-trivial sufficient conditions; but it cannot have both non-trivial necessary conditions *and* trivial sufficient conditions. Thus every concept that has non-trivial necessary conditions must have non-trivial sufficient conditions. The reason, intuitively, is that if this were not so then the analysis of the concept would contain a redundancy—it would have to express the necessary conditions twice over. Put differently, how can those conditions be necessary if they are made redundant by the final conjunct? Why not just make do with the final conjunct? But we already know that the concept also has non-trivial necessary conditions, so we can't do that. If the final conjunct were a non-trivial necessary condition that, when combined with the other conjuncts, gave sufficiency, then all would be clear and unobjectionable. But if we need to add the concept itself to its own analysis, the earlier necessary conditions drop out—the concept alone suffices. Yet that concept contains non-trivial necessary conditions, so they don't drop out. It would be a bizarre concept that contained itself as a component *as well as* an assortment of necessary conditions! Suppose I define "knowledge*" to mean the same as "true, justified belief": then there will be no need to add the concept *knowledge** to that list of necessary conditions—they are by stipulation sufficient. That is a perfectly intelligible concept, intelligibly composed. But a concept composed of truth, justification, belief, *and knowledge* is a kind of monster— with two heads, only one of which is functioning. Surely our concept of knowledge is not like this; surely it is more like *knowledge**—made up of a cluster of non-trivial necessary conditions that are together sufficient. If a concept breaks down at all, it must break down into concepts that do not include itself as a proper part. So there are precisely two cases: simple concepts with no non-circular parts and complex concepts with non-circular parts; there are no complex concepts that contain a circular part as well as non-circular parts. Non-trivial necessary conditions entail non-trivial sufficient conditions. If a concept is indefinable, then it must be *completely* indefinable.[7]

---

[7] Compare molecular analysis: a molecule cannot have an assembly of atomic parts *and* itself as a part. If it breaks down into atomic parts at all, it completely breaks down. The molecule can't be both complex and contain itself as a constituent. The same can be said of an animal body. Knowledge cannot be completely indefinable, i.e., genuinely primitive, and yet also have non-trivial necessary conditions. That would be like a molecule having no analysis into atomic parts and yet possessing some atomic parts; similarly for perception and action.

All the foregoing considerations have a general character. But it would be nice if we could actually *supply* the analysis that I am claiming must exist. What *are* the non-circular necessary and sufficient conditions for knowledge and perception and intentional action? Here I see in my mind's eye a vast stormy ocean of philosophical literature stretching out to the horizon, pullulating with counterexamples, and amendments, restatements, and more counterexamples, and splintered wrecks. Do I really want to set sail on this roiling sea? What tempests might lie ahead of me? Yet I feel an obligation to do so—an urge, an itch. I want to get out on the choppy water and test my new vessel for seaworthiness. Will my chosen analysis float? Have I designed it well enough? There is only one way to find out.

Think back to a simpler, more innocent time, to the days before Gettier darkened the sky; go back even further, when the analysis of knowledge had not even hit upon the notion of justification. Two grizzled philosophers in sandals are meeting to talk about knowledge, having just had the bright idea that concepts might be analyzable into necessary and sufficient conditions (we are going back even beyond Plato). They begin their conversation by catching up on what has been in the newspapers recently. Apparently, there have been some strange reports relating to belief and seeing. Quite a number of people have been forming their beliefs in the usual irrational way, by means of wishful thinking; but instead of forming false beliefs, as has been the rule until now, they have formed true beliefs—and this is a bit of a puzzle (aliens are suspected). Those beliefs, irrationally formed, have just happened to be true—statistically unlikely, but logically possible. In addition, the local opium addicts, who hallucinate liberally, have been finding, to their surprise, and everyone else's, that their hallucinations actually match objects in the surrounding environment, even when they are quite blocked from seeing those objects. Investigation has shown that these cases are complete flukes—just chance matches (so the interfering aliens hypothesis has been ruled out by the authorities). It is all a matter of probabilities, the newspapers report—you are bound to get such matches once in a while, by the laws of chance. Still, it is curious how irrationality and hallucination can be coupled with truth and veridicality—not what you would expect, offhand. Our two philosophers tut-tut over this, bemoaning the state of epistemic virtue, but they see that there is no logical bar to what the newspapers report. They then turn their attention to the primary point of their meeting—the definition of knowledge. They quickly establish that knowledge requires belief, because (they reason) you can't know something unless you have an opinion about it, unless you assent to a proposition. Then how does knowledge differ from belief? After some blundering, they come up with the breakthrough insight that knowledge requires *true* belief. (This was not so obvious, because people who believe things regularly say they know them—they *take* themselves to have knowledge.) The revelation is so overwhelming that they instantly declare analytical victory: knowledge is true belief—that's the definition they seek. But then, calming down for a second, one of them reminds the other of those stories in the newspapers: about irrational beliefs just happening to come out true, and hallucinations just happening to fit the environment. After a few moments they agree that in such cases the individuals in question don't have knowledge or really see things—because it was by sheer chance that their beliefs were true and their hallucinations veridical. It was just a matter of blind luck that their mental states fit the world. If so, true belief is not sufficient for knowledge and veridical experience is not sufficient for perception—though these conditions still strike our two philosophers as capturing the heart of the matter. They then add as an addendum to their fledgling analysis of knowledge: it must not be a *fluke* that the belief is true—a matter of chance or luck or accident or serendipity. They feel well satisfied with their work for the day and agree to return tomorrow for some further adventures in conceptual analysis.

Note that these worthy pre-Platonics said nothing about justification. It is true that the wishful thinkers of the reports had no justification for their accidentally true beliefs, but the two philosophers bypassed that fact and simply required that the truth of the belief not be a fluke. They *might* have added a justification condition to rule out the counterexamples to their true belief analysis of knowledge, but they didn't. That was fortunate because in the distant future a philosopher by the name of "Gettier" would show that justified true beliefs can be true by fluke also. But their simple primitive formula avoided this kind of problem, by inserting the no-fluke condition (as it came to be known) directly into the analysis. Nor did they linger over exactly what a fluke was, how it arose, what might be done to prevent it; they had no *theory* of flukes. But they could see clearly enough that the true belief analysis had to be supplemented with something like this to accommodate the kinds of cases reported in the newspapers. A later disciple formalized their nascent analysis (some time in the Middle Ages) as follows: x knows that p iff x believes that p & it is true that p & it is not a fluke that the belief that p is true. And what is interesting, historically, is that this analysis was not refuted by Gettier's famous examples, since they were precisely cases in which a belief was true merely by fluke. They had been alerted to Gettier-like cases by the newspaper reports and responded appropriately. Such cases were *salient* for them at the moment of analysis.

I am a follower of my two ancient sages. I think they were onto something (and some recent philosophers have had much the same idea).[8] What I particularly approve of is their proposal as an analysis of the *concept* of knowledge. It is admittedly true that they gave no serious *theory* of flukes, but that wasn't their intention: their intention was merely to give conditions necessary and sufficient for the concept of knowledge to apply without circularity. For this purpose they left the fluke concept at an intuitive level, even allowing that it might be vague and context-dependent

---

[8] I am thinking of Unger's 1968 "An Analysis of Factual Knowledge," in which he proposes that knowledge is true belief that it is not true just by "accident"—it is non-accidentally true belief. As he rightly says, this kind of account bypasses theories that insist on a justification condition. Perhaps oddly, the word "fluke" never occurs in Unger's paper, though I am sure it answers well to Unger's intuitive conception.

and uncodifiable. The dictionary suffices to confer content on the notion (*OED*: "an unlikely chance occurrence, especially a stroke of luck; v. achieve by luck rather than skill"). After all, they also provided no theory of truth or belief, leaving these at an intuitive level—though no one seemed to complain about that lacuna. They felt that they had adequately identified the conceptual components of our concept of knowledge, and further inquiries into those components could be left for another occasion.[9] And subsequent disciples noted that the same strategy could be made to apply to certain other problematic cases: such as people with veridical hallucinations and nervous mountaineers. For in these cases, too, it was just a fluke that the "match" came to occur—the sense experience just happened by coincidence to fit the object and the bodily movement just happened to fit the intention.[10] How this notion of fluke might be further explicated, they deferred to others to answer—they were concerned merely with the analysis of knowledge into its component concepts. A notion like *fluke* seemed clearly to be called for, and it completed the analysis without obvious circularity. What more could you ask of a definition?

An analogy between this analysis and that of Suits is instructive. If the aim of belief is truth, then we must not achieve this aim by means of a fluke if belief is to count as knowledge: the truth goal must be achieved in a certain way for the concept of knowledge to apply. Similarly, for an activity to count as a game, its goal must be achieved only in a certain way—with less than maximum efficiency. There must be a restriction on possible means for an activity to count as a game, by the very concept *game*. But, likewise, for a belief to count as knowledge, it must achieve its goal of truth by only a subset of possible means—those that do not involve fluky truth. The means to truth must be of a restricted kind in order that knowledge is the outcome. The abstract structure is the same in both cases. And the idea of skill also plays a role in defining both concepts: skill in using challenging restricted means, and skill in acquiring true beliefs rather than arriving at true beliefs as a matter of luck. And in neither case is it an obligation of the analyst to produce a further analysis of the terms that he or she takes as primitive, though it may be desirable to do so: specifically, the concept of a fluke or the concept of a restriction of means. So long as these are intelligible concepts, and not circular, the job has

---

[9] My global tracking analysis of knowledge in "The Concept of Knowledge" might be seen as an attempt to provide a *theory* of non-flukiness, and so is consistent with the line pursued in this chapter (which had not occurred to me when I wrote that old paper). What I think now is that we can complete the analysis of knowledge without committing ourselves about exactly what conditions rule out epistemic flukes. In fact, the concept of a fluke is often employed in *presenting* the Gettier cases—so that the solution is contained in the statement of the problem.

[10] Notice that artificial aids to perception and action ("prostheses") don't necessarily undermine ascriptions of those concepts, even though they change the nature of the causal chain quite dramatically—as with using radio receivers plugged directly into the brain bypassing the anatomical eyes. What matters is that such devices don't work by chance or fluke—roughly, they are reliable. Having a robotic arm also does not prevent you from acting intentionally with it, even if the device extends right up to your motor cortex.

been accomplished. We know when the concepts apply in particular cases, allowing for vagueness and context-dependence, and that is enough to ground their use as devices of conceptual analysis. It is important for an analysis to be ambitious, but it is also important that it not try to be *too* ambitious—or else we might not recognize a good thing when we see it.[11]

This notion of achieving a goal by skill, not luck, applies to a wide range of cases. Consider scoring a goal in football, curing a disease, and convincing someone of something. One might initially suppose that a bipartite analysis will be adequate to these concepts: an action followed by a change in the world—kicking and the ball going in the net, working on a disease and the disease being cured, arguing with someone and that person's beliefs changing. But it is easy to see that these conditions are not sufficient: we need a *connection*—presumably causal—between the action and the external state of affairs. Your kick must *cause* the ball to go in, your efforts must *cause* the disease to be cured, and so on. That sounds sufficient, but appears not to be so on further reflection, because weird causal routes can bring about the intended effect: your kick trips a wire that causes a cannon to shoot the ball into the goal, your efforts at developing a cure cause someone else to come up with it first, your arguments cause your interlocutor to recall a discussion he had previously with someone else, which convinces him of the truth of the position you are defending. In all these cases, your actions cause the intended outcome by mere luck (good or bad)—so you didn't *score* the goal, *cure* the disease, or *convince* the interlocutor. You merely did something that by luck brought about the effect you intended. So the concepts apply only if the effect did not occur merely by fluke: that its occurrence is not explained by luck or chance or serendipity—but by your skill alone. The correct analysis of goal scoring thus looks something like this: x scores a goal iff x kicks a ball & the ball goes in the net & x's kick of the ball causes it to go in the net & it isn't a fluke that x's kick of the ball causes it to go in the net. More briefly, scoring goals is getting balls into nets without the help of flukes; and similarly for curing and convincing. No doubt we need to be more precise about the role of luck in these kinds of cases, because one can score or cure or convince by luck in *some* sense; but what is ruled out is performing these successful actions when the connection between action and outcome is entirely arbitrary or fortuitous—not used or foreseen by the agent. For instance, I don't think someone can be said to have cured a disease if in a drunken stupor he mistakenly mixes some random chemicals together and irresponsibly injects them into a patient who lo and behold recovers. Nor have I convinced someone of my position if my inept discourse somehow jogs his brain into accepting my position irrespective of the cogency of my argument. Nor can I score a goal if my kick unknowingly disturbs a force field that propels the ball into the goal

---

[11] We should not suppose that the only adequate analysis is a complete or final analysis. There are degrees of analytical depth. There may never be a complete and final analysis of a concept, in which every constituent concept is reduced to its most elementary parts, but that does not imply that we cannot achieve analytical adequacy at a less deep level.

(suppose the ball goes around the earth three times, taking several months, rebounding off assorted objects, and then by massive coincidence goes into the very net at which I kicked it—did I *score* that goal?). So these "success verbs" have a non-fluke necessary condition built in, as consideration of possible cases reveals. But adding this condition secures sufficiency in as strong a sense as we need to complete the analysis. Intuitively, the reason for the success was the skill of the agent, not just happenstance and coincidence. So there is use for the no-fluke condition in a spectrum of cases; and that shows that its invocation in the cases of knowledge, perception, and intentional action is not arbitrary or unfounded. Indeed, it seems like exactly what we need to handle the class of counterexamples that prompt its introduction—since they all involve fluky success. We therefore appear to have produced workable necessary and sufficient conditions for the concepts in question.

That is all to the good, because we earlier saw reason to suppose that all complex concepts *must* have an analysis—the purported analyses could not be irremediably circular. The completing condition need not be (*could* not be) the very concept that we are trying to analyze, but can be just one component of a complex of conditions that together add up to an analysis. Each component is necessary, none alone is sufficient, but in concert they constitute a sufficient condition. The concept can be taken apart, resolved into its elements, and synthesized back into its original unity. The concept is a synthesis of its parts, none of which is that concept itself. This is why we are not surprised or dumbfounded by a successful analysis: we already apprehend our complex concepts *as* complex—though we are unclear about exactly what their components might be. It is not that concepts like *knowledge* project an illusion of simplicity, so that it comes as a shock to find that they resolve into parts; rather, our intuitive grasp of them prepares us for the possibility of analysis. Thus we *recognize* each stage of the analysis as it proceeds, because it answers to something implicit in our ordinary understanding of the concept. Our analyzable concepts present themselves *as* analyzable. We are accordingly not stunned to discover that *husband* can be analyzed into *married* and *man*. On the contrary, this seems like the most natural thing in the world. What *would* be very surprising is to discover that a concept like *knowledge*, with its easily identified necessary conditions (truth, belief), is nevertheless incapable of noncircular analysis. That really would be quite remarkable.[12]

---

[12] It would be very surprising if we had no ability to combine concepts into complex wholes, using our active creative powers, and then express these complex concepts by means of simple words. Surely the human mind has such a synthetic ability—in which case we possess analyzable complex concepts. The mind is a combinatorial organ by nature (language, mental images) and it is inconceivable that it should not use this capacity to manufacture concepts. But if that is so, then those concepts must be capable of disassembly—which is to say that they are analyzable. Conceptual analysis is an inevitable by-product of the mind's capacity for conceptual synthesis. Looked at this way, conceptual decomposition is exactly what we would *expect*.

4 The Paradox of Analysis

The paradox of analysis is as old as Western philosophy, which is not surprising if philosophy *is* analysis (or analysis is a central part of it). It is not a trouble that arose, ominously, when "analytical philosophy" did—with G. E. Moore, in particular. The paradox is already cited in Plato's *Meno*: "A man cannot enquire either about that which he knows or about that which he does not know; for if knows, he has no need to enquire; and if not, he cannot; for he does not know the very subject about which he is to enquire."[1] It is the first part of this ancient conundrum that is most relevant: How can we coherently search for a definition if we already know the definition? Suppose the conceptual analyst produces a definition of a concept and presents his definition to us: How can he *teach* us anything, given that his definition merely expresses what we already knew? How can a definition of a concept be *informative*, given that it must not go beyond what the person who possesses the concept already knows? If I already know that Paris is the capital of France, I will learn nothing by being told that Paris is the capital of France; but don't I already know what I mean by my words—so how can I be informed about this? I know what "game" means, for example, so how can Suits teach me anything by laying out the meaning of "game"? The paradox can be stated in the form of a dilemma: either I don't know what "game"

---

[1] *Meno* 80e. An alternative translation has it that a man "cannot search for what he knows—since he knows it, there is no need to search—nor for what he does not know, for he does not know what to look for." The idea of search suggests that something is lost that must be found, but how can we *lose* our concepts when we indubitably *have* them?

means, in which case I cannot judge that a proposed analysis is correct; or I do know, in which case I cannot be enlightened by an analysis. I certify an analysis as correct by reference to the concept I antecedently possess, in which case the analysis must be identical to the concept, and hence uninformative; but if it is not identical, how can I certify it as correct, that is, as capturing the concept I already possess? To be informative, it must be incorrect; to be correct, it must be uninformative. A correct analysis is, in modern parlance, a tautology; but tautologies are never enlightening, merely repetitive. This is why Frege *contrasted* the informative value of "Hesperus is Phosphorus" with the lack of informative value of "Hesperus is Hesperus": the two names in the former statement have distinct senses, hence the statement is informative; but in the latter statement the two names have the same sense, hence the tedious tautology. The trouble is that in a conceptual analysis the sentences that flank "if and only if" have the *same* sense, and hence should be another dull tautology; on the other hand, if they have different senses, how can we suppose that one gives the sense of the other? How can an analysis *enlarge* knowledge if it merely restates what we already know? An analysis gives us nothing new, just old wine in new bottles—or rather, old wine in old bottles but with different labels attached. An analysis, by definition, must be new *and* old—but that is paradoxical.

Frege was aware of the paradox. In a review of Husserl's *Philosophy of Arithmetic* he writes:

A definition is also incapable of analyzing the sense, for the analyzed sense just is not the original one. In using the word to be explained, I either think clearly everything I think when I use the defining expression: we then have the "obvious circle"; or the defining expression has a more richly articulated sense, in which case I do not think the same thing in using it as I do in using the word to be explained: the definition is then wrong. (225)[2]

If I stick to the original sense, I move in a circle; if I venture beyond it, I am no longer specifying the original sense. Informative definition is therefore impossible—an oxymoron. The paradox is also implicit in this proposition from Wittgenstein's *Tractatus*: "If we know on purely logical grounds that there must be elementary propositions, then everyone who understands propositions in their unanalyzed form must know it."[3] Then why did it take the genius of Wittgenstein to inform them of the fact? Doesn't the master of language already know everything that the philosopher-logician of language might teach her? Yet it seems surprising and substantive that there must be elementary propositions (or that meaning is picturing, or there is a saying-showing distinction, and so on). Everything in the

---

[2] The review can be found in Beaney, *The Frege Reader* (page reference in the text). Husserl was also well aware of the paradox.

[3] *Tractatus*, 5.5562.

Tractatus ought to strike us as trivially true—what we have thought all along. Yet it comes to us like a bolt from the blue. How can mere elucidations seem so novel, so revolutionary? The phrase "the paradox of analysis" was apparently first used by C. H. Langford in application to Moore's conception of analysis, though the concept was not new.[4] (Moore declared himself baffled by the paradox.) Suits considers the problem in an appendix to *The Grasshopper*, citing the *Meno*.[5] It is clearly a problem that anyone devoted to analysis needs to address and, if possible, solve.

In assessing the polemical power of the paradox, it is important to appreciate its scope. It would be quite wrong to suppose that the paradox afflicts some particular type of analysis exclusively, such as giving non-circular necessary and sufficient conditions for the application of a predicate expression (or concept). It does afflict such analyses, but it afflicts much more, too. In the first place, it threatens analyses of logical form: Russell's theory of descriptions, Davidson's theory of adverbs, standard quantificational paraphrases of vernacular sentences expressing generality, modal logic translations of sentences containing "necessary" and "possible," and many more. For each of these purport to spell out the content (the meaning, the sense) of ordinary language sentences in ways that are unobvious to ordinary speakers, often requiring considerable invention and ingenuity on the part of the theorist. The biconditionals that state these analyses of logical form have the very feature that gives rise to the paradox: they are informative and yet (allegedly) faithful to our prior understanding. We judge them to be correct by reference to our antecedent grasp of the expressions analyzed, but then how can they tell us anything we don't already know? The *proposition* expressed by the original unanalyzed sentence is also expressed by the analyzing sentence, so aren't we just being asked to accept an identity of propositions? We already grasped the original proposition, so how can the analysis tell us anything new? If Russell is right about "the," then we already knew that it expresses existence and uniqueness—so why did it take so long for him to discover the analysis? He knew the correct logical form all along! Why then the earlier flirtation with Meinong? He should have seen that Meinong was wrong simply by consulting his preexisting linguistic understanding. And he must have access to this understanding, or else he could not judge that his analysis captures the sense of the original. The analyses of logical form that I have cited purport simply to state what the sentences in question meant all along—but we knew what they meant all along, since they are sentences of *our language*. So it is not just "knowledge" and "game" and "husband" that present a paradox of analysis: it is "the" and "some" and "all" and "slowly" and "necessarily"—there is scarcely a fragment of language that the paradox does not affect. It affects any piece of language for which a philosopher

---

[4] Langford's use of the phrase dates to 1942. Max Black took up the phrase in an article appearing in *Mind* in 1944. I shall not be concerned with the details of their discussion.

[5] Suits, Appendix 1, p. 163. He asks whether the conceptual analyst must always have the definition "tucked up his sleeve" in order to judge that his efforts are correct.

has presented a persuasive analytical paraphrase. Lesson: if you are fond of quantifier paraphrases, don't wield the paradox of analysis against predicate analysis. Logical form analysis is as paradoxical as predicate content analysis.

Nor is the problem confined to formal analyses; it applies equally to remarks about language and meaning stemming from a quite different tradition. Thus: Wittgenstein's *Investigations* is just as vulnerable to the paradox as his *Tractatus*. That may seem a surprising statement, given Wittgenstein's advertised later hostility to classic conceptual analysis; but a moment's reflection confirms it. Wittgenstein's method is to make "grammatical remarks"—observations about the meaning and use of our sentences, with a view to dissolving philosophical confusions. But we already know the "grammar" of our sentences, which is why we can acknowledge the correctness of Wittgenstein's observations—how then can those observations tell us anything new? For example, Wittgenstein believes that "game" is a family resemblance term and he tries to persuade us of that thesis; if he succeeds, it is because we recognize the justice of his observations, but then we must have known all along that "game" is a family resemblance term. We grasped the meaning of the term, and that meaning (let us suppose) is as Wittgenstein claims, so his thesis should have come as no surprise—yet it *is* surprising. Or again, he asks us to consider the "grammatical" difference between the word "understand" and the word "excitement" (also "pain" and "depression"), particularly with respect to temporal expressions, concluding that the "grammar" is quite different in the two cases.[6] But if he is right, it should have been obvious all along, with him merely restating what we already knew; and if we agree with him by reflection on how we understand the relevant words, we should merely be assenting to a trivial truth. Any true statement that Wittgenstein makes about language should be uninformative to us, because it merely records our prior knowledge of language. Even the claim that there could not be a private language should be trivial, since it is part of the very *meaning* of mental words (for Wittgenstein) that they cannot exist without public criteria. The only way in which a statement about word meaning can be informative is by being *false*—but that is not a very appealing kind of "information." So Wittgenstein's observations about meaning, early and late, can only be either trivial or erroneous. The paradox of analysis dogs him from the *Tractatus* to the *Investigations*, so it cannot be used to deplore the former and approve the latter. So, too, weaker notions of analysis, such as Strawson's "connective analysis" (to be discussed more fully Chapter 7), are equally blighted by the paradox, because mere conceptual connections ought to be equally transparent. It is just not classical dismantling analysis but any analysis that purports to spell out our ordinary grasp of our concepts and words: once again, the analysis can only be correct if its restates what we already know, connectively or compositionally—in which case it must be uninformative.

---

[6] The relevant passage is a footnote on page 59 of the *Investigations*, in which Wittgenstein asks whether understanding is a "mental state."

What else would the paradox destroy? Presumably Frege's sense-reference distinction: for this too is a mere analysis of the total significance of a sentence (or Thought). We must already grasp the sense-reference distinction, or else we would not accede to the arguments for it that Frege marshalls: we "see" that he is right to make the distinction, by recourse to how we intuitively understand the sentences in question—but then isn't he just reiterating what we already comprehend? And the same goes for Frege's other characteristic semantic doctrines—truth values as the reference of sentences, the object-concept distinction, existence as a second-level concept, senses as timeless objective entities. For in each case he is (allegedly) simply describing facts about language and meaning that we already grasp, and which we use to verify that his analyses are correct. If his theses *are* correct, then we should be saying to him: "Yes, but now tell us something we *don't* know."

So is *all* philosophy of language doomed by the paradox of analysis, assuming that it is cogent? Isn't it starting to seem that no argument of that form could have such strong consequences? There *has* to be a flaw in the argument somewhere, on pain of junking everything fine and beautiful in analytical philosophy. There may be some out there who see nothing to admire in analytical philosophy anyway and welcome the wholesale destruction wrought by the paradox. But to those skeptics and nihilists we must point out that the wrecking ball does not confine its destructive powers to philosophy: the destruction extends to linguistics. A linguistic theory attempts to formulate the grammar of natural languages—the rules that generate all and only the grammatical strings of the language. We may suppose that it contains a syntactic and a semantic component. But the grammar of our language is precisely what we *know* in being competent in that language: we know the grammatical rules, syntactic and semantic. But then how can the linguist inform us of those rules? She will only be preaching to the converted, bringing coals to Newcastle, throwing pearls before bejeweled swine. We already know what she is so laboriously trying to explain to us. And if we don't, that can only be because she is not restating the rules we have already mastered, and hence is saying what is false. Any attempt by anyone to make us know what we already know will be open to the paradox of analysis. It applies even to phonetics, construed as the theory of how we pronounce sounds: we know the methods of pronunciation because we make sounds with our mouths all the time, with full control and precision, so how can the phonetician tell us anything we don't already know? Phonetics is an impossible science!

I hope that by now the reader will sense a *reductio* of a *reductio*. The paradox of analysis purports to reduce the project of analysis to absurdity, not by questioning specific analyses, but by an abstract general argument whose conclusion is that any analysis must be simultaneously informative and uninformative—which is absurd. But once the scope of the alleged paradox is appreciated, and its potential destructive power reckoned, we must surely feel that there is an absurdity to the paradox itself: How *could* such an argument have such momentous consequences? And isn't it simply *true* that we have many examples of successful analysis, which are both certifiably correct, judging by our intuitive understanding, and significantly informative? There has to be something wrong with the paradox, even if it is difficult to make out what it is (compare the Sorites paradox). We can't just cease our analytic activities in the face of the paradox, or use it as a stick with which to beat philosophical approaches we don't like: it is just far too *undiscriminating*. We need to find out where it goes wrong, not wield it polemically.

Note, first, that the paradox applies not only to the informative pretensions of analysis, but also to other aspects of analyses—that there can be *disputes* about them, that they can be *controversial*, that they can be *mistaken*, that we can be *confused* about our concepts. None of this should be possible if we already know the analysis of our concepts perfectly well. So there has to be a sense in which we *don't* know the analysis of our concepts before undertaking the labor of devising a conceptual analysis. That is, our epistemic state cannot be *identical* before and after successful analysis; something in us has to change. John Wisdom speaks of analysis as producing, not "knowledge of new facts," but "new knowledge of [old] facts";[7] but this new knowledge must differ somehow from the old knowledge possessed before the analysis is completed. The *way* we knew before cannot be indistinguishable from the way we know after. I used to know what a game is in one way, before I studied Suits's book, but afterward I know what a game is in another way. But what is this "way"? What two "ways of knowing" are implicated in conceptual analysis? Here a pair of words spring readily to the lips (and I have struggled to suppress them until now): *implicit* knowledge and *explicit* knowledge. Then don't we have a swift and pithy refutation of the paradox of analysis: the old knowledge was implicit but the new knowledge is explicit? I know the analysis of my concepts (and words) implicitly, but the analyst makes this knowledge explicit—so I enter a new epistemic state. I have "implicit mastery" of the grammar of my language, but the linguist is seeking an explicit formulation of what I know only implicitly. And so on for all the other types of analysis mentioned earlier. Now it is not that this implicit-explicit distinction is unreal or confused—it certainly seems to point us in the right general direction— but so far it is merely giving a label to something that we don't yet comprehend. What *is* it for a piece of knowledge to be "implicit," and what does it consist in for such knowledge to be made "explicit"? How precisely are we to understand the distinction in question? It is no help at this point to appeal to other ways of marking the needed distinction, as with the contrast between "tacit knowledge" and "conscious knowledge" or "pre-reflective knowledge" and "reflective knowledge" or even "instinctive knowledge" and "articulate knowledge": for each of these raises the same question of theoretical interpretation.

I shall quickly run through three models of the distinction in question, showing their inapplicability to the present case, before presenting my own solution, which

---

[7] Quoted in Urmson, *Philosophical Analysis*, 27: "Philosophic progress does not consist in acquiring knowledge of new facts but in acquiring new knowledge of facts."

I take to be pretty intuitive and in conformity with some standard ways of thinking about concept mastery. First, there is Plato's solution to Meno's challenge: all so-called learning is really recollection—the doctrine of *anamnesis* (literally, reversal of amnesia). We once knew explicitly the analysis of our concepts (Plato himself applies the doctrine more widely) but we have forgotten what we once knew, and our memory needs to be jogged—thus the analyst reminds us of what we used to know consciously and explicitly but have now forgotten. I once knew how to solve quadratic equations, but now I would need to be reminded of it—then it would "come back to me." I would dredge up a long dormant memory. On this view, then, I used to know Suits's definition of a game in so many words and he has now reminded me of what I once knew. The problems with this view are obvious: at no point in my past did I ever consciously and explicitly know Suits's definition (no one taught it to me in secondary school, say)—and there is no previous life in which I could have acquired such knowledge. Nor, in encountering Suits's definition, do I have an experience as of remembering what has long lain dormant—as I might when trying to remember something from my distant past and finally forcing it to conscious awareness. The phenomenology of recognizing the correctness of an analysis is not at all like the phenomenology of retrieving an old memory (no "tip of the tongue phenomenon" or anything like that). So Plato's solution, aside from its extravagant mythology, is also psychologically implausible. The mode of knowing that I have when I pre-analytically grasp a concept is not at all like the mode of knowing that I have when I have a dim distant memory buried in my memory banks. I never say to myself: "Now what did I used to mean by 'game'?" I ask instead: "What do I *now* mean by 'game'?"

A second model is suggested by psychoanalytic theory. Sometimes, it is said, I repress things I know quite well, because of their emotional charge. Maybe I push the unwanted knowledge into my "unconscious" or at least I cordon it off from central awareness. I still know it, but the repression has suppressed the knowledge, blocked it from consciousness. The analyst (psychological variety) can release this repression, and the knowledge can flood consciousness, thus rendering what was implicit explicit. The patient then enters a new epistemic state, with the knowledge relocated from its unconscious hiding place into the full daylight of conscious awareness. Making the implicit knowledge explicit is undoing the repression, the reversal of an affectively driven suppressive force. Now, whatever one might think of this general Freudian story, it is surely not appropriate to the case we are considering. We might repress a lot, emotionally delicate as we are, but we surely don't repress what we mean by our words! (A very determined Freudian might speculate that we repress our knowledge of word meaning because language is used for early communication with the mother, and we repress this knowledge because of our sexual desire for her—but I take it that would be farfetched, even by Freudian standards.) The reason we can't just spout Suits's analysis of "game" at will, before ever hearing his definition, is *not* that we have repressed our knowledge of his analysis because we find it emotionally disturbing (reader: add your own exclamation points here). So this can't be what is going on when we find ourselves enlightened by an analysis such as his. Russell's theory of descriptions is not a piece of deft repression-removal directed at our linguistic anxieties (as if existence and uniqueness alarmed us in some way). Logical forms are not stowed out of sight in the unconscious because of their affective negativity.

A third model appeals to attention. Some things occupy the center of attention, while others lie on the periphery. The visual field presents the clearest example of this: things at the center are clearly perceived, while things in the periphery may be only schematically represented (even shape and color can be unrepresented, with only movement detected). Yet unattended objects can have a cognitive impact—they can enter the subject's field of knowledge. They are known about but not with the focus and intensity of objects at the center of attention. And of course we can switch our attention to them, bring them from periphery to center. Thus an object known in one way—peripherally—can become known in another way—focally, attentively. There is a cognitive transition here, from one level of representation to another. Does this model apply to the transition from ordinary mastery of a concept to awareness of its explicit definition? Clearly not: I don't become aware of Suits's definition of a game or Russell's theory of descriptions just by turning my attention to the relevant concepts or word meanings. It is not that I spend my life failing to attend to my meanings, ignoring them, while they hover at the periphery of my awareness, and then the analyst (logical this time) gets me to pay attention to what I have hitherto ignored—and thereupon I grasp the analysis in all its glory. That would make analysis very easy to perform. But even fully attending to my concept (whatever quite that would be) does not disclose its analysis; the procedure for discovering analyses must be quite different. If I say to you, "Please pay attention to the meaning of the word 'game' and then tell me what its analysis is," you are likely to reply, "I'm not sure what you want me to do exactly, but insofar as I can do what you ask I discern no analysis staring up at me from the meaning in question." Analysis does not consist in shifting a concept or meaning from a pre-attentive mode of cognition to an attentive mode of cognition.[8]

I shall approach my own solution by way of analogy. Consider two ways in which you might learn to play tennis: theoretically and practically. In the theoretical way, you sit in a classroom and the teacher explains the rules and the different strokes verbally. Let us suppose that the teacher is explaining topspin forehand: he describes how the racquet face must be angled downward ("closed") and the racquet swept forward from the "preparation phase" through the "point of contact" and finally

---

[8] Although these suggestions are unapt, they do at least alert us to the possibility of different kinds of knowing, where some kinds are more accessible than other kinds. Some of our knowledge may be dormant, repressed, or unattended—in contrast to the kind that is at the forefront of consciousness. Thus informational advance can occur when such "background" knowledge is brought to the center of consciousness, without any new propositional content being superadded.

brought up and over the body in the right "follow through"—all this without actually holding a racquet or even moving his arm. He then explains that the movement so described will impart "topspin" to the ball (he has no actual tennis balls with him) and that topspin consists of the rapid forward rotation of the ball (he speaks of "revolutions per second"), which causes the ball, through air resistance, to curl downward in a loop in the later phase of its trajectory, thus keeping it within bounds. You diligently take notes, memorizing them, having never held a racquet, hit a ball, or been on a tennis court. You are learning something about tennis: some true propositions, some tennis facts. You now know what topspin is and why it furthers your goals as a tennis player; you might even research some of the physics of rotational motion in order to gain a better understanding. When you have finally passed the written examination, you are allowed onto a tennis court with racquet in hand, ready to hit your first ball with topspin. Predictably, you make a complete hash of it, despite your theoretical understanding. You have theoretical knowledge without practical knowledge (as we call it): in particular, you know the correct verbal analysis of topspin but you don't have the ability to hit a topspin forehand. You can talk up a storm about tennis technique but you don't *have* any tennis technique. Perhaps we can say that you have "propositional knowledge" of topspin, but little or no "practical knowledge" of topspin. More technically, we might say that the linguistic and cognitive part of your brain has a symbolic representation of topspin, so that you can state verbally what topspin is, but the motor part of your brain has no module or program or connectionist network for forehand topspin, so you can't actually hit a ball with topspin. You have one kind of knowledge but not the other kind, though both concern the same subject matter.

Now suppose that instead you learn tennis purely practically, with the help of a very taciturn coach. He doesn't explain anything verbally; he simply stands there, swings the racquet, and tells you to copy him. You observe his movement and try to imitate it. When your imitation is defective in some respect, he tries again, perhaps physically moving your arm for you, occasionally grunting, "Not like that, like *this.*" Perhaps he uses a system of reward and punishment in order to "train" you. Let's imagine you are doing this at an early age, before you can even ask sensible questions (you wouldn't even understand "revolutions per second"). He gets you to swing your racquet in a certain way and to strike the ball with a "closed face"—but he never uses that phrase or any other. The ball rebounds from the strings and loops over the net, landing within bounds, though at first it looked as if it might go long (not that you could describe it in these terms). You keep practicing the stroke, being corrected, until you can reliably *hit the ball with topspin.* You now have the ability to hit a topspin forehand, though you have never heard the word and certainly have no verbal understanding of how topspin should be defined. You have practical knowledge without theoretical knowledge: the motor part of your brain encodes the skill in question, but the cognitive part has no verbal representation of the concept *topspin.* If someone asks you why the ball loops as it does, you will have no reply, though you have become adept at making it so loop. You have one kind of knowledge but not the other kind, despite the identity of subject matter.

After some years of playing tennis and beginning to pick up some of the jargon, a well-meaning coach undertakes to explain to you just what topspin is and how you impart it to the ball and why it makes the ball stay in bounds. You listen carefully, as he analyzes the stroke: closed face, brushing up, forward rotation (not like the backward rotation imparted by "slice"), revolutions per second, degree of loop, bounce characteristics. It all makes sense to you: you recognize the correctness of his description by reference to your own actions. You do the thing he is describing. You used to have a kind of intuitive understanding of topspin, inchoate and inarticulate, but now you understand topspin theoretically—you have "propositional knowledge" of topspin. With your newfound knowledge, you go around the courts saying things like, "x has topspin iff x is in a state of rapid forward rotation, where degree of loop is a linear function of revolutions per second." You know the *analysis* of topspin, whereas before you could merely operate so as to produce topspin. Maybe you had learned how to apply the predicate "topspin" to certain ball movements, since such movements have a certain characteristic look; but you hadn't yet been introduced to a conceptual breakdown of the concept you thus applied. You have definitely acquired new knowledge, yet this knowledge merely describes what you had been doing all along. Practical knowledge has been supplemented by theoretical knowledge. There is nothing paradoxical in any of this. Later, you run into a philosopher on the courts and you are discussing your experiences with topspin over the years; hearing your educational history, this philosopher remarks, "You used to have merely implicit knowledge of topspin, but now you have explicit knowledge as well." You nod, thinking that this is perhaps less illuminating than the philosopher seems to suppose, though the facts seem clear enough.

It is easy to see where I am going with this analogy. You could learn a word, say "game," either practically or theoretically—by imitation or by explicit definition. Neither mode of learning entails the other. If you learn the word initially by imitation, your knowledge of its meaning is practical and demonstrative: you learn how to apply it to certain things and not others (those employing restricted means to a goal and not those that use the most efficient means available) and you can express demonstrative propositional knowledge involving the concept ("this is a game," pointing at chess; "that is not a game," pointing at a workman digging a ditch). But you can't specify what it is about the things to which you refer that elicits your use of the term—you just respond. Maybe the practical part of your brain is keyed to the features that make an activity count as a game, but the part of your brain responsible for conscious propositional knowledge has no such understanding. You respond to games in much the same way that a frog responds to a fly: you produce a differential response, which serves your purposes, but you can't explicitly formulate a definition of what you are responding to. Your skill is "sensory-motor" not "conscious-verbal." It resides in the right side of your brain, not the left. It is a different *form* of knowledge from that possessed by the person who can trot out the definition. You can walk without being able to analyze the concept of walking; you can apply the word "game" without being able to analyze the concept of a game. Your knowledge of games is pre-definitional, non-linguistic, tacit. But if someone comes along and presents a verbal definition, you can respond intelligently, because you can see that his verbal statement *fits* your preexisting skill: you are disposed to apply the word to just those things that his definition captures. You can *see* that your verbal aptitudes match the extension that his definition determines. You learn something, yet what you learn merely articulates what you knew before—but in a different way. Your old knowledge is like the "muscle memory" of the practiced tennis player, but the new knowledge of the explicit definition is stored in your verbal memory—quite a different psychological system.[9]

Here is a simple example. You have spent many years uttering words containing the letter "t": you are skilled at enunciating "t" words, learning the skill as a young child, not reflecting on it. Then you take a phonetics class and the teacher points out that the "t" sound is produced by pressing the tongue on the forward part of the roof of the mouth and then quickly releasing it while exhaling air from the lungs. You immediately recognize the truth of this description, though it had never consciously occurred to you before: you start saying things like, "x is a 't' sound iff x is produced by pressing, etc." You now know the analysis of what was previously a tacitly represented ability—and you recognize its correctness by comparison with the ability already possessed. Knowledge that existed in one form (in one part of your brain) now exists in a new form (in another part of your brain). You have acquired, in Wisdom's words, "new knowledge of [old] facts"—a different *type* of knowledge from the type you had before. What an analysis seeks to do, then, is supplement tacit practical knowledge, acquired by practice and imitation, with conscious propositional knowledge, acquired by understanding a verbal formulation. It brings description to what was once more like a reflex. It brings words to deeds. The paradox of analysis only arises if we assume that all knowledge is of the same basic form—specifically, conscious propositional verbally encoded knowledge. If our ordinary grasp of concepts consisted of such knowledge, then indeed no analysis could be both correct and informative; but there are many forms of human (and animal) knowledge apart from that. Much knowledge is habitual, reflexive, unconscious, practical, unreflective, nonverbal, and inarticulate. This variety reflects the varieties of learning: by

---

[9] We might invoke a "vehicle-content" distinction here, assigning the informative value to the change of vehicle, not to any change of content. There are many ways in which a given piece of information may be embedded in the brain, and a change of embedding will affect the subject's overall cognitive state: short-term and long-term memory, focal and peripheral awareness, verbally or perceptually, as a skill or as a conscious thought, in an encapsulated module or as part of the non-modular central system. It is a truism of brain science that the brain transfers information from one part of itself to another, with much duplication of content, and that the same information takes on different functional properties, depending on its location. There are many "vehicles" for a single piece of "content."

imitation, by repetition, by verbal instruction, by trial and error, by intuitions about possible cases, by blind groping. The conceptual analyst is trying to render one sort of knowledge in the form of another sort, and this is why his project is not paradoxical. He is, in effect, enlisting another part of the brain in producing his analysis, not merely evoking activity in the part responsible for our ordinary grasp of concepts and words.

This is why conceptual analysis can be creative, not merely duplicative. The analyst is not attempting to duplicate the very state of mind that the subject is in when he employs a concept—as it were, providing a new version of what is already there. He must produce a new state of mind, a different cognitive representation. When Bernard Suits invented his definition of a game, he was the first person in history to be in a certain state of mind—that of consciously formulating his definition in words. It is not that we had all already been in *that* state of mind and he merely gave us some new labels. He had to create that new state of mind (and brain) *ab initio*. In producing his definition he didn't just duplicate the ordinary person's grasp of "game"; he enlarged it and augmented it, generating a new cognitive representation. That is why his analysis is informative—it creates a fresh psychological reality. But this creativity is compatible with the conservatism required of analysis, because he simply captured in a new form what was anticipated by our ordinary grasp of concepts. He gave, that is, conscious propositional form to unconscious practical know-how. Thus we have the sameness required for analytic fidelity combined with the difference needed for analytic innovation. Note here the sharp contrast between the Fregean account of the informative value of synthetic identities and the present account of the informative value of analytic identities, such as conceptual analyses must be supposed to be. Frege's account proceeds entirely at the level of conscious propositional knowledge, with different senses determining the cognitive difference between (say) "Hesperus" sentences and "Phosphorus" sentences. But the present account invokes different types of knowledge, not different senses—one propositional and the other not. In Fregean terms, "game" and the words of Suits's definition have the same sense, but our knowledge when we grasp "game" in the ordinary way is of a different order from the knowledge we have when we grasp Suits's definition: the state of knowledge I express when I say (pre-analytically) "this is a game" is not the same state of knowledge (or even the same type of knowledge) as the knowledge I express when I say "This is an activity guided by rules, where the rules limit the means that can be used to achieve the prelusory goal of the activity, and where the rules are obeyed so as to engage in the activity for its own sake." The former knowledge relates me to games practically—in terms of my learned propensities to apply the word "game" and in other ways—while the latter knowledge relates me to games theoretically, in terms of verbally specified necessary and sufficient conditions. (Compare the way a frog and an entomologist relate cognitively to flies—yet both "know what a fly is.")

It would not, I think, be too strong to say that once I have absorbed Suits's definition of games, I have *two* concepts of a game—two cognitive structures in my mind-brain. I have my initial concept, acquired in distant childhood, habitual and practical, deployed many thousands of times as I roam around the world; and I have my very recently acquired concept, learned from a book featuring a grasshopper, hard to remember and reproduce, deployed only a few dozen times in strictly academic contexts (I am not using *this* concept—evoking this cognitive structure—when I say, at the end of a tennis match, "good game"). There are two ways that concepts can be two—Frege's way and this way: they can correspond to different senses but be psychologically at the same level, or they can correspond to the same sense but be psychologically at distinct levels. Inside me right now I have two concepts (conceptions?) of games, but the two concepts don't differ in their "content": and this is the explanation of how an analysis can be both informative and faithful to its *analysandum*. The mistake of the paradox of analysis is to assume a fundamentally Fregean model of informative value and try to apply it to conceptual analyses, then fretting that the analysis can never be faithful to the concept being analyzed. But analysis does not employ different modes of presentation of the same thing; it trades on differences in the nature of the knowledge that we have when we possess concepts—in a word, the difference between practical and theoretical knowledge. The informative value of "Hesperus is Phosphorus" and the informative value of "Knowledge is non-fluky true belief" hold in virtue of very different kinds of facts, and we must not assimilate one kind to the other. The former is a function of different senses grasped in the same psychological mode (by conscious apprehension), but the latter is a function of the convergence of two types of knowledge on the same sense (practical knowledge and theoretical knowledge). The important consideration is that we can come to know the same thing in very different ways—whether it is topspin or the correct use of a word: we can come to know it by practical imitation and sensory-motor skill, or we can come to know it by being told about it in language and processing it by means of our ratiocinative faculties. That is what the distinction between implicit and explicit knowledge is all about. This kind of distinction is pervasive in our cognitive lives, not merely when we are pursuing conceptual analysis: knowledge frequently has these two modes, as when I know the way home practically but cannot easily explain it to others verbally. We each of us know many things that have little or no verbal representation. Thus there is no paradox in the fact that a verbal explanation can change our cognitive state. I know what games are by being able to play them, but I know how *game* should be analyzed by following a chain of philosophical reasoning—and these are totally different cognitive achievements. Yet I can recognize the correctness of the latter by reflection on the former: I use my practical knowledge to test whether the theory offered captures the right class of things. Conceptual analysis is thus an intricate interplay between theoretical knowledge and practical knowledge:

both are essential. What is wrong with the paradox of analysis is then that it equivocates on "know."[10]

I want to end this chapter by mentioning another problem about conceptual analysis that I am less clear about, and which is never (as far as I know) mentioned in these discussions.[11] We can call it the "problem of synthesis," or even the "paradox of synthesis." According to the analytic school, complex concepts break down into more elementary constituents. The complex concept is conceived as generated by combining these constituents into a whole. The standard way this is represented is by means of conjunction: x is C iff x is F & x is G & ... That is, the mechanism of synthesis is conjunction. The concept C is thus a whole consisting of a conjunction of parts F, G, and so on. But this seems inadequate to capture the kind of synthesis that is involved: for a conjunction is merely a *list*, an unconnected series of unrelated elements. I could form a conjunction of arbitrary concepts that have no tendency to coalesce into a coherent conceptual whole—such as *man* and *zoologist* and *obese*. This would merely give us the concept of an obese male zoologist, but that is not a unified concept deserving its own specific word; it is just a set of independent attributes conjoined together. This is nothing like the way in which the concepts that make up *knowledge* combine to produce that natural conceptual unity, or even how *male* and *married* conspire to produce *husband*. What is the difference, then, between genuine conceptual synthesis and mere conceptual conjunction? How do the concepts that figure in an analysis of a unitary concept *cohere*? The reason that this can have the look of a paradox is that we have plurality combined with unity: *several* concepts making up *one* concept. If a concept can be exhaustively broken down into separable parts, how can it form a natural unity? Not by conjunction, apparently. Machines and organisms are unified wholes made up of parts, but here we are not so puzzled about how plurality produces unity—by spatial aggregation and organized functioning. But what plays this role for complex unitary concepts? What is the *nature* of conceptual synthesis? By what general principle does it operate? Simple concepts don't have this problem, because they are not the synthesis of independent components; but complex concepts look to be in danger of dissolving into mere lists—beads on a string.

---

[10] Another way to put the point is that pre-analytically I have a "recognitional capacity" with respect to games, which enables me to judge whether an activity is a game, but I don't (pre-analytically) have a "discursive representation" of games—an explicit symbolic statement of the essence of games. Thus I can recognize games by being sensitive to their distinctive features without being able to *state* what those features are—as I can recognize people by their faces without being able to articulate what it is that I am responding to. There is a perceptual *Gestalt* to faces that my cognitive system responds to, and there is a like *Gestalt* to games. None of this may have a verbal representation (compare animals that can recognize faces and instances of play behavior). The young child may know what games are in one way but not in the other way. In fact, there is a whole series of gradations of knowledge as to what games are, as the basic capacity to recognize them is progressively articulated.

[11] Aristotle seems to have been sensitive to the problem, wondering how the "unity" of a definition is possible: see *Metaphysics* 1037, 12.

We may be reminded here of a problem that troubled Frege and others: the question of the unity of a thought (or sentence). Thoughts are complexes of elements, that is, senses, as sentences are complexes of words. How then do they achieve their natural unity? Why aren't they just lists? They certainly cannot be conceived as mere conjunctions, as if each sense (or word) had *&* (or "&") between it and the next sense (or word). Frege toyed with the idea of the function-object model of the unity needed, with his metaphor of "unsaturatedness"; but, however satisfactory (or unsatisfactory) that account may be for thoughts and sentences, it looks distinctly unpromising as an answer to the problem of synthesis for individual concepts. Where do we find the unsaturated concept and its accompanying object in the analysis of *game* or *knowledge* or *husband*? How exactly does "saturation" produce synthesis? In some sense, the constituent concepts in these analyses have an "affinity" for each other, but that seems more like a label for the problem than a solution to it. What is the principle of cohesion here, the agent of synthesis? How does the plurality assemble itself into a higher unity? Is the unity somehow more than the sum of the parts—in which case, where does that leave the project of conceptual analysis? Maybe we can informatively analyze a concept into its parts, where these give necessity and sufficiency, but we still don't understand how the parts synthesize into a whole—so the whole remains mysterious. There seems to be *more* to a concept than its parts collected together; the parts must fuse and transform somehow. They must slot into each other (to use a mechanical metaphor), not merely sit glumly side by side. But what is this slotting, this mingling, this mysterious joining? How is conceptual synthesis possible? We have seen how conceptual analysis is possible, in the face of the paradox of analysis, but now we want to know how its converse is possible. Once the concept has been broken down into its parts, how do we put them back together again? And if no conceivable mechanism of synthesis can be discovered or devised, maybe the reason is that the concept has no parts to begin with— the enterprise of analysis is misguided. I think that would be a gross overreaction to the problem, and to fly in the face of much successful analysis, but it does seem to point to a genuine puzzle—and one to which I at present have no ready answer. Still, it is sometimes the mark of a fruitful approach that interesting new problems are raised by it; so I suggest that we see the present problem in that positive light. The question for further reflection is: How can a concept have natural unity without being primitive?[12]

---

[12] Perhaps the tendency to take complex concepts as primitive stems from the perceived natural unity of concepts of whatever degree of complexity. The concept seems like a unit, not a congeries. There is no problem of unity for primitive concepts, so we mistake unity for primitiveness. But that is really a non sequitur, because there is no logical tension in the idea of a complex unity—as with almost any natural object you care to mention. Unitary things can obviously have a plurality of parts. The problem in the concept case is just that we don't have any good model for how the unity is generated (though we know that it is).

5 Psychologism and the Linguistic Turn

I began this book by stating that philosophy is the a priori search for the essences of things, undertaken in a spirit of play. It is the search for the essences *of things*—not concepts or ideas or words or meanings or senses. Thus its results concern the objective world of non-mental, non-representational, non-propositional entities: *references*, to use Fregean terminology. We are interested in the nature of knowledge and games and husbands—what we refer *to* with the words "knowledge" and "game" and "husband." We seek to discover the essences of those things, employing a priori methods. Thus when Aristotle says, "a definition is an account (*logos*) that signifies an essence," he means the essence of a thing: the definition of man as a rational animal states what is essentially true *of men*—that they, men, are rational animals. There is no reference here to the concept of a man or the word "man" or the meaning of "man": the reference is to a certain species or collection of entities that stalk the world at large—living, breathing beings. Aristotelian analysis is analysis *de re*.

Moore took much the same view in his discussions of moral goodness, writing:

What, then, is good? How is good to be defined? Now, it may be thought that this is a verbal question. A definition does indeed often mean the expressing of one word's meaning in other words. But this is not the sort of definition I am asking for. Such a definition can never be of ultimate importance in any study except lexicography. If I wanted that kind of definition I should have to consider in the first place how people generally used the word "good"; but my business is not with its proper usage, as established by custom.... My business is solely with that object or idea, which I hold, rightly or wrongly, that the word is generally used to stand for. What I want to discover is the nature of that object or idea, and about this I am extremely anxious to arrive at an agreement... Definitions of the kind that I am asking for, definitions which describe the real nature of the object or notion denoted by the word, and which do not merely tell us what the word is used to mean, are only possible when the object or notion in question is something complex. (58–59)[1]

Evidently, Moore is interested in saying what goodness is—what it is for something to be good. Using terminology that is not his, we could say that he is interested in discovering the nature of the *property* or *attribute* that constitutes moral goodness—what we *denote* (his word now) by the word "good." It is unfortunately true that he disjoins the word "object" in the quoted passage with the words "idea" and "notion," thus appearing to take back with one hand what he has just given with the other—since objects and ideas or notions are not the same. We have ideas or notions *of* objects, but objects are not *identical* to ideas or notions (as Moore is generally eager to point out). I find this alternation puzzling, especially with Moore's use of "denote" to express the relation between a word and *either* its object (reference) *or* the idea or notion it expresses. Despite his normal care and clarity, he seems a bit confused here, grievously so. But I take it this must be a kind of slip and his intention is to endorse the Aristotelian view that the kind of definition he seeks is the definition of an object in the ordinary sense—something in reality to which we refer. This object might indeed be a kind or a property, but it is not something that belongs on the side of the mind; it is what Russell would call "a constituent of a fact." He means to adopt what might be called a *realist* conception of definition, not a linguistic or psychological conception. He wants to know what the essence of goodness itself is, independently of thought and language—as we might want to know what the essence of heat or light or water is (or games or knowledge or man). And his position, notoriously, is that goodness is a simple non-natural quality—a primitive property with no parts or internal articulation. He thus provides a *de re* analysis of the object that goodness is—holding that it *has* no dismantling style of analysis.[2] He is telling us what a certain attribute of things consists in—as he tells us what the attribute of being red consists in (not the perception of red or the concept *red* or the meaning of "red"). He concludes: "It [good] is one of those innumerable objects of thought which are themselves incapable of definition, because they are the ultimate terms by reference to which whatever *is* capable of definition must be defined" (61). The *target* of analysis

---

[1] Moore, *Principia Ethica*. Page references are in the text.

[2] There is no contradiction here: an analysis can consist in reporting that a given concept is primitive (the "null analysis"). The analyst can disagree with his fellow analysts by asserting: "My view of this concept is that its analysis is not complex but primitive." The theorist is analyzing the concept *as primitive*. What matters, for our purposes, is that Moore is claiming that the attribute of goodness has no constituent attributes, as a matter of a priori analysis—this is a thesis of *de re* analysis.

is thus, for Moore, an objective worldly entity, not part of our human ways of representing such worldly entities.

Suits's analysis is likewise world-directed. He investigates the nature of games and tells us what a game essentially is; there is no talk of how we use "game" or our idea of games or the sense of "game." He surveys games themselves and generates a set of necessary and sufficient conditions for being a game—that is, properties that an activity has in virtue of which it is a game. The complex property of being a game is shown to be constructed from other more primitive properties—being rule-governed, having a goal, and using inefficient means. There is nothing linguistic about this: it is a claim about the constitution of reality, about what a certain human activity consists in. It is no less concerned with the objective reality of games than is the claim that games are found in all cultures or are good for one's health. These are contingent facts about games, and it is likewise a fact about games (though a necessary fact) that games involve the use of inefficient means. There is no "semantic ascent" or redirection of attention when we seek to analyze games: we are dealing with games themselves. We are analyzing *games*, not mental representations of games or the word "game" or the sense of the word "game." We need to keep this point extremely clear (which is why I have repeated it several times). The target of analysis is the objective world.

But if the objects of analysis are really things in the world, then why analyze *concepts*? If our aim is to discover the essence of things, what are we doing examining concepts? Concepts and things are not the same—concepts are *of* things. It is as if I am suggesting that by looking inside the mind, where concepts are, we can discover the nature of things outside the mind! This seems no better than undertaking linguistic analysis in order to find out about extra-linguistic reality—as if analyzing sentences could tell us what sentences are *about*. It is like trying to investigate a person by inspecting his *name*. So my two recommendations about how philosophy should be pursued seem to be in tension: first I say that we are concerned with the what-it-is-to-be (the *being*) of things, but then I turn around and advocate the analysis of concepts. Which is to be? Is philosophy about things or is it about concepts? I seem to be confusing a hawk with a handsaw. I seem to be guilty of a use-mention confusion on a giant scale. Analyzing concepts *cannot* be the same thing as analyzing reality—that would be to conflate sense and reference, representation and fact, mind and world. Well, if I am guilty of confusion on this point, then so is a vast stretch of analytical philosophy—because conceptual analysis has been generally conceived as a road to knowledge of reality. We find out about things by investigating how we *think* about things. But the challenge is quite natural and needs to be addressed: How *is* it that conceptual analysis can yield knowledge of what concepts are about? Skepticism about analysis is fueled by this worry, as much as by anything: the suspicion that it rests on a kind of category mistake—applying to reality what properly applies to concepts. And a comparison to science underlines the worry: science investigates reality itself, not our concepts of it, given that it is concerned with discovering truths about reality. If philosophy has the same aim, shouldn't it employ the same method—not distract itself with mere concepts? It is simply looking in the wrong place. Look outward, not inward! Keep your eye on the ball; don't examine your own eye! The analytical philosopher seems like a physicist who behaves like an optician—always gazing at the lens when his intended object is the object. The critic might even accuse the conceptual analyst of trafficking in paradox: holding both that reality goes beyond concepts and that there is no more to reality than concepts. How can we resolve this apparent paradox ("the paradox of analytical philosophy")? It is not the paradox of how an analysis can be both informative and true; it is the paradox of how an analysis of one thing (a concept) can yield information about another ontologically distinct thing (the reference of the concept). What justifies the *inference* from concept to fact? Or, why resort to inference at all when you have the object there anyway? Why do concepts come into the picture to begin with?

Good question, plainly put. But like many a paradox, this one is best viewed as an invitation to reflection, not a refutation of the practice in question. The answer to it is twofold. In the first place, we need to be clear what a concept is—what it is *such that* it can be a route to reality. A concept, I maintain, is a reference to a property (I mean this to be neutral between many theories of concepts: concepts as words in the language of thought, mental images, discriminative capacities, brain circuits, eddies in the World Spirit). When you have a concept, your mind refers to a property, if I may put it so: if I use the concept *square* in forming a thought, then my thought (or a part of it) denotes the property of being square. The concept is not the *same* as the property, however: the property can be instantiated by external things, but the concept cannot be so instantiated (though it can be "satisfied"). The property is no more the concept of it than it is the predicate that denotes it. Things were square before there were either concepts or predicates. But the *identity* of the concept turns on which property it denotes; its content is fixed by its reference.[3] There is thus no such thing as analyzing a concept that is not analyzing the property it denotes: to analyze a concept *is* to analyze the property that gives it content. When Suits analyzes games he is analyzing the property of being a game—what it is to be a game—but that is just to analyze the concept of a game, because the property fixes the content of the concept. The paradox is thus resolved by noting that there is no *divide* between concept and thing: the concept is individuated by the property—its content consists in its reference. Thus we are not inferring from the concept to the property; we are analyzing the concept *by* analyzing the property. We analyze the property and *thereby* we analyze the concept. There is no opposition here—*either* the concept *or* the property; rather, the two are inseparable, bound tightly together. If there is any inferring going on, it is from the *property* to the *concept*, not contrariwise: the property is logically prior in the process of analysis. Yet we examine the

---

[3] I argue for this view of concepts in *Mental Content*, chapter one. It is a thesis of "externalism" in one good sense of the term.

property by *means* of possessing the concept: we view the property in the light of the concept (not by experimental means, say). Thus our inquiry is a priori. We view the property under the concept, but it is the property we view. The concept is a (direct) representation of a property, so that investigating concepts is investigating properties; but the investigation takes place under the auspices of the concept, so that the inquiry is conceptual. Put in more loaded language, the concept *incorporates* the property, so that insight into the concept is just insight into the property; but the insight comes from mastery of the concept alone. We learn about reality by analyzing concepts simply because concepts and reality are not separate spheres.[4]

Second, the phrase "conceptual analysis" carries a dangerous ambiguity. If I speak of the "conceptual analysis of objects and properties," I may be thought to contradict myself: I seem to be saying that an analysis of concepts takes the same object as an analysis of objects, but objects and concepts are not the same! In this reading, "conceptual analysis" is synonymous with "analysis of concepts": that is, it refers to the *subject matter* of the analysis. But there is another reading on which "conceptual analysis" refers to the *method* of analysis, not the type of its objects: on this reading, we *can* speak of the "conceptual analysis of objects" and commit no solecism. Compare the phrase "perceptual analysis": it might mean "analysis *of* perceptions" or it might mean "analysis *by* perceptions." The psychologist might undertake the first kind of analysis, but the second kind of analysis is employed by anyone who uses his senses to find out about the world. In the former case, "perceptual analysis" takes psychological objects as target and analyzes them; in the latter case, "perceptual analysis" takes ordinary material objects as target and analyzes *them*—perceptually. One is a type of object of analysis; another is a type of analysis. These are quite different ideas. The same ambiguity afflicts such phrases as "linguistic analysis" and "chemical analysis" and "mathematical analysis": Do we mean the type of object being analyzed, or do we mean the type of method used in the analysis? The adverbial formulation resolves the ambiguity in the direction of method—as in analyzing something *perceptually* or *linguistically* or *chemically* or *mathematically*.[5] Here it is the style of analysis that is being expressed, not the ontological category of its objects (hence a "mathematical analysis" of games or social behavior or evolutionary change). It is the same with "conceptual analysis": we can use this phrase to signify analyzing something *conceptually*—as the case might be, objects and properties. This means that we analyze things *as conceptually represented* (compare

[4] Of course, there is more to properties than what our concepts of them encode, since they participate in synthetic truths of various kinds—as that game playing is rarely practiced in Greenland. But the internal structure of the property is typically reflected in our concept for it, precisely because that property *fixes* the concept (thus the property of games of being rule-governed is reflected in our concept of a game).

[5] Mark Rowlands suggested to me that I am adopting an "adverbial theory" of conceptual analysis, since I think the logical form of "conceptual analysis" is best expressed as "analyze conceptually"—verb and adverb, not adjective and noun.

analyzing things as perceptually represented, as opposed to as mathematically represented). So conceptual analysis need not be taken as specifying a specific subject
matter, namely, concepts; it can be taken to specify a specific method, namely,
examining objects as our concepts represent them (and not, say, experimentally).
And this is surely what a great deal of so-called conceptual analysis does: it tells us
the nature of things—games, knowledge, husbands—*by* employing a particular
method, that is, viewing those things conceptually. On this understanding,
conceptual analysis never even turns its attention *to* concepts and *away* from
things—any more than perceptual analysis of the immediate environment involves
turning away from the environment. Thus Suits undertook a conceptual investigation of *games*, not an investigation of the concept of games (on the other reading of
that phrase)—using, of course, his concept of a game. An empirical investigation of
games would have the same object, but it would use a different method—an a posteriori method. We can analyze games conceptually or we can analyze games empirically: same subject matter but different methods.

If we put together the second point with the first point, then we can say that by
analyzing games conceptually we can gain insight into our concept of a game: first
we find out the structure of the property of being a game by conceptual means, and
then we read this structure into the concept of a game by exploiting the link between
concepts and properties. First the method, then the subject matter: the conceptual
method as applied to games, then the move from games themselves to the concept
of a game. All the while it is the reality out there that is controlling our inquiries.
There is no looking within in an attempt to discover what is outside; if anything, we
are using what is outside to discover what is within. The method is *de re* and concepts themselves are *de re*. So there is no danger of conceptual analysis becoming
sealed off from reality—a kind of shuttered inner toiling. Conceptual analysis is
outer-directed, worldly, objective—just as much as science or history. Thus there is
no tension between philosophy as a search for the being (essence) of things and philosophy as conceptual analysis; indeed, the two ideas complement one another.[6]

Let me be maximally explicit about what I take conceptual inquiry to be. I say that
we investigate things "under" a concept or "by means of" a concept, as opposed to
"experimentally" or "empirically". But what does that distinction come to? The
question brings in the analytic-synthetic distinction, the subject of the Chapter 6,

---

[6] The correct picture, as I see it, is this: things in reality have an essence that is independent of
language and concepts—knowledge and games are what they are independently of our representations of them—but concepts and meanings latch onto these objective essences in their mission of
referring to the things in question, thereby coming to express the essences. Concepts thus track
(objective) essences. As it were, concepts "know" the what-it-is-to-be of things. Language and
thought thus contain information about how the world is just by referring to things in the world:
knowledge is part and parcel of reference. And the knowledge concerns how things are *necessarily*.
You know how games are necessarily, and this knowledge mediates your reference to games with
"game." Linguistic understanding consists in *de re* modal knowledge of definition: you understand
"game" by knowing the correct *de re* modal definition of games.

but let me say something now to allay any fears that I am up to no good here. My view is quite simple: to possess a concept is to have knowledge of its object. When I possess the concept *game* I thereby know what games are—I even know, in a sense, Suits's analysis of games (see Chapter 4 of this volume). To have a concept is to have a cognitive relation to its referent—to know what the referent is. Russell speaks of concepts as "acquaintance with universals," thus introducing an epistemic notion into the description of concept possession;[7] so let us introduce it explicitly— conceiving is a type of knowing. A concept is, or incorporates, knowledge of the referent. To have the concept *red* or *square* is to know what it is to be red or what it is to be square. In consequence, a conceptual investigation is simply one that exploits only the knowledge integral to possessing a concept. It brings in no extraneous knowledge, such as might be gained by experimental inquiry; it uses only the knowledge that comes with possessing concepts as such. When we "consult our concepts," we consult that knowledge: knowing that the concept applies to this kind of thing and not that, that it contrasts with some other concept, that it entails this concept or that, that it refers to such and such a property and not some other one. The results of conceptual analysis are a priori just in the sense that they access this knowledge and not other knowledge that we might have. For example, we know that games contrast with work and that the two presuppose different attitudes toward means, just by virtue of having the concept of a game; we also know that games have a long history and are popular with children, but this knowledge is extraneous (you don't lack the concept just by being ignorant of such facts). Conceptual analysis is simply inquiry that taps into one fund of knowledge as opposed to the other. Analyzing something conceptually consists in using only the knowledge that is integral to possessing the concept. The procedure involves a kind of deliberate restriction of means (and hence is game-like, on the Suitsian conception of games)—not using *all* the knowledge one has of the subject matter. Knowledge *of* a conceptual analysis, in the explicit sense, is thus knowledge of knowledge, arrived at by reference only to the knowledge inherent in possessing the concept. We come to know (in one way) what we already know (in another way), guided only by what we know in knowing the concept being analyzed. Conceptual analysis is coming to have explicit knowledge of what we already know implicitly, guided by what we know implicitly. It is the attempt to arrive at knowledge of knowledge driven by knowledge.[8]

---

[7] See Russell, *The Problems of Philosophy*, especially Chapter 10. Acquaintance, for Russell, involves direct insight into the object of acquaintance, so that we must know the intrinsic essence of universals by being acquainted with them in acts of consciousness. If anyone ever had a paradox of analysis in its purest form, it would be Russell—yet, so far as I know, he never so much as mentions it. How could there be a sense in which we do *not* know the nature of a universal if our acquaintance with it automatically gave us the kind of inside knowledge that Russell assumes? The trouble is that he has a perceptual (indeed, sense-datum) model of concept possession, instead of a practical model (a seeing, not a skill).

[8] If I set out to analyze *C*, I am seeking to discover what I know about *C*-things that constitutes my grasp of *C*. So the knowledge yielded by conceptual analysis is second-order: knowledge of what

We can summarize the previous discussion by saying that conceptual analysis is not guilty of psychologism. It may have appeared momentarily that it could not avoid that sin, since concepts are psychological entities: So isn't inquiry into concepts inquiry into psychological matters? The question is not without point, but we have seen how to answer it. Our interest in games is not an interest in the psychology of games—that is, our psychological representation of games. We *might* be interested in the concept of a game from a psychological point of view—how that concept is realized in the brain, its psychodynamic properties, its development in the child's mind, its potential loss and pathologies, and so on. But that is not the interest we have when we try to analyze the concept of a game philosophically: we are not interested in the concept as a psychological phenomenon. Hence we are not drifting into a regrettable psychologism; we are *objectivists* about analysis, and proud of it. We must not confuse these two ways of being interested in concepts, or else the project of conceptual analysis will seem like an incoherent undertaking: How could the study of concepts as such, considered as psychological states, ever yield information about the non-psychological world? If we were to discover that concepts are symbols in a language of thought or nodes in a connectionist network or eddies in the World Spirit, how could that have any bearing on the Nature of Things? The universe is not in the head! And the answer is that it could not. The concept of a game might be very interesting from a purely psychological standpoint (in fact, as we shall see in Chapter 10, it is arguably the cradle of civilization), but the analytical philosopher interested in the nature of games is indifferent to that question. A concept might even be analyzable into parts *qua* psychological entity—into a string of symbols in Mentalese, say. But that is not object-directed conceptual analysis— which analyzes *things* (properties, kinds) into parts. We can obviously be interested in concepts in very different ways or from many different points of view, as long as we don't confuse them— for example, psychologically, historically, physiologically, culturally, and philosophically. In the last of these, our interest is not in the concept *qua* concept (psychologically) but *qua* guide to reality (ontologically).

I take it that few people would dissent from the point just made. But they might respond to the apparent threat of psychologism by taking a leaf out of Frege's book: we avoid psychologism in the analysis of concepts by denying that concepts are psychological to begin with. What we should be analyzing are *senses*, conceived as abstract non-mental entities; then we will achieve the objectivity we seek in

---

I know. This is not like other conceptions of concept possession, such as empiricist image theories or language of thought theories or pure dispositional theories: for it makes concepts essentially *epistemic* things—bits of knowledge. Accordingly, we can apply the analysis of knowledge to this particular type of knowledge: to have a concept is to have non-fluky true beliefs about its extension. To know what games are, for example, I must have non-accidentally true beliefs (or belief-like states) regarding games. The knowledge is practical, but it is still knowledge, so it follows the general pattern of knowledge. We analyze concept possession as knowledge, and then we analyze such knowledge; thus we provide an informative analysis of the concept *concept-possession*.

conceptual analysis and avoid the dreaded psychologism. Some may suggest that we can preserve the spirit of Frege's anti-psychologism, though not its Platonist letter, by substituting public language for concepts in the psychological sense—thus we secure all the objectivity we need. In my view, these maneuvers do nothing to avoid the underlying problem with psychologism: they merely replace that doctrine with what might be called "abstractism" or "linguisticism." For the fatal problem with psychologism is locating the object of interest in the wrong place—in the mind, instead of the world. We seek knowledge *of things*—of references, objective correlates, Being. But Platonic abstractions and public language are just as much *not* such things as psychological states: How do we find out about things in the world by studying abstract senses or public sentences? That challenge can never ultimately be answered by such doctrines, squirm and obfuscate as they may: somehow we must reach out to the world if we are to uncover *its* secrets. The *object* of our study must be reality if we are to discover anything *about* reality. We must, that is, analyze references—not senses or speech. Analyzing things conceptually is not analyzing abstract senses or public sentences: those are the wrong subject matter, the wrong target, just as analyzing psychological states is a misdirection of theoretical attention. All three views share the same fundamental flaw: they make it impossible to see how philosophical analysis can be about the world. They confine it to another domain—the abstract, the linguistic, the psychological. But these are merely parts of a wider world, and they are not the parts that primarily engage us as philosophers. The philosopher is interested in the *whole* world—but philosophically. In short: to study reality you have to *study reality*. Different methods may be used by different disciplines, some a posteriori, some a priori, but they each focus on the same target.[9]

[9] The point applies equally to the study of language itself: empirical linguistics studies the same object as philosophy of language, but the method is different—empirical and conceptual, respectively. (The same goes for empirical psychology and philosophy of mind.) It is not that philosophy of language studies the concepts of language *as distinct* from language itself; it studies language, the thing, but it does so conceptually. Note, in this connection, the extreme oddity of taking the linguistic turn in respect to the study of language itself—as if we could gain a better perspective on language by studying how we *talk* about language, i.e., sentences that *refer* to sentences. The proponent of the linguistic turn claims that we should study material objects (say) by studying sentences about material objects; just so, that proponent must maintain that we should study language by studying sentences about language (that is, studying a meta-language). But that sounds like a very unpromising project: Why not study language (the object language) if our interest is in language—why study language about language? We are interested in language about the world in philosophy of language, not language about such language. That would give us a double helping of quotation in identifying our subject matter: the linguistic turn advocate is interested in the sentence, "the sentence 'snow is white' contains a mass term and a color predicate." But that is not what we are really interested in; we are interested in the sentence "snow is white"—and saying about *it* that it contains a mass term and a color predicate. Why study the object language by investigating some meta-language? Such a procedure seems utterly bizarre and beside the point. Then why is it a good idea to study *non*-linguistic reality by focusing on sentences about that reality? Language is part of reality, too, and we don't think we need to take a linguistic turn to study it! By studying language we have *already* taken a "linguistic turn."

It is sometimes complained that the conceptual analyst, ensconced in his comfy armchair, never leaving the house, is engaging merely in self-directed introspection, while his scientific colleagues are out and about busily perceiving the world. He is "contemplating his navel," immersing himself in his inner reveries, oblivious to what is happening outside. His attention is fixed on his private concepts, as it might be on his twinges and tickles; he is caught up in his own inward consciousness. And that is no way for someone claiming to be interested in external reality to behave. Introspection can never be a good method for finding out about reality "outside the head." This again is a fair question: Am I suggesting that the proper method in philosophy is introspection? And is this defensible? I do not think it is false to characterize the philosopher's method as introspective, since I think he consults the knowledge he already possesses in virtue of mastering concepts, instead of seeking new knowledge (or knowledge of new facts). His contemplative posture is indeed self-directed; his attention is reflexively deployed ("What do I think about this possible case?"). But we must be careful how we understand this attentive posture: he is not looking within *as opposed* to looking without. The prior knowledge he consults is knowledge *of reality*—it is not purely self-knowledge ("I am a selfish so and so"). For example, he consults his knowledge that knowledge implies truth and belief or his knowledge that games are constituted by rules. He is not gazing at some inner gleaming item cut off from the world outside (the precious stones of the mind); he is accessing his knowledge *of* the world. He consults his "intuitions" about possible *states of affairs*, his ways of classifying different *objects*. Thus his attention is actually pointed outward: he is thinking *about* games and knowledge, as he tests the applicability of his concepts. His intentionality is not directed within, as if at some supposed inner theater—as if concepts were like toy soldiers enclosed in a box. He thinks about his concepts in *relation* to objects, and it is the objects that are his primary concern. He contemplates the reality beyond, even as he reclines in his armchair, conceptually analyzing. There is no question of his being locked up within himself, like some sort of marooned mariner or self-obsessed meditative mystic. These descriptions give quite the wrong image of the nature of his activities. His thoughts are directed at things, as much as those of his scientist friends.

There is a strong association in people's minds between conceptual analysis and something called "linguistic philosophy." Am I supposing that philosophy consists of "linguistic analysis?" Have I made the "linguistic turn"? The alert reader will know that this is not at all my position: I do not think that language is the subject matter of philosophy, or is the method of philosophy, or constitutes the data of philosophy. Philosophy has nothing essentially to do with language, in my view (except, of course, philosophy *of* language). So far as I can see, a species of intelligent beings could engage in philosophy and be bereft of language, as long as they are capable of abstract thought. I don't in general believe that thought requires language, and so I don't think that thinking philosophical thoughts depends essentially on language. A rational reflective being could think about the mind-body problem or the problem of free will or the existence of the external world without having *words* for any of these things. And I am tired of hearing people insist, as if it were a sacred dogma, that there cannot be thought without language (often qualified as no "sophisticated" thought, whatever that may be), when no decent argument has ever been given for that conclusion, when the view is implausible on its face, and when concepts are not in any clear sense inherently linguistic.[10] Language is merely the expression of thought, as common sense supposes, not its *sine qua non* (and how could it be the foundation of thought when it must be *meaningful* language that is at issue, i.e., language that expresses concepts?). In any case, I am far from supposing that philosophy depends on language. Those who do maintain such a view must explain what it is about language that is so central to philosophy: it can't be phonetics, or etymology, or even syntax, let alone sound waves or the larynx. No, it must be language insofar as it expresses concepts; but then it is concepts that are the focus of interest. And that means concepts only inasmuch as they refer to objects and properties, not concepts as such (as psychological—or even abstract—entities). The most that could be maintained is that it is sometimes *convenient* to talk about language when considering concepts, that is, when engaged in a conceptual investigation: but this can never be essential, constitutive, and indispensable. Suppose that I am interested in knowledge and that I seek an account of its essence. I might describe myself as engaged in a conceptual investigation, so as to make it clear that I am not interested in knowledge as a psychologist might be (how it is communicated, how it develops in the child's mind, how it is lost through forgetting). I might even say that I am concerned to analyze the meaning of "know." But these are just ways of indicating the *manner* of my interest, not the *object* of my interest—that my interest is not in contingent, extraneous, inessential features. I may lapse into the "formal mode" for expository purposes, but my underlying interest is best expressed in the "material mode": I want to know what knowledge is, or games, or art, or seeing (the what-it-is-to-be of these things). The idea of the "linguistic turn" is clearly that of turning from one thing to another—from the world to language, obviously. I do not

---

[10] Here we should distinguish two sorts of the alleged dependence of thought on language: the language of thought hypothesis and the claim that thought depends on a public communicative language. If the former is true, then indeed there cannot be thought without language—but this view does not make thought depend on a public language used for communication. I am not opposing *this* type of view in the text. I am opposing the latter type of view: that there cannot be thought without the expression of thought in public speech—that there cannot be *thinking* without *talking*. That is: no one can have a thought unless he or she has the capacity to communicate that thought in speech. I discuss and reject such claims in *The Character of Mind*, Chapter 4. One thing that makes it so implausible is that the brain mechanisms for thinking and speaking are quite distinct (speaking is a motor capacity, after all). I therefore have no objection to the claim that it is impossible to think philosophically without an internal language of thought (the notorious Mentalese), but I see no good reason to insist that philosophical thought is impossible without the practical capacity to produce speech acts. This is really no more plausible than the idea that sensations and emotions are logically dependent on language ability—or digestion and reproduction for that matter. We are simply dealing with distinct psychological and biological systems within the human organism.

believe that such a turn is required or beneficial (or even, in the end, coherent). In fact, in practice the turn is purely rhetorical, since the philosopher continues to be interested in the *reference* of linguistic expressions. Language is useful for talking to other people about philosophy, and putting things on the board, but it is not what philosophical thought is *about*—or the necessary method for reasoning philosophically. It is no more constitutive of philosophy than it is of physics, where again language has its uses as a vehicle of expression. A physicist may say that he interested in the reference of "charge" or "electron," as a stylistic variant on saying that he is interested in charge and electrons; but no one in his right mind would conclude that this physicist has taken the linguistic turn. It is really no better to describe a philosopher this way who says that he is interested in what "know" stands for. The reference to language here is entirely superficial. And if a philosopher were to insist that he really was interested in the word "know," then the natural response would be to retort: "Good luck with that, but I am interested in knowledge, thank you very much." In the end, only linguistic idealism could justify the linguistic turn—the doctrine that the world consists of words. Then, indeed, an investigation of language is an investigation of the only reality there is. But anyone with a firm grip on the distinction between language and reality will view the "linguistic turn" as a perverse decision to look in the wrong direction.[11]

Someone may concede that language is indeed neither the subject matter of philosophy nor its method, but assert, nevertheless, that it can supply the *data* for conceptual analysis, conceived non-linguistically. Can't we ask "what we would say" in certain situations in trying to arrive at a conceptual analysis? That is, we imagine a possible case and then ask ourselves how we would *describe* the case—whether we would apply a certain word to it. But it is easy to see that the reference to language here is quite inessential: we could equally ask whether we would *judge* that a certain concept applies. For example, do we judge that a person knows that p in a situation in which she is less than certain that p or in which she has arrived at the true belief that p via invalid reasoning? And this is a far more accurate way to put the point, since we can have all sorts of reasons for *saying* that p independently of whether we judge that p. Saying that p is neither necessary nor sufficient for judging that p. Questions of conversational implicature, politeness, fatigue, reserve, and laziness

[11] In the old positivist days, when the necessary, the a priori, and the analytic were deemed to result from "linguistic conventions," one can understand how someone might advocate the linguistic turn—because philosophical theses were taken to be linguistically grounded, like all necessary and a priori truths. That is, philosophical claims were (disguised) meta-linguistic claims, like other a priori necessities. But those days are long gone and contemporary proponents of the linguistic turn (like Michael Dummett) do not subscribe to such positivist views (at least overtly). So there is no longer this kind of basis for supposing that philosophical propositions are geared toward language. Yet perhaps the conventionalist linguistic account of the a priori still exercises subliminal attraction and suggests that philosophy has an essentially linguistic subject matter. If that is part of the thinking behind the linguistic turn, then proponents of it should ask themselves whether they favor such a turn for the case of mathematics, which is also an a priori discipline.

affect the first question, but not the second. What speech acts we would perform in a given situation are a very unreliable guide to what is true in that situation (or what we take to be true)—and conceptual analysis is only concerned with what is true. It wants to know whether a concept really applies in a certain possible case, not what our verbal proclivities might be in such a case, since these depend on so many things other than what we judge to be the truth. Our intuitive judgments function as data for conceptual analysis, but our acts of speech are beside the point and are potentially quite misleading. Thus it is a complete mistake to suppose that conceptual analysis is responsible to "usage" or people's speech habits. The most we can say is that linguistic dispositions constitute (highly defeasible) *evidence* for what people believe about various actual and possible situations, and it is this latter that forms the basic data for conceptual analysis. This is why there is no contradiction in the idea of a race of people thinking philosophically but having no linguistic dispositions, because they lack language in the ordinary sense (maybe they have a language of thought just in virtue of being thinkers). Such philosophical thinkers could not appeal to the linguistic data of common usage, there being none such, but they would be no worse off for that. Their concern is with the a priori essence of things and they use conceptual analysis to satisfy their curiosity, but language never comes into the picture for them. I suggest that for us likewise language comes in only adventitiously: *qua* philosophers, language plays no crucial role (as is also the case for us *qua* physicists or *qua* geographers). Its chief role, for us humans, is as a vehicle of communication, but surely only the most unregenerate die-hard will insist that it is logically impossible to be a philosopher without being a communicator of philosophy. In fact, I believe that the whole idea of the "linguistic turn" has done great harm to the reputation and status of philosophy in contemporary intellectual life, and I would like to do what I can to stamp it out. I also think it is deeply confused and wrongheaded.[12]

I therefore see no internal connection between conceptual analysis and "linguistic philosophy." I don't even think that there was a "conceptual turn" at some point around the beginning of the twentieth century. Ever since Plato and Aristotle, philosophers have been searching for essences and definitions, guided by their concepts of things. Twentieth-century analytical philosophy simply continued that tradition, with no fundamental reorientation of method or subject matter. The most important innovation was the development of formal logic, which opened up the domain

---

[12] The view is often associated specifically with postwar Oxford philosophy (philosophy as "linguistic analysis"), rightly or wrongly, but one had supposed that it was defunct by now. However, Dummett appears to be endorsing a version of it, now seen through the lens of Frege's philosophy; obviously, I am strongly disagreeing with such a meta-philosophy. I think it not merely false but also pernicious—a threat to philosophy as a viable sustainable subject. And it does the image of philosophy in the broader intellectual world no good at all. Fortunately, it is an incoherent idea in practice, a mere notational substitution of the formal mode for the material mode, but that doesn't prevent the preaching of it from sowing confusion and doing harm.

of logical analysis. But I don't think that philosophers like Moore and Russell, who spearheaded the movement, ever turned from the world to our concepts—indeed, in their writings they consciously opposed such a turn. It is true enough that analytical philosophy has taken a pronounced interest in the philosophy of language, but it is a very different thing to claim that this area constitutes the very essence of philosophy in general. Even Ryle, whose most famous book is called *The Concept of Mind*, is fundamentally concerned with the *nature* of mind—with what psychological states and processes *are*. Talk of concepts here is just a *façon de parler*.[13] I see a straightforward continuity of method and subject matter in the history of philosophy, not a sudden *volte face*, as if the newer philosophers woke up one day and exclaimed: "By Jove, we used to think that philosophy is all about the world, but now we see that it is about concepts—thus I must turn my face away from reality and toward concepts of reality!" Such a sentiment strikes me as a sad tissue of confusions and misconceptions—about concepts, method, and subject matter. We need a better meta-philosophy than that.

---

[13] Wittgenstein might look like an exception, in view of such remarks as "All philosophy is a 'critique of language' (though not in Mautner's sense)": *Tractatus*, 4.0031—as well as his later views about the nature of philosophy as linguistic therapy. But on closer inspection these doctrines arise from very specific features of Wittgenstein's philosophy and do not transfer beyond that context. First, there is the "linguistic tautology" conception of the necessary a priori in the *Tractatus*. Second, there is the idea that language is the cause of philosophical puzzles, expounded in the *Investigations*. Neither of these views is now widely accepted, so they cannot be the basis for endorsing the linguistic turn. There is nothing here to warrant a general methodological prescription to turn toward language, enforceable even on those who reject such specifically Wittgensteinian doctrines—and that prescription is not in fact ever based on those particular doctrines. Let me repeat: philosophy has nothing intrinsically to do with spoken language—with the system of signs that we use to communicate with each other.

6 The Analytic-Synthetic Distinction

If a concept has an analysis, then a statement connecting the two will be analytically true—it will be true just in virtue of the correctness of the analysis. If the concept *husband* is correctly analyzable as *male and married* (these provide necessary and sufficient conditions), then the proposition expressed by "a husband is a married male" will be analytically true. The truth of the statement is guaranteed by the correctness of the analysis. By contrast, the truth of the statement "husbands have higher life expectancy than bachelors" is not guaranteed by the analysis of *husband*, but depends on certain extraneous facts about husbands—facts extraneous to the analysis. There are definitions and there are empirical facts. These observations appear rock solid, scarcely rationally disputable. If there are correct conceptual analyses, then there are analytically true statements—and there are correct conceptual analyses. Thus there is an analytic-synthetic distinction. The distinction here seems as firm and beyond contention as any devised by a philosopher—like the use-mention distinction or the type-token distinction or the necessary-contingent distinction. And indeed the analytic-synthetic distinction, once Kant had explicitly formulated it, was unquestioned by philosophers until Quine began to cast aspersions on it in the middle part of the twentieth century; maybe there were some quibbles about formulation, but the existence of the distinction was not seriously disputed. If the distinction turns out to be spurious, then many astute philosophers, belonging to widely varying schools, have been dramatically and shockingly mistaken. Kant made a whopping blunder; he didn't put his finger on an important self-evident truth. Contraposing, if there is no analytic-synthetic distinction, then there are no analyses: no concept breaks down into constituents, with the accompanying necessary and sufficient conditions. All concepts ("meanings") turn out to be primitive, or there are no concepts ("meanings"): some adopt the former view; Quine adopted the latter. Both views seem utterly extraordinary to the naïve viewpoint—like being told that all linguistic expressions (including phrases and sentences) are primitive or that there are no linguistic expressions. Can't we just *see* that some concepts are complex and have analyses, and hence that there is an analytic-synthetic distinction? To hold that there *is* no analytic-synthetic distinction is apt to strike the traditional philosopher as like holding that there is no subject-predicate distinction or no true-false distinction. He or she will want to hear a pretty convincing argument before going down that path. In this chapter, I shall consider whether there is such an argument.

I begin by quoting extensively from Kant. In section III of *Critique of Pure Reason*, entitled "Philosophy Stands in Need of a Science Which Shall Determine the Possibility, Principles, and Extent of Human Knowledge *a Priori*," Kant writes:

> A great part, perhaps the greatest part, of the business of our reason consists in the analyzation of the conceptions which we already possess of objects. By this means we gain a multitude of cognitions, which although really nothing more than elucidations and explanations of that which (though in a confused manner) was already thought in our conceptions, are, at least in respect of their form, prized as new introspections; while, so far as concerns their matter or content, we have really made no addition to our conceptions, but only disinvolved them. (LIII)[1]

We can see the paradox of analysis lurking just below the surface of this passage, with Kant's talk of the "confused manner" in which our conceptions include their constituents, though he is apparently untroubled about its potentially subversive power: analyses, for him, clarify what was previously confused. He has no doubt that our "conceptions" admit of "elucidations" that provide "introspections" that consist in the "content" of the conception becoming "disinvolved"—in other words, decompositional analysis. This plea for the importance of analysis is then closely followed by section IV entitled "Of the Difference Between Analytical and Synthetical Judgments," which unfurls as follows:

---

[1] I quote from the translation of the *Critique* by J. M. D. Meiklejohn, who in his Preface remarks of Kant: "He had never studied the art of expression. He wearies by frequent repetitions, and employs a great number of words to express, in the clumsiest way, what could have been enounced more clearly and distinctly in a few. The main statement of his sentences is often overlaid with a multitude of qualifying and explanatory clauses; and the reader is lost in a maze, from which he has great difficulty in extricating himself" (XV). The translator explains these defects of style by observing that Kant wrote the book in five months. Seldom have I read such a candidly negative assessment by a translator of any work, still less one as celebrated as Kant's *Critique*. Page references to that (lamentably expressed) work are in the text.

In all judgments wherein the relation of a subject to the predicate is cogitated (I mention affirmative judgments only here; the application to the negative will be very easy), this relation is possible in two different ways. Either the predicate B belongs to the subject A, as somewhat which is contained (though covertly) in the conception of A; or the predicate B lies completely out of the conception A, although it stands in connection with it. In the first instance, I term the judgment analytical, in the second, synthetical. Analytical judgments (affirmative) are therefore those in which the connection of the predicate with the subject is cogitated through identity; those in which this connection is cogitated without identity are called synthetical judgments. The former may be called *explicative*, the latter *augmentative* judgments; because the former add in the predicate nothing to the conception of the subject, but only analyze it into its constituent conceptions, which were thought already in the subject, although in a confused manner; the latter add to our conceptions of the subject a predicate which was not contained in it, and which no analysis could have discovered therein. For example, when I say, "all bodies are extended," this is an analytical judgment. For I need not go beyond the conception of *body* in order to find the extension of body connected with it, but merely analyze the conception, that is, become conscious of the manifold properties which I think in that conception, in order to discover this predicate in it: it is therefore an analytical judgment. On the other hand, when I say, "all bodies are heavy," the predicate is something totally different from that which I think in the mere conception of a body. By the addition of such a predicate, therefore, it becomes a synthetical judgment. (LIV)

Kant goes on to note that synthetic judgments are made on the basis of sense experience, while analytic judgments require no such basis and are therefore a priori.

Let me make three observations about this famous passage. First, there is no mention of synonymy or meaning or language in the account of analytic truth: it all proceeds at the level of judgments, conceptions, and cogitation. Analytic truth is *not* defined in terms of sentences and synonyms, but in terms of conceptual containment. The reference to sentences is purely for expository purposes; the underlying distinction is drawn in terms of "conceptions" (there is no linguistic turn here). Second, Kant's terminology is not ideal, since *both* kinds of judgment involve synthesis, that is, the bringing together of concepts into a unified whole. Indeed, the relation between a complex concept and its constituents is precisely one of synthesis: thus a conceptual analysis might well be called a synthetic judgment! We could express such a judgment by saying, "the concept of body is a synthesis of the concepts of extension, impenetrability, and shape" (since Kant holds that all three concepts are contained in our conception of body). The concepts of analysis and synthesis are not antithetical but complementary: what is analysis in one direction is synthesis in the other. But the terminology is now entrenched and no better suggests itself. We could replace it with the alternate terminology that Kant introduces, speaking of the "explicative-augmentative distinction," but this is a mouthful and it is too late now—though it is worth bearing this alternate in mind when one hears the phrase "analytic-synthetic distinction." Third, Kant picks a particularly bad example of a synthetic judgment to contrast with his analytic judgments: "bodies are heavy." This is bad because heaviness is close to mass and mass arguably *is* definitive of body—a body is that which resists motion to some degree or contains a variable "quantity of matter." He would have done better to choose something like, "some bodies are painted red" or "Descartes had a theory about the essence of body"—these are highly "augmentative." What may also be noted in this passage is its unbuttoned appeal to consciousness, properties, and what "I think in a conception"—as opposed to the descriptive austerity that has become habitual since Quine "deplored" such things. Without Kant's richer repertoire of conceptual resources, it is indeed hard to capture the phenomenon he is interested in—namely, providing a *definition* that makes us *conscious* of the *properties* that we *think* in having a *conception* of something. Part of reviving the analytic-synthetic distinction requires becoming more tolerant of such notions in the face of Quinean "misgivings." We should certainly not be lulled (or gulled) into rejecting that distinction because of misguided anti-mentalism. Since I myself have no sympathy for Quine's "desert landscapes" and desiccated theoretical Puritanism, I am ready to articulate the analytic-synthetic distinction in terms that he would find distasteful, following the example of Kant. Specifically, Quine's outdated and extreme behaviorism should not be taken as a given in this debate. Taking the analytic-synthetic distinction seriously involves taking the mind seriously.[2]

The analytic-synthetic distinction, as Kant understands it, presupposes a mereological conception of conceptions: conceptions have parts, and these parts can be separated out in a conceptual analysis. An analytic judgment is one that merely articulates the parts of a concept; a synthetic judgment is one that does not merely articulate the parts but adds something from outside—properties and relations of a non-mereological kind. So an analytic judgment is a part-whole judgment, while a synthetic judgment is not a part-whole judgment: part of what it is to be a husband is being married, but it is not part of what it *is* to be a husband to live longer than a bachelor (this is not part of our conception of husbands as such). Concepts have parts and so there is a distinction between saying what these parts are and saying other kinds of things. And given that concepts have parts, there *must* be such a distinction. I think it is very important here to note that exactly the same thing is true of things that are not concepts. Consider chemical analysis: breaking

---

[2] Eliminativism about all things mental will inevitably spill over to the analytic-synthetic distinction, since it can only be adequately formulated in frankly mentalistic terms. The same can be said of such distinctions as the conscious-unconscious distinction, the belief-desire distinction, the active-passive distinction, the perception-imagination distinction, and many others. Quinean skeptics about the analytic-synthetic distinction might want to ask themselves whether they wish to reject these other distinctions, too. I suspect that Quine himself would be resistant to all these distinctions, because of their mentalistic nature; but others may be reluctant to be so sweeping in their condemnation.

substances down into their molecular parts. Chemistry is deeply mereological—it tells us what chemical compounds are made of (as well as how they interact). A typical statement of chemistry is the philosopher's chestnut: "water is H_2O," that is, water is composed of two parts hydrogen to one part oxygen. This statement is not analytic in the philosopher's sense (it isn't even a priori), but it *is* chemically analytic—that is, it reports the results of chemical analysis. Water decomposes into hydrogen and oxygen; these are its constituents. Such a statement of chemical analysis contrasts sharply with other statements we can make about water, such as "water covers two-thirds of the earth's surface" or "there is no water on the moon": these latter are not chemically analytic—they are chemically synthetic. So chemistry employs an analytic-synthetic distinction: there is a clear distinction between statements that record the composition of chemicals and statements that record other kinds of facts about chemicals—part-whole statements and non-part-whole statements. So far, so banal—who would question such a distinction? And obviously the same kind of distinction crops up in anatomy, geography, physics, and linguistics, since there is, in all these areas, a clear distinction between mereological facts and non-mereological facts. In linguistics, say, we distinguish between statements that tell us what parts a sentence has (verbs and nouns, say) and other facts about sentences—when they are uttered, how they are pronounced, how they function socially. There is a linguistic analytic-synthetic distinction. Clearly, there is a pattern here—a universal, one might say. Across the board, we find a distinction between two kinds of statement, defined in mereological terms. And this is because there are two kinds of facts in the world: part-whole facts and other kinds of facts. (Is there a planet somewhere on which a philosopher has denied this general distinction? There are no truths about the parts of anything. What is his reputation, up in Twin Harvard?)

The moral is that the analytic-synthetic distinction for concepts is just a special case—another instance of the universal, entirely predictable, not at all controversial. If concepts can have parts, like other things, there must be an analytic-synthetic distinction for them. Kant is assuming that they do have parts, so the distinction he draws is unproblematic for him. The entire question, then, depends on whether concepts have parts—and cannot be sensibly debated independently of that. Do we need seriously to defend the proposition that concepts have parts? Why should we? What argument is there against the supposition? As far as we can tell, every domain of inquiry consists of complex objects that divide into parts—chemistry, physics, anatomy, psychology, geometry, arithmetic, and linguistics. Complete thoughts divide into parts, corresponding to their constituent concepts. Why suppose that concepts alone are an exception to the rule? Why should concepts be essentially indivisible, universally atomic? It would clearly be an extremely bad argument for this claim to point out that the linguistic expression of a concept like *husband* is syntactically simple—so that we should immediately infer conceptual simplicity. Many things look simple on the surface but turn out to be incredibly complex, with a great many interlocking parts: surface appearance is no guide to underlying complexity.[3] Also, the simplicity of the expression syntactically is plausibly explained, not in terms of the simplicity of the underlying concept, but in terms of economy and brevity—we don't want to waste our breath giving the whole definition of "husband" whenever we want to say that someone is a husband ("this is my married male, John"). And obviously we can stipulate abbreviation for just that reason, with no shrinkage of the concept involved—as when I tell you that I shall henceforth abbreviate "person with a pronounced uneven tan" by the word "striper." Thus there is no reason of principle why simple words should not express complex concepts—one feels embarrassed even having to argue the point. Moreover, there would appear to be a great many examples where precisely this situation obtains—where simple predicates have complex analyses: "game," "husband," "know," and so on.[4] Concepts patently have constituents; if so, there is a distinction between saying what they are and making other kinds of statements. How could that *not* be so?

Someone might protest, limply, that concepts cannot have parts literally, since all parts must be spatial. Such a protestor is evidently not thinking very hard. Sentences and thoughts have parts, but they are not spatial objects either, as commonly understood; indeed, concepts are parts of thoughts—so it is hard to see how concepts themselves are excluded from having parts. And, of course, some concepts have their parts clearly displayed in the sentences that express them: the parts of *single white male* are transparently on display in the sentence "single white male seeks single white female for fun encounters." Mathematical objects have parts, too, since numbers break down into constituents. Events have (temporal) parts. Parthood is just another name for complexity, and complexity is everywhere. Being laid out in space is clearly not a necessary condition for having parts (what about *n*-dimensional geometry?). And anyway, concepts might turn out to have spatial parts, if they are

---

[3] Isn't this one of the main general lessons of natural science—that things are frequently much more complex than they appear? Our senses simplify and condense, for obvious evolutionary reasons (only reveal as much complexity as you need to). There is more to almost everything than what meets the naked eye. Wouldn't we expect the same thing to be true of concepts—that they have more inner complexity than we might naïvely suppose? The brain is certainly a lot more complex than unaided perception reveals, including the parts that underlie conceptual thought. Perception itself is far more complex and fine-grained than simple introspection discloses. Are we then to suppose that *only* concepts are as simple as they naïvely appear? Isn't it more likely that our conceptual scheme is vastly more complex and decomposable than casual inspection would lead one to suspect?

[4] The same is true for "the," "some," "quickly" and other logical form analyses: the analysis always introduces more complexity than initially appeared—new elements enter the picture. That is not at all surprising, since spoken and written language is inherently abbreviative, because of its demands on the speaker's time and energy: Why spend more time and energy when you could get by with less? Thus we favor condensation, short cuts, ellipsis, and other verbal economies. Language therefore disguises the full complexity of thought, the better to speed communication. The thinking process itself may also operate by a kind of abbreviation, synthesizing a plurality of primitive concepts into one more manageable by the mechanisms of thought. The mind economizes on time and energy, too.

brain states of some sort—since brain states have spatial parts. There is no objection from the meaning of "part" against the idea that concepts have parts. But if concepts have parts, there must be a distinction between statements that record what their parts are and statements that do not—however precisely we conceive the part-whole relation in their case.[5]

There is a definite danger in rebutting imagined opposition to a thesis one takes to be self-evident that the thesis will start to look questionable, precisely because one is defending it by appeal to wider considerations, when the proper response is just (following Moore) to hold up one's hands and say "here are two hands." I feel inclined to hold up a concept or two and say "these are complex," instead of trying to respond to the over-scrupulous scruples of a concept skeptic. So let me just add, for what it is worth, that I feel myself to be in the position of someone trying with all his might to defend the claim that "bachelors are not bachelors" is a contradiction against a querulous skeptic. If you can't see it yourself, or refuse to own up that you can see it perfectly well, then there is not much I can do to help you.

It has become customary to think of analyticity in terms of synonymy: an analytic truth (a statement that expresses an analysis) is a statement that contains synonyms—in the simplest case, the predicate expression is a synonym of the subject expression. Thus "A is B" is analytic iff "A" and "B" are synonymous. It seems to me that this is quite wrong, in any ordinary sense of "synonymy." Synonymy is neither necessary nor sufficient for analyticity, and is anyway a red herring in this debate. Doubts about synonymy, whether well founded or not, are therefore beside the point. The lack of equivalence between the two is most glaringly seen by considering indexical expressions. Suppose I say today "today I am a husband" (perhaps I got married yesterday). Tomorrow you say, referring to me, "yesterday he was a married man" (I got precipitously divorced overnight). The sentence you uttered is not synonymous with the sentence I uttered, but it qualifies as an analysis of what I said. Likewise "here" is not a synonym of "there," but the two words can be used to express the same proposition—which is what is needed for analysis. What matters is what is said, not the lexical synonymy of the words used.[6] Further, dictionaries give directions for the use of words by providing synonyms, but they don't generally supply conceptual analyses: you will search in vain in the *Oxford English Dictionary* for Suits's definition of a game. This is why Moore, in searching for a definition of "good," dismisses "the expressing of one word's meaning in other words" as mere

---

[5] I am not intending to suggest that there are no serious philosophical questions about how concepts have parts—on the contrary. But this should not incline us to doubt that concepts have parts—any more than the mind-body problem should incline us to doubt that we have minds. The question of the nature of conceptual part-hood is no doubt closely connected to the question of how whole thoughts have parts—itself a non-trivial issue.

[6] I am here adverting to the kind of distinction captured by Kaplan's content-character distinction, where character is close to linguistic meaning and content resembles the classic notion of a proposition. The distinction pulls proposition (statement) and lexical meaning apart.

"lexicography," of no philosophical interest (58);[7] and also why Kant never even mentions synonymy. The aim of the conceptual analyst is not to substitute one word with another that people use with the same meaning—words that they use interchangeably. The aim is to explicate conceptions, articulate essences, give the what-it-is-to-be of things; how people use words interchangeably is irrelevant. Language isn't even the object of the exercise, let alone the hunt for synonyms. Searching for synonyms is certainly *not* the essence of philosophy.

You can see how far philosophers have departed from the ordinary meaning of "synonym" by looking at some actual synonyms. Here is a list of typical synonyms: "large" and "big," "shun" and "avoid," "help" and "assist," "gift" and "present," "blend" and "mix," "rich" and "wealthy." Now imagine using these terms in an analytical biconditional, for example, "*x* is rich iff *x* is wealthy." That is not at all what you would expect of a successful conceptual analysis, though it does give a priori necessary and sufficient conditions for the concept on the left in other vocabulary. Why? It is because it provides no conceptual breakdown—no *analysis*. It simply repeats the concept in unanalyzed form by using a synonymous word. It is entirely trivial, merely verbal. So synonymy is not sufficient for analyticity (giving an analysis). Neither is it necessary: "married man" is *not* a synonym of "husband," since they are not usable interchangeably (you would get some funny looks if you described your sister's husband as her "married man").[8] Plainly, too, a traditional definition of "knowledge" does not provide a synonym, nor does Suits's definition of "game." It is not a matter of stylistic variation, verbal equivalence; it is a matter of digging into the underlying structure of the property denoted. As the typical philosopher today uses "synonym," it is not synonymous with the ordinary word "synonym." The ordinary meaning corresponds to a kind of practical equivalence, a fact of sociolinguistic usage, conversational parity. But this "folk" notion is not the one we need for serious philosophical inquiry—any more than the ordinary person's use of "force" is the one we need in physics. In fact, the whole tradition of using "synonymy" as the purpose of analysis arises from the positivist attempt to domesticate the a priori; it has no historical or vernacular warrant. The fact that Quine linked the two in an effort to discredit both simply reflects his intellectual context—his opposition to Carnap, the positivist, basically. But this is a distortion of the original distinction Kant introduced (or named), and we do well firmly to dissociate the two. It may well be that the "folk" notion of synonymy is a frail reed on which to secure such a profound

---

[7] *Principia Ethica*. His general point is that he is not concerned with a mere "verbal question"; he wants to know the essence of goodness itself, not what people might mean by "good" (they may have all sorts of erroneous ideas).

[8] Compare the two sentences "I am going out with my husband tonight" and "I am going out with my married man tonight." The latter is compatible with going out with somebody *else's* husband, but the former surely is not. One word is not just a stylistic variant of the other, having no differential impact on the meaning of sentences in which it occurs. In fact, I don't think "husband" has a real synonym in English, if we exclude such contractions as "hubby." By contrast, there are many synonyms for "father": "dad," "daddy," "papa," "paterfamilias."

distinction, being far too vague and context-dependent and pragmatic; but that is no count against the distinction itself, its rationale or its definition. We need more technical terms, designed for a theoretical purpose (hence Kant's "explicative" versus "augmentative"). It would be silly to try to discredit the physicist's notion of force by cavils directed at the unscientific character of the ordinary person's use of the word "force."[9]

Someone might object on epistemological grounds to what has been said so far: How do we *tell* that a concept has parts—what is our evidence? I seem to be relying on the thinker's own intuitive judgments—how he or she responds to possible cases. But isn't this unreliable, unscientific, subjective? I shall be discussing this kind of point in Chapter 9, but let me make one reply now—namely, that we are not confined to such first-person information. The issue of conceptual analysis is not the *same* as the issue of using intuitive judgments from a first-person perspective. In addition to using my own intuitions about possible cases, I could consult the intuitions of others. In fact, this is part of standard philosophical practice: solitary contemplation is often allied to vigorous dialogue. One asks one's colleagues or students what *their* intuition is on a certain matter—would they count such and such a possible case as an example of *C*, where *C* is the concept being analyzed? In principle, this could be extended into a more rigorous survey of the kind regularly undertaken in the social sciences, complete with statistical analysis and even experimental design (such philosophical surveys have been carried out, though whether they meet scientific standards is another matter). But another kind of method is in principle possible, which I would not disdain—brain scans. Suppose you want to know whether concept *C* contains concept *F* as a constituent. Your experimental procedure is then as follows: present subjects with words for the two concepts, or possibly instances of them, and see whether the same part of the brain "lights up" in the two experimental conditions. For example, you present "husband" and "married" and see whether there is overlap in the parts of the brain that "light up." If so, you have evidence that *married* is part of *husband*; if not, the two concepts are unrelated, or not constitutively related. I am not saying this would be easy to do, only that it is in principle the kind of neurophysiological evidence that might be brought to bear on questions of conceptual constituency. Suppose you found that whenever the *game* part of the brain lights up, it overlaps with the part that lights up when the concept of *restricted means* is employed: that would confirm Suits's thesis that the latter concept is a necessary condition of the former. The brain correlate of *game* embeds the brain correlate of *restricted means*. And obviously the same could be done with the concepts of knowledge, perception, art, and so on. Here is an experimental way to gauge whether a proposed conceptual analysis is correct; it might supplement the

---

[9] The same is true of almost every other technical term of philosophy that one can think of: "necessary," "contingent," "entailment," "theory," "quantifier," "modal," "utilitarianism," "rigidity," and so on.

deliverances of first-person intuitions. We might be able to decide between Russell and Strawson on definite descriptions by seeing whether the existential quantifier part of the brain is activated when a person understands "the king of France is bald"! That would tell us how the speaker understands the sentence in question—what conceptual resources she brings to bear. Conceptual analysis naturalized! One wonders what Quine would have made of this suggestion—making a science out of "synonymy." Would he accept brain scans as providing an experimental criterion of conceptual containment? In principle, we could test for the analytic-synthetic distinction using this kind of method, because it gives us an empirical criterion for ascriptions of concept identity. Enunciate "husbands are married males" to the subject slowly and see whether the same part of the brain lights up at the end of the sentence as lit up at the beginning; then try the same experiment with "husbands live longer than bachelors." I wouldn't mind betting on how this experiment would turn out (assuming we could eliminate the experimental bugs). I can see the paper title now in the *Journal of Neurophilosophy*: "A Magnetic Resonance Imaging Study of Kant's Analytic-Synthetic Distinction."

Anyone in the current period wishing to defend the analytic-synthetic distinction must contend with the arguments presented in Quine's "Two Dogmas of Empiricism," since it is the dominant source of skepticism about that distinction.[10] There is a slight problem about this procedure, however: there are no arguments—good, bad or indifferent—to that effect in that famous paper (though the page fairly bristles with tendentious rhetoric). There is nothing in there to get one's argumentative teeth into. Quine's reiterated complaint in the paper is that analyticity depends on synonymy, but synonymy is unclear. He looks at various attempts to clarify the notion, finds none of them satisfactory, and declares that the lack of clarity has not been remedied. Curiously, though, at one point he concedes that synonymy does make sense in one special case: "the explicitly conventional introduction of novel notations for purposes of sheer abbreviation. Here the *definiendum* becomes synonymous with the *definiens* simply because it has been created expressly for the purpose of being synonymous with the *definiens*. Here we have a really transparent case of synonymy created by definition; would that all species of synonymy were as intelligible" (26). In this special case, Quine evidently takes synonymy to be perfectly clear, when it results from abbreviation by conventional stipulation. Presumably, then, he would have no complaint about the synonymy of "husband" and "married male" *if* the former term had been explicitly introduced in the past as an abbreviation of the latter, even if the stipulation has long since been forgotten. What if it actually *was* so introduced? On discovering this, would Quine cease his complaints of lack of clarity at least in this case? Can't we imagine a language in which all such linguistic pairs *are* linked by explicit stipulation? Wouldn't that language look and sound just like ours? What if we *now* stipulate that any such pairs in our language, antecedently claimed

---

[10] "Two Dogmas" is reprinted in *From a Logical Point of View*. Page references are in the text.

to be synonymous, shall henceforth be regarded as standing in the abbreviation relation? Would Quine's misgivings be wholly allayed? Consider the pair "avoid" and "shun," commonly regarded as synonyms: Quine finds this synonymy claim obscure (what does he find *not* obscure?). Couldn't we patch things up for him by explicitly stating that the latter is short for the former (by one letter)? That seems a very quick and easy way to resolve his skepticism. Once the stipulation is made, he is evidently prepared to allow that "to shun someone is to avoid him" is analytic, because it is guaranteed by a "transparent" (his word) synonymy. And isn't it really true, as a matter of etymological fact, that such synonymies often exist precisely because of a (possibly tacit) stipulation?[11] It certainly *could* be true.

What about Quine's celebrated confirmation holism? Here the obvious reply is that no defender of analyticity is going to accept that analytic statements face the tribunal of experience at all; the holism applies only to synthetic statements. Quine fudges this by defining analytic statements as "a limiting kind of statement which is vacuously confirmed, *ipso facto*, come what may" (41). But why assume that statements like "husbands are married males" or "to shun someone is to avoid him" face the tribunal of experience at all? That is the very point at issue. It is simply a "dogma of holism" to insist that every statement should be vulnerable to empirical confirmation or disconfirmation (a second dogma of holism is that confirmation has anything to do with meaning). At the conclusion of all this, Quine laconically remarks: "I hope we are now impressed with how stubbornly the distinction between analytic and synthetic has resisted any straightforward drawing" (41). What is remarkable to me (though not impressive) is how stubbornly inattentive he is to Kant's original formulation, which strikes me as a quite "straightforward drawing," though not one that respects behaviorist dogma and positivist revisionism. All he says about Kant's formulation is that "it limits itself to statements of subject-predicate form, and it appeals to a notion of containment which is left at a metaphorical level" (21). The first defect is easily remedied to fit a logical theory more recent than the subject-predicate logic that Kant was working with, such as predicate calculus.[12] The second complaint is not clearly correct as a description, given that the meaning of complex expressions can contain the meanings of their parts (doesn't a conjunction contain each of its conjuncts, non-metaphorically?); and it leaves open the possibility of explaining containment in terms of necessary and sufficient conditions. Certainly, Quine's quick dismissal of Kant's careful classic formulation is quite inadequate as

---

[11] Suppose I make a habit of using "shun" and "avoid" interchangeably, just for purposes of stylistic variation, and that I make this apparent to my hearers: Am I not tacitly stipulating that in my idiolect "shun" and "avoid" are synonyms? There are tacit promises and tacit agreements, so why not tacit undertakings to use words synonymously? Isn't this, in fact, part of regular linguistic practice? If so, stipulated synonymies abound—and Quine apparently has no serious objection to them.

[12] Instead of analyzing "All *F*s are *G*" as a subject-predicate proposition, we analyze it in the familiar form "For all objects *x*, if *Fx* then *Gx*": then instead of saying that the predicate is contained in the subject, we say that the consequent is contained in the antecedent. So that limitation is readily remedied.

serious criticism. The notion that Quine *refutes* Kant in "Two Dogmas" strikes me as sheer fantasy, ideologically motivated.[13]

But there is another way to assess the cogency of Quine's critique, and that is to look at his treatment of paraphrase in *Word and Object*.[14] For the tension between "Two Dogmas" (1951) and *Word and Object* (1960) is unmistakable, despite Quine's sporadic and sketchy attempts to reconcile the two. Turn to Chapter 5, "Regimentation," to find Quine's maturing views on the virtues of paraphrase as a philosophical method. We there read that departures from ordinary language have been recommended as "aids to understanding the referential work of language and clarifying our conceptual scheme" (158). (Isn't the latter exactly what Kant was advocating when he spoke of "explicating" our "conceptions" in order to resolve "confusions"?) Such departures, Quine says, also enable "simplification of theory" (158). What do such departures consist in? They consist in "paraphrasing ordinary language" into "canonical notation" (159). The judge of the paraphrase is to be the speaker himself, because he can "judge outright whether his ends are served by the paraphrase" (159). Let us note parenthetically that the *Oxford English Dictionary* defines "paraphrase" as follows: "express the meaning of (something) using different words, especially to achieve greater clarity." And we soon find Quine availing himself of this common understanding, writing: "S' might indeed naturally enough be spoken of as synonymous with the sentence S'' of semi-ordinary language into which S' mechanically expands according to the general explanations of logical symbols" (160)—where S' is a sentence in canonical notation (logical symbols) and S'' is its rendering into stilted ordinary speech ("every object x is such that x ..." and so on). We are then told, however, that there is no need to speak of synonymy as between the logical formula (or its stilted articulation) and its ordinary language original; the relation between the two is merely that "the particular business that the speaker was on that occasion trying to get on with, with help of S among other things, can be managed well enough to suit him by using S' instead of S'' (160). For "the notion of their being a fixed, explicable, and as yet unexplained meaning in the speaker's mind is gratuitous. The real point is simply that the speaker is the one to judge whether the substitution of S' for S in the present context will forward his present or evolving program of activity to his satisfaction" (160). I pause to observe, bemusedly, that these are curious remarks in a number of ways, but let us press on before subjecting them to criticism. Next we read: "On occasion the useful degree of analysis may, conversely, be such as to cut into a simple word of ordinary language, requiring its paraphrase into a composite term in which other terms are compounded with the help of canonical notation" (160). In other words, a simple expression of ordinary

---

[13] I cannot refrain from noting how astonishing it is to me that people will confidently cite "Two Dogmas" as having decisively refuted the analytic-synthetic distinction, when it is so patently question-begging, obscure, and devoid of cogent argument. I cannot think of a less inherently convincing influential article (except perhaps "Epistemology Naturalized").

[14] Page references to this work appear in the text.

language may be analyzed into a complex expression of logical notation (as "all men are mortal" becomes "every object x is such that if x is a man then x is mortal"—with the former considerably expanded and enriched). The paraphrase discerns more semantic structure in the original than appeared to be there:

Among the useful steps of paraphrase there are some, of course, that prove pretty regularly to work out all right, whatever plausible purposes the inquiry at hand may have. In them, one may in a non-technical spirit speak fairly enough of synonymy, if the claim is recognized as a vague one and a matter of degree. But in the pattest of paraphrasing one courts confusion and obscurity by imagining some absolute synonymy as goal. (161)

Evidently, we may enjoy the benefits of synonymous paraphrase without commitment to synonymy construed as "some absolute synonymy." The reader may blink and rub his eyes at this point. There is apparently good synonymy and there is bad synonymy, and we should embrace the former and "eschew" the latter. Quine goes on to praise the powers of canonical notation: "Each reduction that we make in the variety of constituent constructions needed in building the sentences of science is a simplification in the structure of the inclusive conceptual scheme of science" (161). So canonical paraphrase, which may be regarded as a species of (good) synonymy, enables us to simplify and organize the "conceptual scheme" of science. He concludes: "The quest of a simplest, clearest overall pattern of canonical notation is not to be distinguished from a quest of ultimate categories, a limning of the most general traits of reality" (161). The enterprise of paraphrase, then, has as its goal and result new insight into the nature of reality—the reality referred to by the vernacular sentences that we systematically paraphrase. Having thus resoundingly laid out the motivation for paraphrase and logical analysis, Quine goes on to offer a number of examples of its clarifying power: the handling of generality by means of quantifiers, the use of parentheses, scope notations, Russell's theory of descriptions, the treatment of tense, the recasting of names as predicates, analyses of the notion of an ordered pair. He does not shrink from using the word "analysis" to characterize his paraphrastic activities, though he always insists that no notion of (bad) synonymy is entailed. When addressing the question of when an analysis is a good one (he avoids calling analyses correct or incorrect), he dwells on pragmatic factors: "A paraphrase into canonical notation is good insofar as it tends to meet needs for which the original might be wanted" (182). An analysis is subject only to the test of whether it "fulfills those functions" (259) that were fulfilled by the original. Analyses, paraphrases, synonymies, notational expansions, ideal symbolisms, clarifications of our conceptual scheme, ultimate categories, the speaker's aims—all these are evidently perfectly legitimate notions as far as the Quine of *Word and Object* is concerned.

A number of questions are prompted by these passages. First and foremost: Are they compatible with the rejection of the analytic-synthetic distinction as advocated in "Two Dogmas"? They are not. Here Quine speaks of analysis as something to be judged by the speaker's pragmatic purposes: a statement can record such an analysis, and it will be judged acceptable by criteria that make no reference to empirical confirmation. A paraphrase as such makes no empirical claims: it is a claim about a particular piece of language—to the effect that the paraphrase can serve the purpose of what it paraphrases. In effect, Quine accepts a "paraphrase-synthetic distinction," because a statement of paraphrase is a statement of pragmatic equivalence (in some sense) as between linguistic expressions—it is not a claim about non-linguistic empirical reality.[15] The reason that we accept quantifier notation paraphrases, say, is that this clarifies vernacular sentences and simplifies inference; it is not that the empirical evidence from science has confirmed this notational way of describing the world as superior. Since Quine himself accepts some kinds of synonymy, he would not disagree on principle: *these* synonymies are not just another kind of synthetic sentence, vulnerable to empirical refutation. Holism does not extend to paraphrase. And how *could* paraphrase be confirmed or disconfirmed by our experience of the course of non-linguistic nature? How could discoveries in physics or biology undermine, say, the utility of parentheses in keeping track of scope distinctions? We don't judge analyses by reference to empirical data about non-linguistic reality, and neither does Quine, sensibly enough.

Second: conspicuously absent from Quine's account of paraphrase is any mention of necessary and sufficient conditions for the truth of a statement. It would normally be assumed that if S' is a paraphrase of S then the truth of S' is necessary and sufficient for the truth of S. That is the minimum that would be required. Quine surely believes that vernacular sentences may be true or false, and just as surely thinks the same of sentences in canonical notation; and he also thinks the latter can paraphrase the former: Does he not then believe that the latter are necessary and sufficient for the truth of the former? If not, what use are they as substitutes? The two sentences must at least have the same truth conditions; their truth conditions cannot be simply disconnected. But this truth-conditional relation is not the same as pragmatic equivalence. It is, in fact, much more like the classic notion of analysis. So evidently Quine does believe in the notion of analytic truth in one sense: a biconditional linking the vernacular sentence with the sentence of canonical

---

[15] The logical form of "S' is a paraphrase of S" is evidently the same as "S' is synonymous with S"—that is, a two-place relation between sentences. The relation expressed is thus entirely intra-linguistic—no reference to the world. The former sentence is accepted because (Quine says) S' can serve the same purpose as S for the speaker, not because it is confirmed by empirical data from beyond the speaker. Thus a paraphrastic sentence does not "face the tribunal of experience": it faces only the tribunal of the speaker's purposes, and such criteria as simplification and clarification. It no more faces the tribunal of experience than sentences affirming synonymy do. If that is a defect in synonymy, it is also a defect in paraphrase. Paraphrases clearly play the same role in Quine's overall conceptual scheme as synonymy sentences do for the traditional believer in the analytic-synthetic distinction. In neither case are they touched by confirmation holism; they are not just one more empirical sentence in the total web of belief.

notation that paraphrases it will be true in virtue of the fact that the latter gives necessary and sufficient conditions for the truth of the former. In other words, the two are *truth-conditionally equivalent*. But this is just the classic notion of analysis, and of analytic truth. So Quine accepts a general analytic-synthetic distinction, formulated his way.

Third: Quine clearly needs to find some interesting relation between the paraphrasing sentence and the paraphrased sentence, short of (bad) synonymy—this is why he brings in the idea of serving the same purpose as the original. But why does it serve the same purpose? He had better not say that it does so because it has the same meaning. So sameness of purpose must be divorced from sameness of meaning. But surely then it is hopelessly insufficient as a criterion of good paraphrase: I can achieve a result with one sentence that I can also achieve with another without these sentences standing in the paraphrasing relation. I want to get your attention, so I shout "Hey, you!," but I could have achieved the same result by saying "Excuse me, sir, may I have a word with you?": Is the latter a paraphrase of the former? Or I might wish to insult you and hesitate between calling you a pig and calling you a dog— both would serve my purpose admirably: so is "you are a pig" a good paraphrase of "you are a dog"? Clearly, the relation needs to be much more intimate than merely that of one sentence "meeting the needs" of another for the speaker on a particular occasion: it needs (to beg the question for a moment) to be the relation of *propositional equivalence*. Russell's analysis of descriptive statements aims to capture the proposition expressed by the vernacular sentence; it is not enough that his paraphrase can do the same "business" as the original on some occasion—whatever this means exactly.[16]

Fourth: the idea of serving the same purpose smuggles in a relation of identity between propositional attitudes. Suppose we say that a given paraphrase can fulfill the speaker's intentions in using the original, and this is *why* it counts as a paraphrase. Then we presuppose sameness of intentions: But isn't that one of Quine's taboo equivalence relations? Yet if we try to purge the formulation of such illicit content, then we get only a pallid simulacrum of the intuitive notion of sameness of purpose—presumably, something about the *effect* that utterances of the two sentences have. And now we are back to the problem of insufficiency: two utterances can have the same effect without standing in the paraphrasing relation. Indeed, all utterances have the same effect with respect to *some* effect—such as making the

---

[16] We might well, in a Quinean spirit, quiz Quine (querulously) in the following *ad hominem* manner. What exactly is the definition of the vernacular phrase "manages the same business" that is supposed to hold between a sentence and its canonical paraphrase? The phrase is hardly vouchsafed by science, and seems perilously vague, context-dependent, obscure, and psychologically loaded. How can a sound philosophy of language be built on a notion so nebulous, so poorly understood? Apparently, it can't even be defined in terms of the notion of synonymy! What, too, are the identity conditions of "businesses"? Do we really want to quantify over them, accepting them into our ontology? They seem like "creatures of darkness." We do well to "eschew" them.

hearer's eardrum vibrate. Now every sentence paraphrases every other sentence! Clearly we need a mentalistic notion of purpose to get anything close to the ordinary notion of paraphrase.

Fifth: Quine frequently notes that paraphrases into canonical notation may be revisionary, cleaning up the original, even having entailments the original lacks. He concludes that synonymy is not the goal of analysis (in these cases, anyway). The two statements are clearly *not* synonymous in these cases. Thus he expresses a judgment of *difference* of meaning: he knows the meaning of the original and he knows the meaning of the paraphrase, and he can see that they have different meanings. But how is it possible to make judgments of differences of meaning without being able to judge *identity* of meaning? If differences of meaning can be clear enough to allow for a confident verdict, how can identity of meaning be so unclear as not to allow for rational determination? The two come hand in hand. If antonymy is clear, how can synonymy not be? If *any* relations of meaning admit of rational assessment, then sameness of meaning ought also to admit of it. If Quine can tell that one statement is not synonymous with another, why can't he tell when they are synonymous? The statement "a rich man is not a poor man" is analytically true because "rich" and "poor" are antonyms: Does Quine also think this is a dogma to be discarded? Why pick on synonymy?

I think it is quite apparent what is going on here. Quine is rightly impressed with many of the analyses that have been proposed by philosophers and logicians over the course of the twentieth century. He does not want to junk all this good stuff. But he disbelieves in synonymy and allied semantic notions, officially anyway; he thus (ostensibly) rejects the analytic-synthetic distinction. But how can you keep those wonderful logical analyses while rejecting analytic truth? You have to try to maintain a notion of paraphrase that shuns (synonym: avoids) any notions like synonymy. But that is none too easy a thing to do. The result is a text that seems to vacillate and waver, with many a hollow disclaimer and obscure qualification. In particular, no serious effort is made to explain just how paraphrase can work without the officially taboo notions. In some sense or other, the paraphrase must capture the content of the original in order to *be* a paraphrase, but Quine cannot allow himself to say that outright—so we get obscure gestures in the direction of pragmatic equivalence. Is this meant to be a *theory* of sameness of content or a *rejection* of sameness of content? If a theory, then (1) it needs to be worked out and defended, and (2) it will ground a traditional analytic-synthetic distinction. If a rejection, then with what right does Quine employ the notion of paraphrase ("expressing the meaning of (something) using different words")? Let me put it this way: if you substitute "paraphrase" for "synonymy" throughout "Two Dogmas," you disturb the flow very little. Thus: How are we clearly to *define* "paraphrase"? Can paraphrases be substituted for each other in all contexts *salva veritate*? What is meant by "true by paraphrase alone"? How are paraphrastic statements consistent with confirmation holism? Isn't it very difficult to judge when we have a good paraphrase? Isn't the idea of "managing the same bit of business" as obscure and unscientific as the notion of paraphrase itself, and hence unhelpful as clarification? Isn't it objectionably mentalistic to judge the merits of a proposed paraphrase by reference to what the speaker "had in mind" in using the original statement—his purposes, intentions? How do we settle what these are? Aren't they too removed from publicly observable use? The whole notion of paraphrase is mired in obscurity and dubious associations. We do well to "eschew" it. So a strict adherent of "Two Dogmas" might say in response to the position of Quine in *Word and Object*. The tension between "Two Dogmas" and *Word and Object* arises because you can't have it both ways: you can't embrace the analytic delights of canonical notation while rejecting analytic truth. The analytic-synthetic distinction is actually alive and well and living in *Word and Object*, despite the rhetorical assault it received in "Two Dogmas." The later work is the more mature production, in my view, despite some lingering echoes from the young firebrand of the earlier work. There was nothing in that earlier work to threaten the analytic-synthetic distinction anyway, so Quine could succumb to its attractions once he turned his attention to the virtues of logical paraphrase. Ironically, Quine emerges as an exponent of conceptual analysis, complete with an analytic-synthetic distinction.[17]

---

[17] If you see Quine as a hybrid of Skinnerian behaviorism and Russellian logical analysis, you begin to see the deep tension in his intellectual allegiances: for there are no propositional attitudes to analyze in the Skinnerian scheme. What then are we analyzing? Behaviorism empties mind and language of content, but then the Russellian program loses its footing. Behaviorism destroys the analytic-synthetic distinction, because there is nothing left to analyze (no "judgments" and "beliefs"); but that distinction (with its defining concepts) is required by Russellian analysis—so we need to find some other way to conceive of analysis. Quine's wavering and unstable position on logical paraphrase is the symptom of this irresoluble tension. He is trying, vainly, to Russell his inner Skinner (or skin his Russell).

7 The Whole of Philosophy

The thesis of this book is that philosophy is the a priori search for the essences of things (undertaken in a spirit of play) by means of conceptual analysis. It may reasonably be complained at this point that I have said nothing to justify such a sweeping claim. All I have argued so far is that *one* task of philosophy is the discovery of essences by conceptual analysis—that this is a legitimate enterprise *within* philosophy. I have not produced any defense of the claim that this is *all* that philosophy does or can do. And that claim might well seem exaggerated at best and ludicrous at worst. In this chapter, I shall contend that analysis is indeed the sole occupation of the philosopher, though I will now broaden the conception of analysis somewhat (but not in a way that falsifies any earlier claims). My general intent is to show that this contention does not require any undue narrowing of the domain of philosophy, or any downgrading of its importance; quite the opposite in fact. We simply need a suitably capacious understanding of what conceptual analysis can aspire to be.

The type of analysis so far considered consists in decomposition: we extract the necessary conditions that together suffice for the concept to apply. We identify the constituents of a concept. We unpack the concept. We can do this for "know" as well as for "the." Thus I do not sharply distinguish ascriptions of logical form from classic decompositional analysis (in giving the logical form of general statements, we break the word "all" down into a longer string of words, as in "every object x is such that x...."). Thus we supply necessary and sufficient conditions for the statement we are analyzing, avoiding circularity. We provide an equivalent statement, the parts of which correspond to the underlying parts of the meaning of the statement being analyzed. We are spelling out internal structure, not revealed in the form of the original (which is typically syntactically simple). We can call this "decompositional analysis," because it breaks a composite concept down into its constituent parts. But not every conceptual question of interest to the philosopher has this dismantling character: sometimes we want to know what *kind* of thing a given entity is—what its general nature is. I shall call this "category analysis." In this kind of analysis, we typically employ specialized terms of art, invented or co-opted by philosophers—highly general categories. The following provides an illustrative but incomplete list: mental, physical, abstract, particular, universal, analytic, synthetic, necessary, contingent, a priori, a posteriori, meaningful, nonsensical, categorical, dispositional, objective, subjective, cognitive, non-cognitive, fact, value, teleological, mechanical, natural, non-natural, factive, non-factive, internal, external, deterministic, non-deterministic, substance, event, verifiable, unverifiable, real, unreal, projected, independent, analyzable, primitive. A characteristic philosophical debate will revolve around whether some entity or phenomenon or property or process belongs in one or other of these general categories. The categories typically come in pairs and they define particular doctrines or schools of thought. I need not elaborate examples, since any experienced philosopher will be very familiar with these hardy dichotomies and the doctrines that they encode. Sometimes it is claimed that everything falls into a particular category and nothing into its paired contrary—as it might be, everything is natural and nothing is non-natural. Sometimes the question is just whether a controversial case goes one way or the other—say, whether beliefs are dispositional or categorical, and similarly for sensations. Sometimes a given region of thought is contended to be of one category as opposed to another—for instance, is ethics objective or subjective? What makes these questions distinctively philosophical is that there is no empirical criterion for deciding them—so they are not like the question of whether something is animal, vegetable or mineral, or whether a platypus is a mammal. We are asking a question about essence (or we think we are; see below), but it is general essence—*genus* essence. We can thus ask whether knowledge is a "mental state" or whether pain is a "physical state," and these are not questions of conceptual decomposition in the narrow sense. We can ask whether the property of being red is subjective or objective, while agreeing that it *has* no decompositional analysis. We are asking about what the philosopher would call "metaphysical type/category." This is still a question of conceptual analysis, though, determined by a priori reflection; empirical information will not settle the question.[1]

---

[1] One lesson we can already draw is that conceptual analysis is not committed to the dismantling model, which some find dubious (though not for any convincing reason): there are questions of category analysis that do not involve mereological decomposition. The word "analysis" can be misleading in this broader framework, because of its connotation of breaking a composite entity into its constituent parts; we could just as well speak of conceptual elucidation or explication or articulation or plain conceptual truth. An analogy would be investigating the anatomy of an animal as contrasted with discovering its zoological genus: what is its constituent makeup and what is its general type—its parts versus its general classification. Conceptual dismantling is the anatomy of concepts; category analysis is concerned with taxonomy (groupings, co-classifications).

The positivists would declare such questions meaningless for that very reason—they are not empirically verifiable. So we need to add the category of "category analysis" to the "decompositional analysis" already recognized. It is a distinct variety of analysis, not reducible to the dismantling style of analysis.

Two points should be briefly noted about category analysis. First, unlike decompositional analysis, it employs special philosophical concepts: we can decompositionally analyze "game" and "knowledge" without going beyond our ordinary pre-philosophical concepts, but when we come to ask about metaphysical type, we inevitably lapse into technical terminology (or ordinary terminology used technically). Second, and in consequence, such questions carry a distinct risk of falling into vacuity or confusion or sheer nonsense—of being, in short, pseudo-questions. For the alleged category distinctions might not be well defined or capable of coherent interpretation. I think this about questions concerning whether something is mental, physical, or abstract—since I hold that these alleged category concepts, as they are used by philosophers, are not properly defined (see Chapter 11). Quine thinks that this is true of the analytic-synthetic distinction. Others have questioned the fact-value distinction. Some find the distinction between particular and universal unclear. Almost anyone should find the natural–non-natural distinction problematic. Words of ordinary language have been plucked from their normal context and pressed into special philosophical employment, and it is not clear that their meaning has survived the transition (you can think this without being a Wittgensteinian). The category concepts themselves need to be analyzed and scrutinized to make sure they have real content, before we start wondering how they divide the world up. Philosophy has to be careful and self-critical about the conceptual tools of the trade.

In addition to these two categories of analysis, we need to acknowledge what I shall call "compatibility analysis." As the name suggests, this type of analysis inquires into whether two things are compatible with each other. Sometimes this is far from obvious, and it takes some analysis to decide the question. The classic example is free will and determinism: Are they compatible? It depends on the analysis of the two concepts. It depends, in particular, on what free will *is*—on its nature or essence or what-it-is-to-be. If its nature consists in the agent being able to do otherwise, then we have a prima facie inconsistency with determinism. Again, I need not elaborate. Another example is skepticism: Is knowledge of the external world compatible with the fact that our justifications for belief fall short of absolute certainty? To answer this question, we need to know what the necessary conditions for knowledge are—in particular, whether knowledge requires certainty. It also depends on the nature or analysis of justification. A third example might be whether the motivational force of moral reasons is compatible with the objectivity of such reasons: again, we need to know what the motivational force of reasons consists in, as well as what the objectivity of such reasons involves. Finally, we might wonder whether an object's being transparent is compatible with its being white—and the answer might not be immediately apparent, requiring some further insight into what it is to be transparent and what it is to be white.[2] These kinds of consistency problems are very characteristic of philosophy; they are bound up with "how-possible" questions. How is it possible to be free in a deterministic universe? How is it possible to know in the face of uncertainty? How is it possible to be motivated by something that exists outside you? The answer to each of these questions might be: it is not possible. But the questions demand that we think harder about the analysis of the relevant notions. The questions, in effect, concern relations between essences: whether the essence of one thing is compatible with the essence of the other. Hence we need compatibility analysis, perhaps based on a prior decompositional analysis, or even a category analysis. We might first analyze free will as "the ability to do otherwise" and then ask whether that is compatible with determinism (and this will require that we have a good analysis of determinism). So, we pursue "how-possible" questions by conducting compatibility analysis, and this is a distinct type of analysis. Thus we can include such questions under our general meta-philosophical scheme, but we must extend the types of analysis recognized in order to accommodate them.

We must also include what Strawson calls "connective analysis." Strawson contrasts this with the "dismantling model" and writes: "Let us imagine, instead, the model of an elaborate network, a system, of connected items, concepts, such that the function of each item, each concept, could, from the philosophical point of view, be properly understood only by grasping its connections with the others, its place in the system—perhaps better still, the picture of set of interlocking systems of such a kind" (19).[3] He gives the example of the connection between the concept of knowledge and the concept of sense experience, where neither concept can be understood independently of the other, but where neither reduces to the other. To grasp one concept requires grasping the other, so that one concept is analytically connected to the other, but neither concept is a *component* of the other. Other examples (not given by Strawson) might be the connection between "good" and "right" and also the connection between "law" and "cause." Moore may well be right that no dismantling analysis of *good* can be given—it has no more primitive parts—but it may yet be true that to grasp this concept requires understanding *right* as an attribute of actions; and the same might be true of grasping *right*, with its dependence on *good* as an attribute of states of affairs. Surely it is part of understanding "good"

---

[2] The example comes from Wittgenstein, *Remarks on Color*. I discuss it in *The Subjective View*. Another example would be whether the nature of consciousness is consistent with the possibility that it emerges from the brain, with *its* distinctive nature: could the "subjective" arise coherently from the "objective"? Descartes analyzed the mind as essentially a thinking thing and analyzed body as essentially an extended thing, and he took these to be incompatible essences—no one thing could be both. Materialists have contended, to the contrary, that nothing about the analysis of mind precludes its unification with the body. This is all what I am calling compatibility analysis: whether the concepts of mind and body allow for their harmonious integration or not. (Note that these debates do not proceed by empirical observation of mind or brain.)

[3] Strawson, *Analysis and Metaphysics*. Page reference in the text.

that one appreciates that if a state of affairs is good then one ought *prima facie* to bring it about—that it would be right to do so and wrong not to do so.[4] Similarly, grasping the concept of cause requires understanding that causation exemplifies laws, and grasping the concept of a law requires understanding that laws describe causal sequences: but these two concepts need not be *constituents* of each other. At a very broad level, the concepts *body, space, causation, event,* and *time* might be interdependent and locked together; but no dismantling analysis will find one of these more basic than the others. Or again, one might hold that *red* is a primitive concept, with no compositional analysis, and yet there are conceptual truths about *red* linking it to other concepts, for example, "red is closer to pink than it is to blue." These truths might reasonably be called analytic, in that they record relational conceptual connections revealed by a priori reflection; but they are not analytic in the Kantian "containment" (dismantling) sense. Concepts can be analytically related to other concepts without being mereologically related to them. So we need to add connective analysis to our growing list of types of analysis.

We may as well throw in what I shall label "contrastive analysis." Sometimes we succeed in sharpening or elucidating a concept by indicating what it *contrasts* with. Here we are using a negative condition to articulate a concept: for example, we might explicate what a universal is by saying that it is *not* a particular, or that a value is *not* a fact, or sense is *not* reference, or that immaterial substance is *not* material substance. We take the more obscure term of a pair and we contrast it with what is clearer and antecedently understood. No doubt this is a pretty cheap maneuver, and tends to signal desperation, but it seems to me that it sometimes goes on and can confer content on a notion that is hard to convey. Then our understanding tends to be negative in content—we have little or nothing in the way of positive analysis. If I am asked to explain my concept, I reply sketchily that its opposite partner is such and such. Often the framing thought is that the obscurer notion is *like* the clearer notion, except that it is *not* that other notion: thus sense is like reference in being semantic, but it is *not* reference. Often, too, we can *point* to instances of the clearer notion, whereas that is not possible for the more obscure notion (e.g. value and fact). For the sake of completeness, at least, we may as well add this type of "contrastive analysis," marginal and jejune though it may be. It can certainly be an analytic

---

[4] Moore contended that "good" could not be defined as "productive of the best consequences," because of the open question argument: that is, the concept of goodness does not break down into the concepts expressed by that latter phrase. But this is consistent with allowing that there is *some* conceptual connection here—that in grasping "good" we see that such goods as happiness and knowledge are relevant and indeed crucial. Thus Moore's own utilitarianism can be regarded as conceptually grounded, even though it does not provide some sort of analytic reduction of goodness to consequences. (The same point might be made about right action and duty: we cannot exhaustively analyze the former by means of the latter, but nevertheless there might be a conceptual connection here.) In general, the notion of a web of concepts is not like the notion of a breakdown of concepts. Hence the notion of a conceptual truth is broader than that of a conceptual breakdown.

truth that a given concept contrasts with another concept—being that concept's logical opposite.[5]

Sometimes an analysis is intended to free us of unwanted assumptions or excess baggage, simplifying our ontology. We don't decompose the concept, dissecting out its parts; instead, we replace it with something that is more to our liking. We lose no important truths thereby, but we shrink our ontological commitments, for reasons of economy or suspicion. The classic model is Descartes' analytic geometry, in which the ontology of Euclidian figures is reduced to arithmetic and algebra by use of numerical coordinates; we then solve mathematical problems by means of equations. Here we are not saying that figures are *made* of numbers, or that geometrical concepts *are* arithmetical concepts, but only that we can find a numerical proposition for every geometrical proposition and operate with it instead. Nor are we claiming that this is what people mean by the geometrical sentences. Analytic geometry simplifies by unifying two branches of mathematics into one, allowing a single set of methods to cover both. No such neat example exists in philosophy (isn't that always the way?), but we do have something similar in (for example) phenomenalism, behaviorism, and reductive views of the self and social reality. The first two doctrines, symptomatic of empiricism, seek to explain propositions purportedly about material objects and the mind in terms of sense experiences and episodes of behavior—generally prompted by the supposed "inaccessibility" of the entities being analyzed. The thought is that our ordinary sentences express a content in excess of sound epistemology, so we should replace them with sentences that keep within empiricist bounds: these new sentences act as substitutes, not duplicates—they improve on the original. The second two doctrines proceed from the conviction that selves and nations cannot exist "over and above" mental facts and facts about individuals, respectively. We don't want selves and nations to be irreducible entities that exist in *addition* to mental states and individual people, so we attempt to reduce them to what we already acknowledge to exist at a "lower level." This kind of ameliorative analysis is aptly described as "reductive," because it spares us ontology that we would be happy without. It is to some extent revisionary, not merely descriptive, because it doesn't merely attempt to spell out our ordinary concept; it recasts our ordinary way of talking in a new conceptual framework. It exhibits ontological preference, not merely neutral articulation. But the line between reductive analysis and dismantling analysis can be blurred, since it is not always clear what the commitments of the *definiendum* concept are. Some would say that our ordinary psychological concepts are *already* behaviorally understood, and Berkeley thinks he is merely spelling out what the "vulgar" spontaneously think about the so-called material world. On the other hand, those who think that ordinary thought is in error

---

[5] What is Wittgenstein's notion of *showing* in the *Tractatus*? It is what *cannot* be said—what contrasts with the class of things that can be verbally stated. That is contrastive analysis at its purest (and most blatant).

about reality will regard their analyses as rectifying our naïve conceptions, by offering something less suspect but equally effective. What is important, from the present point of view, is that reductive analysis is another form that analysis can take, and that it introduces a revisionary theme into the picture. Not all analysis seeks modestly to bring to light what is already implicit in ordinary thought.[6]

And here we may encounter another potential objection to conceptual analysis. For some may quarrel with what they perceive to be the *quietism* of conceptual analysis—its merely descriptive and conservative quality. Should philosophy be concerned only to put into clearer language what we already think? What about the idea of criticizing what we think? What about replacing what we think with something better? This, again, is a reasonable qualm. But there are two responses to it. The first is that analysis is not confined to the terms and concepts of ordinary talk and thought; it also covers the conceptual apparatus of science and other specialized subjects (law, aesthetics, history). The full range of concepts marshaled in physics, biology, and psychology are also available for analysis, of all the varieties mentioned so far. And these concepts are often pitted against ordinary concepts (consider the concepts of space, time, matter, and causality embedded in current physics). Thus conceptual analysis can be as revisionary as the science it analyzes; it is not confined to obsolete common sense. It is quite consistent to be a committed conceptual analyst and entirely to reject common sense (though I do not myself commend such iconoclasm). Second, much standard analysis is revisionary in intent and upshot: it seeks to correct and improve, not merely to record and describe. Quantifier notation tries to straighten out the confusing ways that we express multiple generality. Conflations of word and object are cleared up by rigorous attention to use and mention (sometimes with specially invented devices of quotation). Russell's theory of descriptions deplores the ordinary grammar of statements containing "the," ruthlessly recasting them into a new form. Suits's definition of games detects error and sloppiness in what we habitually *call* games. Analysis is often corrective and revisionary; indeed, clarification itself is a kind of revision—replacing unclear thoughts with clear ones. Compatibility analysis can lead us to discover inconsistencies in our ordinary thought, with the result that important parts of our conceptual scheme are

---

[6] Often the form of the reductive analysis consists in preserving some of the content of the original concept and ditching the rest—one part deemed acceptable, the other suspect. For example, the reductive functionalist might hold that the functional content of psychological concepts is worth preserving, but the "qualia" component needs to be jettisoned. Both aspects are admitted to belong to the ordinary concept, but only one of them meets a particular standard of respectability. The functionalist analysis is thus revisionary of the ordinary concept. (Much the same might be said of the phenomenalist analysis of material object sentences.) We can thus claim to be analyzing our ordinary concept as well as taking a critical attitude toward it—keeping the good, cutting out the bad. This might be called "subtractive analysis." In principle, someone might adopt a subtractive analysis of knowledge, on the grounds (say) that the notion of truth is suspect, holding that knowledge is non-fluky *useful* belief or some such. Of course, if the subtraction becomes too extreme, we sacrifice our right to the original concept.

put under pressure and may have to be abandoned—such as free will or knowledge of the external world. Conceptual analysis is not necessarily conservative and uncritical. It is certainly not uncritical of *other* analysis: analysts fight fiercely among themselves. Accordingly, we must make room for "revisionary analysis" alongside "descriptive analysis," analogously to Strawson's revisionary and descriptive metaphysics.[7] Indeed, there is no sharp line between the two distinctions, since revisionary analysis can give rise to revisionary metaphysics—as with Berkeley's analysis of "there is a table in front of me" (despite Berkeley's own professed conservatism). And, to go back to the first point, an analysis of the concepts used in quantum theory, say, might well lead to a profoundly revisionary attitude toward our commonsense view of the physical world. The conceptual analyst can be a revolutionary, too. In fact, we probably do well to allow for a spectrum of revisionism, and sub-varieties of it, according to the type and depth of the revision being proposed: some revision is quite minor (quantifier notation), but some is pretty extreme (panpsychism, four-dimensionalism).[8]

The general lesson, from a meta-philosophical perspective, is that there is more to conceptual analysis than meets the eye. There are more ways in which we can get at concepts (and hence reality) than by dismantling them (worthy as that enterprise is). Analysis can take many forms and serve many purposes. Once these forms are assembled, the scope of analysis emerges as large and ambitious. In fact, I cannot think of an area of philosophy left uncovered once all the forms of analysis have been enumerated: metaphysics, epistemology, ethics, philosophy of mind, language, logic, art, mathematics, physics, biology, law, politics. In all these areas, we engage in one kind of analysis or another, often using several kinds simultaneously, in an effort to discover the essence of things. We don't do any experiments (though we are happy to analyze the results of other people's experiments and bring them to bear on contentious issues). We recline in our armchairs, reflecting, introspecting, often conversing with colleagues in other armchairs, enjoying lively discussions, laboring to discover the what-it-is-to-be of things—though we may well be fresh from a scientist's lab or recently steeped in history or art or legal proceedings. Our job is to analyze what we know—to organize and order this knowledge, simplify and systematize, describe and revise, dismantle and connect, resolve and repudiate, create and

---

[7] Strawson, *Individuals*.

[8] In more extreme cases, it is natural to speak of an "interpretation," not an "analysis": we are imposing something on our discourse, not merely exposing what is already present (the logical notion of an *interpretation* is apt here). Thus we can have a four-dimensionalist interpretation of our talk about physical objects and time, and a panpsychist interpretation of particle physics. Russell always insisted on an interpretation of talk about continuant particulars in terms of sequences of events, because of his horror at the old notion of substance. These kinds of proposals are still exercises in conceptual inquiry, substituting one sort of ontology for another, for reasons of economy or metaphysical suspicion. We might call them "interpretative analyses." Their characteristic form is: it is a conceptual truth that we can preserve such and such aspects of the original discourse using only an ontology consisting of so and so things.

destroy. We are not just twiddling our thumbs as we wait for fickle intuition to strike. Our efforts are difficult and lengthy, surprising and sometimes disturbing, fraught with hope and disappointment, rigorous and convoluted. We cover a vast range of topics, as best we can, with nothing off limits. But, if I am right, our method is always conceptual analysis, broadly construed. I therefore boldly conjecture that conceptual analysis covers the *whole* of philosophy—and this should not seem surprising once we take the full measure of that method and not fixate on narrow paradigms. Every question in philosophy is a question of conceptual analysis in the end. Philosophy is the theory of reality *from a conceptual point of view*. It is the study of what there is from the perspective of our elaborate and ramified system of concepts, old and new, simple and complex, opaque and transparent. There is nothing parochial or blink-ered about a study so conceived. It is merely to note the difference between the dis-cipline of philosophy and other disciplines. As physics differs from geography, as psychology differs from biology, so philosophy differs from all these disciplines.[9]

But am I not privileging one style of philosophy over all other styles? Am I not asserting that analytical philosophy is the only kind? And isn't that restrictive and chauvinist, favoring one particular tradition over all others? I am asserting that all philosophy is analytical philosophy, but I am not asserting that all analytical philos-ophy is "analytical philosophy." I mean my conception to be maximally inclusive, as I have been at pains to make clear. I certainly include Plato and Aristotle; indeed, they are my exemplars, my analytical heroes. Plato sought definitions and analyzed the world into particulars and universals, always distinguishing and dividing: he asked what is virtue, knowledge, the ideal political state. Aristotle seeks the analysis of *de re* essence, and a hierarchical ordering of all reality based on what-it-is-to-be: the essence of species, the four types of cause, the nature of the virtues, and so on. Aristotle distinguishes the inquiry into being *qua* arena of change and motion (which is physics) from the inquiry into being *qua* being, that is, what makes a being the being it is (which is philosophy proper—metaphysics).[10] Thus he delineates

[9] What philosophy is not is every discipline but in some watered down or etiolated fashion. It is not a less rigorous way of doing what the other disciplines do. The whole idea that philosophy asks the same sorts of questions as science but in a sloppier way, awaiting replacement when the science matures, is woefully wide of the mark. Philosophers are not like amateur scientists, but lacking in labs and grants, a sort of intellectual Everyman, neither one thing nor the other. They are narrow specialists in their way, rigorous within their domain, working in a very specific manner: their con-cern is with the analysis of concepts (analyzing reality conceptually). They may roam widely in their objects of interest, but they are confined in their *modus operandi*—they are experts in a single field, i.e., the field of concepts. A philosopher is no more a physicist or a psychologist or a geographer than those three are each other. She takes an interest in those fields, to be sure, but *her* field is orthogonal to theirs: their field is empirical investigation of reality; her field is conceptual investigation of reality. The philosopher is not some sort of all-purpose, free-ranging, ill-equipped promiscuous seeker after knowledge of all kinds; the philosopher is a tunnel-visioned specialist, like everyone else. How could she not be?

[10] Aristotle's "being *qua*..." well captures the identity of subject matter, but variety of interest, that characterizes the different disciplines. The physicist abstracts away from many aspects of his subject matter, being interested only in change and motion (whether the object is animate or

philosophy as the search for intrinsic essence. That is more or less the conception of philosophy that I am advocating. I see both Plato and Aristotle as arch analytical philosophers: they break things down, look for common patterns, and provide necessary and sufficient conditions. And, as I explained in Chapter 1, subsequent philosophers, treading in their footsteps, also took the analytical path (there was no "analytical turn"), up to the empiricists and rationalists of the seventeenth and eighteenth centuries. Locke and Hume analyzed ideas, assuming an analytic-synthetic distinction (though not so naming it); and Leibniz and Descartes also analyzed and defined, assuming a distinction between "truths of reason" and "truths of fact." Kant kept on in the same vein, analyzing Newtonian science and the basic categories of human thought, insisting firmly on the analytic-synthetic distinction. He analyzes the faculties of the mind and the fundamental structure of reality, all at an a priori level. The period of Frege, Russell, Wittgenstein, Moore, Carnap, Quine, Strawson, Ryle, Davidson, Kripke, and countless others is all analytical philosophy all the time—despite some minor skirmishes over what approach to analysis might be the most fruitful (Austin is as much an analyst as Russell). And so it continues to the present day: we are still analyzing.

But what about so-called Continental Philosophy—is that conceptual analysis? Yes it is: Hegel, Husserl, Heidegger, Sartre, even Nietzsche, are all conceptual analysts in my capacious sense (they had better be, or they aren't doing philosophy). For they are all concerned with the discovery of essence a priori. Speaking very roughly, Hegel is analyzing the course of history (thesis, antithesis, synthesis), tracking the development of the World Spirit; Husserl is analyzing intentionality (using "phenomenological intuition" to "intuit essences"); Heidegger is analyzing *Dasein* (finding being, time, and instrumentality); Sartre is analyzing consciousness and freedom (the being of consciousness is defined as Nothingness); Nietzsche is analyzing conventional morality (finding it to be guilty of "slave morality" and suggesting a revised morality). They are all claiming that a certain phenomenon has a particular essence or nature, and they arrive at their position by reflection on knowledge already possessed. Hegel is not a historian, Husserl is not an empirical psychologist, Heidegger is not an anthropologist, Sartre is not a psychiatrist (despite his concern with *angst*), Nietzsche is not a biblical scholar or religious historian. All these philosophers proceed at a meta-level, examining our given conceptual scheme, trying to grasp the general character of some particular discourse or domain. Sartre's existential philosophy might be thought furthest away from other analytical philosophers of other

_____

inanimate is irrelevant—only mass and other physical quantities count). The psychologist is not interested in the ballistic or gravitational properties of his objects of study. The philosopher focuses on the a priori essence of his objects of interest—of games, knowledge, art, causality, necessity, identity, persons, and so on. But this difference of interest does not signify a retreat from being, i.e., from reality as such—as if language (or even thought) had abruptly replaced reality as his focus and passion. To paraphrase Aristotle: philosophy is concerned with the what-it-is-to-be of the what is—with being *qua* being.

persuasions, because of his practical and political engagements. But actually nothing could be further from the truth (and I know quite a bit about Sartre, unlike some of the others sketchily mentioned): Sartre's early work on the imagination is a model of analytical philosophy (quite close to Wittgenstein); he has an abstract philosophical analysis of the emotions; and his masterwork *Being and Nothingness* is a prolonged attempt to work out the significance of his basic thesis that the essence of consciousness is nothingness. First, he analyzes consciousness in terms of intentionality, and then he argues that intentionality necessarily involves a positing of its object as what it is *not*—so consciousness never contains in its own being what it posits in intentionality. Consciousness is analyzed by Sartre as pure intentional positing. This is straightforward analytical philosophy, despite the exotic idiom (to philosophers raised in a different tradition). Sartre may be using a different style of conceptual analysis from that employed by (say) Frege and Austin (who differ between themselves too), but he is using recognizably the same analytic approach: he is trying to uncover the essence of consciousness as it is contained in our ordinary conception of consciousness—consciousness *as such*. His approach is explicative, to use Kant's term, not augmentative. There is nothing to prevent Sartre from stating his central thesis in the familiar biconditional form: x is consciousness iff x is a being such that it is what it is not and it is not what it is (i.e., there is no more to it than what it posits in intentionality, and yet it is not identical to what is so posited). You may not find this analysis easy to understand, or you may dissent from it, but it surely is an analysis—an a priori account of essence. It is not a bit like saying, "there is no consciousness on Mars" or "consciousness in humans depends on the reticular formation" (which are plain synthetic propositions). All the "continental" philosophers cited are concerned to enunciate necessities (though they may not say as much)—that is, constitutive essences, not just accidental facts. Hegel is telling us what history necessarily is, explicating its essential dynamic, not just recording some contingent fact of history; and the same for the others. Seeking necessity is the mark of the conceptual analyst—aiming for the very heart of the thing in question. By this criterion, all the philosophers cited are rightly designated as conceptual analysts.[11] The only people regularly labeled "philosophers" who are not philosophers by my criterion are those twinkly individuals who offer sage advice, in vague and general terms, about such practical matters as human relationships, health tips, and "positive

[11] It might be asked whether the philosophers cited are not better characterized as seeking *theories* rather than *analyses*—as with Hegel's dialectical theory of history. But this distinction is not a deep one. Frege and Russell proposed a "theory" of number, as Wittgenstein proposed a picture "theory" of meaning, as Tarski proposed a "theory" of truth. In all these cases, however, we can happily substitute "analysis" for "theory": the word "theory" merely suggests a speculative quality, not a fundamentally different kind of project. In each case we have a conceptually driven "account" of some particular object of interest—number, meaning, truth. Thus we also speak of the "redundancy theory" of truth or the "correspondence theory," but that is just a stylistic variant on "analysis." Certainly, it would be a mistake to think that the emphasis on analysis precludes the search for philosophical "theories": but they would be *philosophical* theories, not empirical scientific theories. (Of course, there is also a good deal of scientific "analysis.")

thinking." I might wax "philosophical" about my life hitherto, bemoaning my laziness and fecklessness, undertaking to mend my ways, but I am not thereby a philosopher in the sense defined here—an a priori seeker after essences by means of
conceptual analysis. But I take it that this is a desirable result, since it is only by
courtesy that such ruminators are styled "philosophers." The natural kind *philosopher* includes the central figures mentioned in this book, but not just anyone who in
ordinary speech is *called* a philosopher. The a priori essence of the philosopher,
arrived at by conceptual analysis, is someone who searches for the a priori essence of
things by conceptual analysis. (This book is a conceptual analysis of the concept *philosopher*.)[12] It seems to me that this definition includes all the right people and
excludes the wrong people (such as barroom ramblers and maudlin motto makers).
Rightly seen, "analytical philosopher" is a pleonasm. Necessarily, there is no other
kind of philosopher. I might even say that "philosopher" *means* "conceptual analyst,"
since that expresses my analysis of what a philosopher is: the sentence "a philosopher
is a conceptual analyst" is *analytic*.

Distinctions are very important in philosophy. Philosophical ability largely consists in the ability to make distinctions. But distinctions are the bread and butter of
conceptual analysis; they are what "intuitions" are all about. To see that knowledge
is not just true belief, you have to be able to *distinguish* situations in which someone
has knowledge from situations in which she has mere true belief. We arrive at such
distinctions by doing analysis, particularly by considering possible cases: we ask
whether it is *conceivable* to have one thing without the other. Descartes sought clear
and *distinct* ideas, and ideas are seen to be distinct by pulling them apart: the idea of
knowledge is distinct from the idea of true belief because we can conceive of cases in
which the latter idea is instantiated but the former idea is not. As Hume said, what is

[12] As the philosopher has an essence, so the geographer has an essence—her essence is to seek
knowledge of the layout of land and sea. So also the physicist has an essence—to discover and formulate the laws governing the motion of bodies. And so on. Meta-philosophy is, in effect, the inquiry
into the essence of the philosopher: what the philosopher is by definition, in his core, constitutively.
His a priori essence, I claim, is to seek a priori essence—but the a priori essence of other inquirers is
not to seek a priori essence. The a priori essence of the philosopher defines him, makes him what he
is. He is not lacking in essence, a kind of intellectual odd-job man, a jack-of-all-trades, now a physicist, now a psychologist (but without the specialized training and expertise). This is why I say that
"analytical philosopher" is a pleonasm—as "empirical philosopher" is an oxymoron. The latter
phrase is like "a priori geographer" or "concrete mathematician." But the associations of "analytical"
are by now so strong that this claim is apt to seem like a willful misuse of language, and I risk alien-
ating my reader by appearing extremist. I could say instead that "explicative philosopher" is a pleonasm or "elucidatory philosopher": that makes the inclusion of the Continentals less
artificial-sounding. According to the *OED*, the word "analysis" comes from a Greek word meaning
"unloose," and "explicate" derives from a Latin word meaning "unfold." These are suggestive associations: the image is that of something tightly packed or wrapped, which then becomes shaken loose
or opened up. The jammed together and folded up is separated out and expanded, so that the air can
get in and the darkness exposed to the light of day. The concept becomes less condensed, less tightly
wound, as its inner being is revealed in an amplified form. The conceptual analyst loosens, unpacks,
unfolds, prizes apart. He unfurls the coiled, eases into the hidden interior. And he does it by pure
thought.

distinct is what can be conceived apart. But distinctions are not always self-evident; sometimes they are hard to perceive. A potent source of philosophical error is failure to see distinctions. (I don't think this has much to do with ordinary language being misleading; it simply comes from the actual *similarity* of two ideas or their close connection). Progress in philosophy often results from making new distinctions, the failure to see which has snarled up previous efforts. Everyone has their favorites, but the following would appear on many lists: the use-mention distinction, the type-token distinction, the implication-implicature distinction, the name-quantifier distinction, the fact-value distinction, the analytic-synthetic distinction. To my mind, all of these hard-won distinctions are pure gold; and all result from careful patient analysis of the relevant concepts. Thus Grice taught us that the conversational appropriateness of a remark is neither necessary nor sufficient for its truth (these two things have different essences or analyses). It is neither necessary nor sufficient for using a word that one mentions it (again, different essences). We should not confuse types with tokens because it is in the nature of types to be general and to recur, while tokens are localized, fleeting, and unrepeatable. If we confuse analytic and synthetic statements, we will not see that some statements can be true by definition alone; we may then mistakenly suppose that *all* experience confirms them. It is conceptual analysis that yields these priceless distinctions—the sharp tools of the philosophical trade. That there are these distinctions is not a discovery of science or lexicography; they result from conceptual insight, the teasing apart of ideas easily conflated. To suppose that conceptual investigation reveals nothing of intellectual value would be to consign these distinctions to the scrap heap. But, in fact, honing one's analytic skills and training in the appreciation of distinctions are vital to philosophical competence. All philosophy depends upon the appreciation of distinctions, no matter what the school or style; so all philosophy requires skill in conceptual analysis. Indeed, the seeing of conceptual distinctions *is* a type of conceptual analysis.

It used to be said, in the heyday of "linguistic philosophy," that all philosophy is really *logic*, since it is concerned with the logical analysis of language. Wittgenstein proclaimed, in much the same spirit, that all philosophy is really "grammar." Does anything survive of these sentiments in a conception of philosophy like the one presented here? Certainly, I reject the notion that philosophy is about language, or even *about* concepts (as contrasted with reality), but I nevertheless take it to consist in conceptual analysis (analyzing things conceptually). And, in fact, I do think it is not false to characterize philosophy as logic, as long as "logic" is properly understood. For I think that philosophy is concerned above all with *entailments*, this being what necessary and sufficient conditions amount to. It is concerned, that is, with conceptual connections (or connections conceptually revealed). It is not concerned to discover nomological connections or other empirical connections (like physics, history, geography, and so on). So it is a species of logic, widely construed. We might even call philosophy "the logic of concepts" and violate no historical or semantic precedent (though we might court misunderstanding). Clearly, the thought here is not to reduce philosophy to one or other of the current logical systems, as it might be first order predicate calculus; that would be preposterously narrow. But if logic is to include all types of entailment, from the decompositional to the connective, then I do not demur from the label "the logic of concepts." The logic of concepts, in the intended sense, is not to be distinguished from the a priori search for essences—investigating the world from a conceptual point of view. Here I agree with the spirit of Quine's famous remark: "The quest of a simplest, clearest overall pattern of canonical notation is not to be distinguished from a quest of ultimate categories, a limning of the most general traits of reality" (161)[13]—except I would prefer to speak of a quest for the logical structure of our conceptual scheme and of a limning of the essences that compose reality. And, in the same spirit, I would insist that logic is not to be distinguished from ontology, in the sense that to analyze a concept is to engage in a specific ontological inquiry—discovering the nature of the thing being analyzed. So all philosophy is both logic *and* ontology, with nothing to separate them: finding out what something is by means of tracing out entailments and other conceptual links—knowledge, perception, games, art, goodness, free will, consciousness, and so on. In a clear sense, then, logic and ontology are jointly the most basic part of philosophy—and these together give us metaphysics. Even in ethics and aesthetics, we are doing logic and ontology—analysis and essence. We want to know (say) what right action is, and we establish this by analyzing the concept of right action (which involves thinking systematically about the class of right actions). Thus we may arrive, for example, at consequentialist or deontological theories (analyses) of right action. We are therefore simultaneously engaging in logic and ontology. That activity, I contend, is the whole of philosophy. Philosophy is "the logic of concepts," which is to say a priori ontology.[14]

---

[13] From *Word and Object*.

[14] It is important to look beyond the labels here and fix on the underlying meaning. The labels are technical inventions aimed at capturing certain general features of intellectual inquiry. Words like "logic" and "ontology" and "analysis" occur in some philosophical traditions more than others, and so they tend to connote specific aspects of those traditions. But the underlying traits they are used to denote can be common to many traditions, though not always so labeled. This is why we can describe a phenomenologist as interested in the "logic of concepts," so long as we interpret that phrase as it is intended and not get hung up on provincial associations. Sartre speaks of "immediate structures of the for-itself" and tries to articulate what these are: he is actually inquiring into the "logic of concepts," but he doesn't describe his activities that way. He is concerned with what is entailed by the very idea of consciousness—the essence of consciousness as we conceive it. So my advice is to try to see beyond the labels and to focus on the underlying features—the fundamental divisions and contrasts within the entire field of intellectual inquiry. Then the affinities will emerge, though initially disguised by style and vocabulary. For a penetrating examination of the deep commonalities between so-called analytic philosophy and Continental philosophy, see Amie Thomasson's "Phenomenology and the Development of Analytic Philosophy" and other works.

8 The Sense of Names

Now we must descend from the heady heights of meta-philosophy to the low slopes (I will not say "gutter") of proper names. But our eyes will be kept on the cloud-encircled peaks, even as we labor in the scrub of the lowlands. For names offer one of the strongest challenges against the position taken in this book, both in themselves and in the general moral that they seem to imply. In the old days, proper names were taken to express descriptive concepts: we could analyze a name by means of a definite description. Thus we could write down something of the form: x is a iff x is the F, where "a" is a name of x and "F" is a predicate that only x satisfies. For example, someone is Bertrand Russell if and only if he invented the description theory of names (assuming Russell uniquely did so). In other words, "Bertrand Russell" expresses the same concept as "the inventor of the description theory of names." But this theory has come under sustained attack, and many have become convinced that names have no such analysis; instead, they are to be regarded as semantic primitives, simply denoting their bearer. They have no analysis, no conceptual complexity, and no implicit content. Yet they refer to things that are by no means ontologically simple—complex human beings, in fact. So there need be no reflection at the level of meaning and thought of complexity in the object of reference. A word (and its associated concept) can be a simple label of a complex entity; there is nothing conceptually present here to dismantle. But if this is taken as a model for language in general (and the extension of the point to natural kind terms encouraged the supposition), then words can label entities without any complex conceptual structure coming between the two. Predicates can simply *name* kinds without their meanings having any internal structure; and if the meanings lack structure, then the associated concepts do too. Every (syntactically simple) predicate might be a mere name of a kind or property that conveys no underlying conceptual complexity—a semantic primitive. Thus, on this model, no predicate has an analysis, in the classic sense. That is the tempting generalization that may be derived from the demise of the description theory of names. If names can refer without having any analysis, why can't other syntactically simple terms do the same? Problems in devising an analysis can then be easily attributed to the fact that the word in question is really name-like—a device of "direct reference." Someone impressed by Wittgenstein's position on "game" might accordingly conclude that "game" is just a name for a type of activity that has no underlying analysis; it is a semantic primitive. The words "knowledge" or "good" might be natural kind terms that have no a priori necessary and sufficient conditions—just like "water" and "tiger." There is no analytically equivalent sentence that can be substituted for sentences containing these words, just as sentences containing proper names are not equivalent to sentences containing definite descriptions. Thus we arrive at a "Millian" theory of meaning and concepts in general: all (syntactically simple) words are just unanalyzable labels for objects or kinds. Nothing has an analysis. To suppose otherwise is to hold a "description theory of meaning," but that theory has been refuted for its most favored case, that is, ordinary proper names. Instead, we should hold something like a "causal theory of meaning": terms refer to objects and kinds via causal links between their use and those objects and kinds. For instance, "game" refers to certain activities because it is causally linked to those activities and not others; it does not refer to them by being synonymous with a complex description that is satisfied by all and only games—as it might be, "the rule-governed activity that consists in using restricted means to achieve prelusory goals." It is not that a speaker refers to games with "game" because he has such a description "in mind" and all and only games satisfy it; he does so because of certain causal-historical connections with actual games or with other speakers who refer to games. The name-bearer model is now the paradigm of reference and meaning, and names have no analysis—they are just empty labels, mere tags. The general project of conceptual analysis is therefore misguided as a matter of deep semantic principle. Meaning something just doesn't work that way.

I daresay that some philosophers have been seduced by such a line of thought, and it does admittedly have a certain tinny appeal. But the more cautious and astute investigators have recognized that the situation is more problematic: for the "Millian" theory of names runs into well-known and intractable problems, namely, the problems of existence and identity that so troubled Frege and Russell.[1] I shall not rehearse

---

[1] Kripke, in *Naming and Necessity*, does not explicitly endorse the "Millian" theory of names, noting the difficulties raised by identity and existence statements; he is rightly cautious. However, he clearly rejects the description theory and is strongly attracted by the "Millian" theory.

this familiar story, merely noting that no convincing solution to these problems from within a "Millian" framework has ever been produced. So we are faced with a nasty dilemma: the description theory looks to have been refuted, but only it can solve the problems of existence and identity that plague "direct reference" theories. So what are we to do? Should we conclude that reference by names never takes place at all—that names of objects are impossible? But don't we use names every day? Don't most of us *have* a name? We cannot just casually drop the description theory and carry merrily along our way, because the problems for the alternative theory are so severe. Maybe, then, we should retrace our steps and try to determine whether the objections to the description theory are as powerful as they have been cracked up to be. Could it be that another version of the description theory can evade those objections?[2] That is the line I shall pursue in this chapter. My point so far has been that the stakes are high and the presumption in favor of the description theory strong. Everything would be just so much easier if proper names turned out to have a descriptive analysis after all.

Suppose we try to define a name "a" by means of a description "the F" where the description records a famous deed performed by a or a well-known fact about a. Then we immediately run into trouble stemming from the rigidity of "a": in worlds in which someone else b performed that deed or participated in that fact, we shall have to say that "a" denotes b. For example, if "Plato" means the same as "the inventor of the theory of Forms," then in a world in which Thales invented the theory of Forms, "Plato" must refer to Thales. But it doesn't, referring rigidly to Plato. The problem is obvious: we have picked on a contingent property of Plato and have tried to elevate it into the definition of "Plato." The property, being contingent, is neither necessary nor sufficient for being Plato: he could exist without inventing the theory of Forms, and someone could be the inventor of that theory without being Plato. You can't get rigidity out of contingency. Compare trying to define "knowledge" as "the trait most prized by Socrates" or defining "game" as "the most popular leisure activity in America." Suppose these descriptions are in fact true of knowledge and games, so that in the actual world they tie the reference down in the right way. But now consider possible worlds in which the associated properties are differently distributed: a world in which Socrates is a very different kind of man and prizes drunkenness above all else, and a world in which TV watching is the most popular leisure activity in America. Then with respect to these

---

[2] Kripke leaves the door open for such a possibility, though he does not pursue it, in note 38, page 88, of *Naming and Necessity*: if any version of the description theory is defensible, it "must be one of a completely different sort from that supposed by Frege, Russell, Searle, Strawson and other advocates of the description theory." I think he is right to say this, and the theory I propose in this chapter is of a completely different sort—though still a description theory. Perhaps Kripke senses that there may yet be life in the description theory, despite the inadequacies in the versions heretofore presented. As he also remarks, the description theory can seem well nigh inevitable in *some* form.

worlds, "knowledge" refers to drunkenness and "game (playing)" refers to TV watching—which is absurd. The trouble is obvious: we have tried to define knowledge and games in terms of contingent properties, and so the rigidity of the corresponding terms cannot be respected. And why on earth would anybody try to do anything so silly? You need to define knowledge and games by means of their essential constitutive properties—their necessary and sufficient conditions—not by merely accidental facts about them. What kind of *definition* would that be? At most, it determines the right reference in the actual circumstances: but that is hardly an *analysis* of the concept of knowledge or a game. Analyses provide essences. Well-known facts about things do not constitute necessary and sufficient conditions for being those things, so it is hopeless to define the corresponding terms by reference to such facts. This, surely, is painfully obvious, excruciatingly so. But that is exactly what the classical description theory criticized by Kripke and others attempts to do: it picks a famous deed or well-known fact and uses that to define a person's name. The result is a complete failure to handle counterfactual situations correctly—predictably enough. What we need is a genuinely necessary and sufficient condition for being the person in question, so that in any world, whoever satisfies that condition will be that person. We need, in short, an individual essence—just as we need a kind essence for "knowledge" and "game." If we don't have that for names, the description theory doesn't stand a *chance* of working—it is disqualified before it even gets out of the blocks. It is a complete non-starter.

Historically, it is curious that the inventors of the description theory—Frege and Russell—should have designed their theory so perfectly in order to engineer its inadequacy. For both philosophers are well aware of the rigorous standards set by a search for analysis. Neither would have dreamed of defining "two" to mean "the number of cats owned by so-and-so," even if so-and-so does in fact own two cats: first, that is no kind of analytic definition of a number word; second, it runs into trouble in worlds where so-and-so has no cats or has three (the rigidity of "two"). It takes something a lot more stringent and penetrating to *define* a proper name of a number! A description like "the class of all couples" is the kind of thing we need. So why were these two great philosophers so cavalier about defining names of people, using only contingent empirical facts about people in the definition of their names? That obviously wasn't going to fly. If they had thought harder about what it takes to define a term, they might not have come up with anything as vulnerable as the "famous deeds" theory of names. Famous deeds may redound to a man's credit, but they hardly define his essence—his what-it-is-to-be. People don't *necessarily* do what makes them most famous.

How do we remedy the early theorists' evident oversight? The answer is obvious: we construct a proper definition of the relevant concepts, observing the usual standards of correctness. The relevant concepts here are what are often called "individual concepts"—concepts of individuals, such as the concept *Plato*. This kind of concept applies uniquely to a particular person, so what we need is an analysis of persons specialized to this one case. We need, in other words, an *analysis of personal identity*—necessary and sufficient conditions for being a particular person. And where do we look for such an analysis? Why, the branch of philosophy concerned with personal identity, obviously. In other words, the meaning of "Plato" is to be given in terms of the correct analysis of personal identity as applied to Plato. That is where we *should* have been looking all along, not at mere famous deeds or well-known facts. The case is no different in principle from the case of "knowledge" and "game" (or "husband" for that matter: you can't *define* this word by use of the predicate "person whose marital status is the same as that of Barack Obama"). In the literature of the theory of personal identity, as everyone knows, we find a number of different suggestions about what constitutes a person: her body, her brain, her memories, her character, her individual consciousness. Thus Cleopatra might be identified with a particular biological entity (there are variants of this type of theory), or she might be individuated by her memories (whoever has these memories must be Cleopatra), or she might simply be a particular center of consciousness (an irreducible mental subject). Considering the question from a first-person perspective, I might formulate these theories as follows: either I am *this body* or *this brain* or I am the bearer of *these memories* or I am identical to *this consciousness*. I use a demonstrative plus a sortal term to pick out what I take to be the essence of myself as a person. Now it is a controversial question which of these theories best captures our concept of a person—this is philosophy, after all—and I do not wish here to take a stand on the substantive issue; my point is just that *whichever* of these theories (or others) might be true, *that* is what constitutes the analysis of personal proper names, that is, individual concepts like *Cleopatra*. For ease of exposition, however, I shall assume that the bodily theory is true (this also fits nicely with the way in which we recognize other people as the same and hence with our actual practice of name application in interpersonal situations). So I shall say that a particular person *a* is identical to whoever has body *b*, where *b* is the body that person *a* actually has: for instance, I am identical to the person who has *this body*, referring to the body I now have. Each person has a certain actual body *b*, and they are defined as (in all worlds) whoever has *b*. The essence of a person is her body (including also her brain, so as to get over certain potential counterexamples).[3] Thus this theory might allow that someone can be me without having my memories or character and possibly without even having the individual consciousness that now dwells in my body (the person Colin McGinn might underlie a succession of such centers of consciousness housed in a single enduring body-brain). The theory then says that the correct analysis of a personal proper name is given by a description of the form "the person with body *b*." This is

---

[3] The counterexamples concern brain swaps and suchlike oddities. Let us circumvent them by including the brain in the reference of "that body," or we could just formulate a straightforward brain theory of personal identity and use the description "the person with brain *b*" (or "the person with the bodily part most central in fixing someone's psychology").

not a specification of contingent famous deeds but of constitutive essence, that is, identity conditions.

We can immediately see that this theory will have no problem with rigidity, because the descriptive condition is necessary and sufficient to be a particular person (by stipulation, as we are assuming the correctness of the theory). We have simply defined the name by reference to the individual essence of its bearer. Kripke himself believes in such individual essences for persons (and other things), holding that a person necessarily has his actual origins: "the person with origin o" is a rigid designator, for Kripke, and so co-denotes across all possible worlds with a name "a" that actually refers to the person with origin o. The difference is that such an individual essence does not result from a priori analysis of a person's name: it is a case of empirically discovered essence (sperm and eggs in the human case). But the point about conceptual analyses of persons is that they are a priori, since they exploit only our ordinary concept of a person (without needing to know things about sperm and eggs, say, or DNA): just by mastering the concept of a person, we know that persons are individuated by their bodies, and our grasp of individual concepts of persons includes knowledge of their bodies. I understand names of people by means of my acquaintance with their bodies (but not with sperm and eggs). I have a conception of the bodies of people whom I know, and I use this to confer descriptive content on their names—I think, "Jones is the person with body b," where "b" expresses a concept I have of a particular body. When I meet Jones I apply the name "Jones" to him because I recognize him to have a particular body, the one that I associate by definition with "Jones." My concept of Jones thus includes my concept of his body (and this is not true of his remote biological origins). Thus the bodily condition of personal identity is an a priori essence (the same would have been true of the memory condition or the individual consciousness condition). Granted that status, there can be no issue of non-rigidity or of a merely synthetic identification: so we have in one fell swoop remedied the glaring defect of classical formulations of the description theory. We have given an a priori analysis of personal identity and then imported it into the sense of names—just as Suits gave an analysis of games (arrived at a priori) and then imported it into the sense of "game." The sense of the expression has been excavated and articulated by providing a straightforward conceptual analysis of its referent.[4]

Do not object that the speaker cannot produce the operative description on demand, so that it can't give the meaning of the name. For that is true of any conceptual analysis—analyses are not automatic and obvious from the start. That is

---

[4] That is, we give a *de re* analysis of what an individual person is—her individual essence—and then we read the analysis into the definition of the name denoting that person. The person is analytically identified with a particular biological entity, and we incorporate a description of that entity into the definition of the name. Thus ontology feeds into semantics, metaphysics determines meaning. It is the same pattern of reasoning that defines "game" by reference to the essential metaphysical nature of games. Reality comes first; meaning follows.

why they can be informative. Why can't the analysis of names be similarly difficult to articulate and make explicit, though we have implicit knowledge of the analysis? Maybe the descriptions favored by Frege and Russell can be brought quickly to mind by a competent speaker (though memory knowledge can often be difficult to access), but it would be arbitrary to impose this as a condition of adequacy on *any* description theory. It would cripple all conceptual analysis, and also make analyses all too obvious if correct. The conceptual analysis of names might well require the kind of analytic creativity required by conceptual analysis elsewhere. Our semantic knowledge here, as elsewhere, is implicit, and it takes some effort and ingenuity to dig out—but that is no count against its existence. By all means let us allow, then, that the description theory of names can permit the descriptions to be known only implicitly—and that it may take substantive philosophical analysis to make this implicit knowledge explicit. No one ever said that conceptual or semantic analysis had to be easy. We might say, in recognition of this, that the *deep* sense of a name is given by an analysis that makes explicit what is only implicit in the ordinary understanding of the name.[5]

Peter Geach maintained, with some plausibility, that proper names analytically imply sortal concepts.[6] Thus names of people, like "Plato" and "Cleopatra," entail the sortal concept *person*. This sounds convincing, as a description of how we ordinarily understand names—and it is totally inconsistent with the pure "Millian" theory. It fits well, however, with the approach that I am advocating: for I maintain that implicit in every personal proper name is a description of the form "the *person* with body *b*." We use the general sortal concept, and we tie it down to a particular by use of the "*b*" term. So our understanding of the name has some conceptual complexity: we need to grasp what a person is, and what a body is, and what the relation denoted by "with" is. There is a good deal of conceptual infrastructure here. Our grasp of a name is not some sort of blank unconceptualized staring or beholding or pointing. Moreover, each of the constituent concepts can be further analyzed in its turn, with more complexity exposed. Thus we can define a person in the manner of Locke's famous definition: he says that a person is "a thinking intelligent being, that has reason and reflection, and can consider itself as itself, the same thinking thing in

---

[5] Presumably, Frege needs the notion of deep sense too, in order to account for the informative content of his definition of number—it is not as if speakers know the logicist definition of numerals off the top of their heads. There is the sense people explicitly attach to a numeral—what they would say about its meaning if asked—and the sense the numeral actually has, which may not be available to the naïve speaker. It is the same with proper names of people. Thus we need to distinguish superficial sense from deep sense, or "speaker sense" from "semantic sense"; and both need to be added to reference (along with force and tone). For example, the name "Hesperus" may have the superficial speaker sense *the evening star*, since that is what the speaker will produce if queried; but it may also have the deep sense that is revealed when the predicate "star" is analyzed (or "evening"). Compare: "chess" has the superficial sense of "the game terminated by checkmate," but it also has the deep sense revealed by Suits's definition of games. In other words, there are layers of sense beneath what the speaker would say if asked to whom or to what he is referring.

[6] The view can be found in Geach's 1957 *Mental Acts*.

different times and places; which it does only by that consciousness, which is inseparable from thinking, and as it seems to me essential to it: it being impossible for anyone to perceive, without perceiving that he does perceive"(302).[7] This is Locke's analysis of the general concept of a person, and it evidently employs a rich range of concepts, all of which are implicit in our ordinary understanding of "person" (assuming we follow Locke's lead). If we combine Geach and Locke, we reach the result that grasp of personal names rests upon a complex conceptual foundation; and if we add in the connection between persons and bodies, certified by the bodily criterion of personal identity, we get something ever richer. All this is contained in the (deep) sense of a name, and hence in our practice of using names to refer to people. Thus the proposition expressed by "Plato wrote the *Republic*" will contain all this conceptual material just waiting to be brought to the surface—and not merely (or at all) the individual man Plato (as in "direct reference" theories). There is not just a confined little definite description in the proposition; there is a whole world of conceptual complexity, some of it deep and philosophically contentious. There is accordingly nothing "simple" about the meaning of proper names. And the same basic picture applies to other sorts of names—as in names for cities, countries, planets, and so on. Here again we have an implied sortal concept and an associated criterion of identity, with all the complexity that comes with that. For example, London falls under the concept *city* (sortal), and cities are entities of such and such a type (here we give our conceptual analysis of cities); and London is the city that uniquely has feature F, where F individuates particular cities (as it might be, geographical location or historical origin or legal fiat). The name "London" implicitly incorporates all of this, being synonymous with "the city that has location l," where each of the elements here can be analyzed in turn. This is not just a description theory of names; it is a *philosophical* description theory of names.[8]

The dialectical position we have reached is this: we need a description theory in order to avoid the problems about existence and identity that plague theories that identify the meaning of a name with its bearer; but we also need a theory that avoids the problems about rigidity that Kripke brings up; we now have a description theory that avoids these problems. So are we home free? Not quite yet, because there are some objections that need to be addressed, and some refinements and extensions are required. The problems that I have in mind center around the "b" term in the analysis (analogous problems will center around a like term in alternative analyses of personal identity). What kind of singular term of natural language will substitute for

---

[7] Locke, *Essay*.

[8] I am well aware of how much I am kicking against the pricks in these remarks: not just a description theory but a *hypertrophic* description theory—a description theory on steroids, all pumped up and rippling with conceptual muscle. Underneath the smooth syntactic skin lies an articulated world of conceptual flesh and bone. There is a veritable conceptual *scheme* embedded in the meaning of a name—a ramifying conceptual web or matrix. There is not a simple denoting relation unconnected to anything else, causal or otherwise. The sense of the name is *thick* and *deep*.

the "*b*" term in "the person with body *b*"? It can't be a term like "the body belonging to person *a*," because that will produce a vicious circle in the alleged analysis: it is no use defining the name "*a*" to mean "the person with body *b*" if we then turn around and define "*b*" to mean "the body belonging to person *a*." There has to be another way to identify the relevant body apart from assigning it to a particular person, that is, using the name of the person whose body it is. Are substitutions for "*b*" then proper names *of bodies*, understood independently of the names of the persons whose bodies they are? But we don't *have* proper names of bodies to fall back on here—we don't name people *and* their bodies. It is not that for any personal name I grasp, I have a paired name of that person's body—so that for the name "Barack Obama" I have in reserve the name (say) "Indiana Jones" that I use to name Barack Obama's body (and how would the reference of *that* name be determined?). I might, in principle, have a purely general definite description of each person's body that does not incorporate the name of the person concerned ("the body at such and such coordinates" or "the body with such and such a distribution of freckles"), but it is generally very difficult to come up with such a description. What I will typically have is a *demonstrative* term for the body in question: John Smith is the person with *that body*. So when I understand a sentence such as "Smith is tall," I interpret it to mean, "the person with that body is tall," referring demonstratively to a perceptually presented body. But now the problem is obvious: my friend Smith is not always available to be the referent of such a perceptual demonstrative; he may be skulking elsewhere when I understand an utterance about him. Worse, he may not even exist at the time at which I understand an utterance containing his name—he may be dead and gone. How then can I understand the name by means of a demonstrative reference to his body? Yet I typically have no other way to identify the bodies of people (except the circular way). So this simple description theory won't work: the name cannot be equivalent to a definite description embedding a perceptual demonstrative.[9]

How to fix it? Fortunately, it does not take much ingenuity to devise a reply to the objection: all we need to do is recognize demonstratives that are not based on perception of what they refer to—and there are many such. We have Quine's "deferred ostension," as when looking at a footprint I say, "That man is heavy." We also have memory demonstratives, as when I think back to a past encounter and comment to

---

[9] Notice that the famous deeds theory avoids this kind of problem, seeming well suited for handling reference to the long deceased and perceptually remote. It sounds a lot less appealing as applied to people of our close acquaintance whom we see every day: I hardly refer to my friends by way of knowledge of their famous deeds! I think of such people in the obvious way—as they are perceptually presented to me, i.e., by way of their body as a perceptual object. And when I think of myself, using my name, I don't identify myself as the author of this or that book: I think of myself as *this* person—the one presented to me in that special first-person way. The famous deeds theory starts with the remote and must work back to the proximate (and notice how the authors of these theories never talk about names of friends and family), while my approach starts with the close and expands out to the remote. That seems to me the natural way to proceed.

myself, "She was nice." And we have testimony demonstratives, as when I listen to what you are telling me about someone and remark, "He sounds like a nasty piece of work." These all involve indexical ("deictic") reference to persons, but the same kind of demonstrative reference can work for physical objects like human bodies: "that body" can be used to refer under all sorts of conditions, often involving extreme remoteness in the object referred to. So when Smith is not present, I can rely on my memories of perceiving his body to anchor the reference of "that body"—and isn't this pretty much exactly what I do when I use the name of an acquaintance who is not then perceptually present? But what about when the named person is not and never has been an object of my acquaintance, say Plato? Can I not name Plato? Here we must appeal to testimony-type demonstratives. Suppose that you are speaking to me of a city long since destroyed, based on your knowledge of historical documents, and I remark, "That city sounds idyllic," referring precisely to that now extinct city. We might reasonably expand such a demonstrative to the description "the city you are speaking of now," or a little more theoretically "the city at the origin of the long chain of speech acts the latest of which is that utterance." We might even abbreviate the description as follows: "the city at the origin of *that* causal chain (of speech acts)." Now we can go back to names of people and their bodies: when I use the name "Plato," the description that is implicit in my understanding is "the person whose body was at the origin of that causal chain," where with the demonstrative I refer to the chain of speech acts that originates in the baptism of Plato (his little baby body squirming there) and continues on through the centuries to the uses of "Plato" today. The "*b*" term is thus "that body," where "that body" here is equivalent to "the body at the origin of that causal chain." So I do have a non-circular way of referring even to Plato's body—by exploiting the causal-historical link between that body and the speech acts I now perceive. This is, indeed, how in general I refer to physical objects that no longer exist, given that I have neither names nor non-testimonial pure descriptions to fall back on. In other words, we incorporate the existent causal chains involving uses of names into a demonstrative description of such chains and then identify that description with the sense of the name.

Kripke considers this theoretical possibility at one point. He cites a footnote from Strawson's *Individuals* that proposes a view very like the one I have just sketched. Speaking of how one speaker's reference can derive from that of another, Strawson says: "The identifying description, though it must not include a reference to the speaker's own reference to the particular in question, may include a reference to another's reference to that particular. . . . So one reference may borrow its credentials, as a genuinely identifying reference, from another; and that from another. But this regress is not infinite" (181).[10] In effect, Strawson is proposing a kind of historical chain description theory, to deal with cases of reference to long dead individuals whom we cannot otherwise identify: "the person at the origin of the historical chain

---

[10] Strawson, *Individuals*.

of references leading up to *that* reference." Kripke's reply to this theoretical possibility is not to deny that we have thoughts about such chains or to claim that these thoughts will not be individuating; it is to point to the distinction between the *existence* of such a chain and our having *descriptions* of it. For Kripke, it suffices that the chain exists; for Strawson, we must have a way of describing the chain (since he is incorporating it into an extended description theory). Kripke's response to that Strawsonian move is that the speaker might misremember from whom he got the name: "If the speaker has forgotten his source, the description Strawson uses is unavailable to him; if he misremembers it, Strawson's paradigm can give the wrong results. On our view, it is not how the speaker thinks he got the reference, but the actual chain of communication, that is relevant" (92–93). This objection to Strawson's proposal strikes me as minor. To be sure, the speaker might misremember from whom he derived a name, thinking he got it from Smith when he actually got it from Jones; then he will pick out the wrong object if he uses the description "the object Smith was referring to yesterday." But there is no necessity for the speaker to commit himself so strongly to the identity of his source and he would be rash to do so: better for him to use the description "the object referred to by whomever it was that I picked up the name from." Suppose the speaker feels a bit hazy about his source—it might be Smith or it might be Jones (he was speaking to both yesterday)—and he wants to explain to someone else what he is referring to by the name that has lately come into his possession. Being unsure he says, "By 'Plato' I mean whomever it was that the person I was talking to yesterday was referring to by that name"; and if he can't remember when, either, he can be similarly non-committal about the time. If he insists on committing himself, then his error will clash with the perfectly true description still at his disposal—the less committal one. But there is nothing to prevent him from not risking such errors, and he can still achieve a determinate reference.[11]

This brings us to the question of errors of description, also used by Kripke to undermine the description theory. I may pick up a name in conversation, referring to its communally recognized bearer, but may form false beliefs about that bearer (as in Kripke's Godel-Schmidt example). In such a case, though I would proffer the description in question if asked to whom I am referring by the name, I do not actually refer to the person who satisfies that description. So the description I "associate"

---

[11] Thus the description theory can deal with all the cases just by picking the right backward-looking non-committal description, trading on the "causal chain" that exists from referent to current use of the name. We have no case in which the speaker refers to the bearer of the name with the name and yet has no description available that uniquely identifies that bearer. As Kripke himself notes, *any* theory of reference for names will lend itself to this kind of description theory, because it will specify necessary and sufficient conditions for something to be the referent of a name, which can then be incorporated into a description. The only obstacle to such a move would be if the theory relied on facts totally unavailable to the speaker's knowledge: but speakers are actually well acquainted with the uses of names from which their own uses derive—they know they are links in a referential chain.

with the name is not what determines its reference on my lips; instead, the reference is fixed by the linguistic community of which I am a member. Therefore, Kripke contends, the description theory is false. This type of objection, if sound, applies as much against the kind of description theory I favor as against the classical version, since speakers may make mistakes about whose body is whose. Suppose at a party I form the false belief that the person whose body is in front of me is Jerry Fodor—I have never met Fodor but have heard some things about his body and I have reason to believe he is at the party. The person whose body is in front of me is in fact Noam Chomsky (actually they resemble each other very little—but never mind). Thus I associate with "Jerry Fodor" the description "the person with the body now in front of me." Do I then refer to Chomsky by "Fodor" when I utter that name? Intuitively, no, because the name "Fodor" is independently anchored in the community use of the name in which my use is embedded. My body-based description refers to Chomsky, but the name refers to Fodor, despite my mistake. Does this argument refute the description theory? It does not, because there is nothing to stop us from formulating that theory *at the level of the community*. What we have here is a case of linguistic deference or community dominance or division of linguistic labor: it is what the community means that fixes what I mean—I refer to what *they* refer to.[12] But their reference can be fixed by an accurate definite description, possibly going back far in time. If most people mean by "Fodor" "the person with body b," where b is in fact Fodor's body, then a minority can make slips and still manage to refer to Fodor, because they are connected to the majority. Thus it is not necessary for an individual speaker to possess a true description of the reference of a communal name in order for that individual to refer to the object in question; here, as Kripke says, the existence of the chain can be enough. But the name still has a descriptive sense as a name of the communal language—and must do so. Compare the following two cases, concerning "game" and "DNA." A person may pick up the word "game" from others and have a very imperfect grasp of it, thinking perhaps that TV watching is a game (it is a type of leisure activity): but it doesn't then, in his idiolect, have an extension that includes TV watching, because the community understanding exerts a strong pull on its sense in his mouth. It would be quite misguided to object to Suits's definition of "game" on the basis that this errant individual is referring to games even though his description of games is erroneous; for the analysis is to be given by reference to people's general understanding of "game." In the case of "DNA," people may use the term and have all sorts of wrong ideas about its referent; yet we don't think that when they utter "DNA" they refer to whatever their wrong ideas may best describe. The reason is that the community understanding of the term, rooted in the knowledge of experts, fixes its reference in their mouth, too. But it would be wrong to conclude from this that "DNA" has no descriptive sense: it has

---

[12] This kind of point has been well made by Putnam, Dummett, Burge, and others. I will not spell it out at length.

a precise scientific definition, in the English language, even if many people don't know what it is. Not everyone needs to know the definition of a term for it to have a definition. Thus mistakes about definition are just that. The term "DNA" has an exact descriptive sense ("the complex molecule responsible for inheritance composed of deoxyribonucleic acid") even though many people do not know that definition. Similarly, a proper name of a person can have a precise descriptive definition ("the person with body b") even though many people might not know this definition and might even have erroneous idiosyncratic ideas about it. Kripke's error cases thus merely show that the description theory needs to be applied at the community level, not that it is misguided as a matter of deep principle. In other words, there are experts and amateurs in the use of proper names, and the experts get to fix the sense. Put simply, *somebody* has to know which body is Fodor's in order that "Fodor" should refer to Fodor. There can't be *universal* error about the correct reference of "Fodor": it can't be that "Fodor" refers to Fodor even though every single application of "Fodor" has been to Chomsky, including the initial baptism.[13]

So we can accommodate rigidity (a modal notion) by recourse to descriptions of individual essence, and we can accommodate error (an epistemic notion) by recourse to communal descriptive meanings. We can then enjoy the benefits of the description theory in respect of existence and identity statements without incurring the kinds of objections brought by Kripke and others. And this implies that names have an analysis after all; they are not mere empty labels. This, I think, gives a better "picture" of names than either the "Millian" picture or the classical Frege-Russell picture. The latter makes the cardinal error of choosing contingent empirical descriptions; the former can't handle existence and identity statements, and makes the relation between name and bearer into a kind of bare confrontation unmediated by concepts. Instead, the analysis of names corresponds to the essence of what they denote—just as with "game," "know," "husband," and so on. The sense of the name "Aristotle" expresses the what-it-is-to-be of Aristotle—which is just what you would expect. This what-it-is-to-be (we are assuming) consists in possessing a particular human body (and brain). On alternative theories, it is held to consist in having certain memories or having a certain specific consciousness—in which case, the sense of "Aristotle" would be expressed by a description like "the person with these memories" or "the person with this consciousness." (Such theories seem well designed to capture what one might mean by one's *own* name.) This seems to me

[13] That is, it couldn't be that Noam Chomsky's baby body was in the crib and was baptized "Jerry Fodor" and every subsequent use of the name "Jerry Fodor" was in application to Noam Chomsky—*and yet* "Jerry Fodor" refers to Jerry Fodor and not to Noam Chomsky. That is not a coherent world. Roughly speaking, the reference of the name is fixed by the community's practice in applying the name, so that the community can't be wrong in its applications—but it is possible for a particular individual to misapply the name because of faulty information. Descriptive errors rely upon descriptive accuracy for the most part. What I refer to by a name on an occasion is not fixed by the description I now associate with it, but by the description my community associates with it—in which case descriptions are still the mechanism of reference.

like a very natural way to look at it, an appealing "picture," and it has the notable theoretical benefit of avoiding the nasty problems besetting "Millian" theories.

It is very important to notice that Kripke's model of name reference relies on mediating descriptions at a crucial point, namely at the point when the name is introduced. Many kinds of description could in principle be used at this point, but it is surely natural to suppose that a central kind is of the form I have identified. Thus, when naming a child, we are in effect saying, "let the person with that body (now pointing in the direction of a certain human body) be henceforth called 'John.'" We pick out the person by reference to the body and introduce the name thereby; after all, it is the body that is most saliently *there*. Our reference to persons (other than ourselves) is mediated by reference to their bodies (Strawson called this "identification-dependence"). And it is necessary that we use such a descriptive mode of name introduction: mere recitation of the name in the presence of the object will never suffice to confer reference on it, nor will saying "that" while pointing into space. We need an individuating sortal predicate and a way to tie this predicate down to a particular case—hence the use of "person" and "that." No name could acquire reference except via such conceptual mediation; certainly mere causal connection will not suffice to confer determinate reference. Kripke does not dispute any of this; in fact, he more or less insists on it—rightly so. Names enter the language via other referential expressions, particularly demonstratives.[14] But his notion of "fixing the reference" is apt to encourage what seems to me to be an illusion: namely, that once the description has done its reference-fixing work it can somehow drop away and leave the name to survive on its own. Like a parent, it brings the name into existence, but once the name is set in motion, it no longer needs the parent to keep operating as a name. This is what I think is an illusion, borne perhaps of misleading analogies. It is like supposing that I can elevate a book by setting it on a table, but then thinking that it will stay elevated if the table is removed. For how can the name continue to refer to a given person if the prop of the description is removed? The name will become an empty sound, signifying nothing. The original description must somehow still be operating as the name is passed down, or else the name loses the only thing that keeps it tied down to a specific object. The description must either be preserved in the speakers' minds as the name pursues its career, or it mysteriously operates from the past to fix the reference of later uses; in either case, it still exerts its reference-determining power.[15] What cannot happen is that the name

---

[14] I discuss this in "The Mechanism of Reference."

[15] If uses of a name have no currently available reference-determining description associated with them, then they rely on the links in the "causal chain" that terminates in the descriptively mediated introduction of the name. In this case, the remote description is responsible for securing reference for the name initially, and later uses depend on links with that description. Without the introducing description, no name reference would be possible, and current uses have not somehow broken free of that description: they only refer now because it fixed the reference then. The reference is *still* descriptively mediated. The name cannot semantically bypass the description and hook onto

becomes utterly detached from the introducing description (without being replaced by a new reference-fixing description): it cannot pick out a determinate object without some kind of descriptive mediation at some point. It cannot have "bare reference." If it could, then it could have been introduced barely—but it is agreed on all sides that that is impossible. If it needed a descriptive prop then, it needs one later—it cannot just shed the introducing description like an old skin. It cannot dissociate itself from that description (any description) and hope to keep on functioning as a name of a determinate thing. The name cannot just "go it alone," leaving what brought it into existence behind. The mistake is to think that the description is not a permanent attribute of the name, while accepting its necessity to get the name going. It will become a mere meaningless sound, devoid of reference, if there is nothing descriptive to mediate its reference. Causal relations by themselves can no more confer determinate reference on the name at a later time than they can at the time of baptism, and for the same reason: they are far too undiscriminating. There are just too *many* objects implicated in the causal chain that could be the reference—not just a particular person, but his body, his (undetached) torso alone, a time slice of his body, the light reflected by his body, the image on the speaker's retina produced by that light, and so on. This is why we need a sortal concept like *person* to home in on the right object. The concept must be doing its reference-determining work at any phase of a name's career, not just its introduction. The name must exploit the introducing description retrospectively, if it does not rely on contemporaneously associated descriptions. It typically does so via the speaker's intention in using the name: the speaker intends to refer to the same *person* to whom his source was referring in using the name. We cannot accept the necessity for descriptions as devices to bring names into existence, but then turn around and jettison them once their procreative work is done. Names either need descriptions to refer, or they do not. It is untenable to think that they do not at the point of introduction; but if they need them then, they need them always. Thus the description theory *has* to be true in some form, even on Kripke's own account, on pain of the impossibility of names. Name reference must always proceed ultimately through descriptive reference (and this holds for all names, logically proper or not). The descriptive reference will typically take a demonstrative form ("that human being," "this city"), but it must contain descriptive content; thus it must be conceptually mediated. Accordingly, the sense of the name will be subject to conceptual analysis.[16]

---

the reference autonomously; there is no description-independent mode of reference determination. Thus, at some level, a description theory of names is inevitable: it follows from the fact that names cannot refer *ab initio*—they must be linked with other referential devices in order to gain a reference in the first place. Names lack semantic autonomy.

[16] This does not apply to primitive predicates: they have no analysis, but express unanalyzable concepts. They do not refer to the property denoted via descriptive concepts, i.e., by uniquely satisfying a descriptive condition. Thus, "red," say, directly designates the property of being red; the word does not mean "the color that is *F*," for some concept *F* that only redness falls under (as it might be, "the color nearest to pink"). Such a predicate functions like a Russellian logically proper name, a

Just as description theories have been rejected for proper names, so they have been rejected for natural kind terms. This is potentially more worrying for the proponent of conceptual analysis than the case of proper names, because natural kind terms are predicates—and then the conclusion might spread to other predicates. Are such predicates non-descriptive labels for kinds, primitive and indefinable, despite a long tradition of thinking otherwise? To show that they are not, we need to be able to specify "nominal essences" for them, that is, necessary and sufficient conditions arrived at a priori by conceptual analysis. One approach that is doomed fastens onto the *appearance* of natural kinds—how they strike us perceptually. This won't work because of perceptual illusions, hallucinations, and the general gap between appearance and reality. It is only contingently true of a particular natural kind that it has a specific sensory appearance: in other worlds, some other kind might have that appearance and the original kind have a quite different appearance. This would be no better than defining proper names by the appearance of the body of the bearer: one person could appear to have the body of another, and two people might have the same bodily appearance. We need to specify personal identity, not by the appearance of a body, but by the body itself. Likewise, two natural kinds could have the same appearance and one might look like another because of sensory illusions or some such. Thus it is neither necessary nor sufficient to be water that a liquid should have the appearance of water—that is, produce sensory experiences of the kind characteristic of water. No sensible person would deny this. But that is very different from defining water by its observable properties—by properties that it objectively has. Suppose we define water as the liquid that is colorless and tasteless, can be used to wash things, boils when suitably heated, causes certain things (e.g., salt) to dissolve in it, and flows in certain ways. This seems to capture our ordinary conception of water. It is a statement that is importantly different from such statements as "there's some water in my glass now" or "water is my least favorite thing to drink" or "there is a lot of water in Holland." The latter are decidedly synthetic, but the former is arguably necessary and even analytic. Someone who did not grasp these things would not know what "water" means.

It might be objected that water is essentially H_2O, so that if we encountered a liquid that was H_2O but lacked the properties cited in this definition, it would still

---

"Millian" label. It may connote a sortal concept like *color*, so that in grasping it we know a priori that redness is a color, but otherwise there is no expressed property beyond the referent itself. Nor was the predicate introduced by means of a description (and there would be an obvious regress if it had to be). Primitive unanalyzable predicates are the strongest candidates for directly referential devices—basic bits of language that merely latch onto a worldly entity. In other words, we can't give a description theory of the reference of (primitive) *descriptions*. And much the same is true for logical terms like "and" and "not" and "some": these are conceptually primitive, and hence "directly referential" (i.e., their extension is not fixed by a descriptive condition such as "the most common truth function"). Proper names are never "logically proper names," but expressions of other categories may be—which is to say that proper names cannot be semantically autonomous, yet other expressions often are.

be water. My problem with this objection is that I don't think it envisages a coherent possibility: nothing *could* be H_2O and lack all these properties (contrast *appear* to have these properties). For there is a necessary connection between the "real essence" of water and the "nominal essence" of water as so defined: chemical composition and chemical behavior are yoked inextricably together.[17] Observable properties are linked necessarily to hidden properties. So there can never be a conflict between what real essence suggests and what nominal essence suggests. If so, having the nominal essence that I have specified is necessary and sufficient for being water, that is, H_2O, and this essence is part of our common conceptions, not a result of arcane scientific discovery. Therefore "water" has an analysis. There will be no counterexamples stemming from the rigidity of "water" and the non-rigidity of the description capturing the nominal essence, since that description is itself rigid—as with the proper names case. Cases of error can be handled in the same way in which I handled the like problem for names, that is, by appeal to community sense. If someone knew nothing of the observable properties of water, then she would not understand the term as we do, by any reasonable standard of understanding (but she could be quite unaware of the plenitude of water in Holland without detriment to her linguistic understanding). And the same goes for other natural kind terms: all natural kinds that we refer to have observable or manifest properties that together define the term, and these properties are necessarily linked to the real essence of the kind—as the phenotype of an animal is linked to its genotype. The phenotype of cats defines "cat" and it flows from the genotype of cats: nothing can be a cat and lack that phenotype and anything with that phenotype is a cat.[18] Of course, something might *appear* to have that phenotype and not be a cat—a rat might in some circumstances produce the sensory experiences typically produced by cats. But actually having the phenotype involves a whole complex of anatomical and behavioral properties that are inseparable from being a cat. If someone were to suggest that a creature could fully have the phenotype of cats and yet not have the genotype of cats, I would wonder how the creature came to have that phenotype except by having that genotype. The phenotype includes all the physical and behavioral characteristics of cats—shape, size, furriness, carnivorousness, being warm-blooded, reproductive habits, purring, scratching, and so on. These cannot be divorced from genotype (from

---

[17] See my 1975 paper "A Note on the Essence of Natural Kinds" for more about this. As I point out there, Kripke does *not* maintain that chemical essence and observable properties are only contingently related, as a matter of metaphysical modality.

[18] We could, if we like, relax this a little, to say that cats (necessarily) *characteristically* have a certain phenotype, to allow for genetic accidents and strange deformations. Still, even cat monsters, with three legs and two heads, will have many of the phenotypic traits of cats, because the genotype will find expression somehow. And if by some bizarre freak of nature a cat were to give birth to an animal with the genetic and phenotypic traits of a lizard, that animal would not be a cat—it would be a lizard born to a cat. There is a definite limit on how much of the phenotype of a cat can be removed and we still have a cat left.

the hidden real essence).[19] The "cluster" of these phenotypic traits seems to me to define the nominal essence of cats, and hence provide an analysis of the concept *cat*. Again, such a definition is very different from synthetic statements about cats, such as "I own two cats" or "cats are common in Cairo." If someone knew nothing of the phenotypic traits of cats, perhaps thinking that cats are rubbery things that float in water and are inflated with air, then he would not understand "cat." There may be some looseness in the definition, and some variability between speakers, but grasp of some significant portion of it is necessary to understanding "cat." Thus a description theory of the meaning of "cat" is indicated, as against a "direct reference" view—we need connotation as well as denotation. And all the same points about reference fixing apply here too: if "cat" needs to be introduced via description, for example, "the animal with *that* phenotype," then it cannot continue to refer to cats without benefit of such a mediating description. It cannot function independently of the concepts that gave it reference to begin with. A pure "Millian" view of natural kind terms cannot work as a matter of principle, as well as not being forced on us by any cogent argument. Accordingly, conceptual analysis is appropriate for natural kind terms as well as proper names.[20]

Let me make one final point. I have claimed that our proper names and natural kind terms express the essence of their referents (though deeply)—their what-it-is-to-be. But what if things had no essences—would that mean they could not be named? What about a possible world where people had no individual essence—must they be nameless in that world? No description would be available, by hypothesis, to capture their essence, so no description could tie the names down in the right way, conferring rigidity on them. But couldn't we still name these objects? Two replies may be made to this query, a superficial one and a deep one. The superficial reply is that we could always avail ourselves of a formal trick like adding an actuality operator to contingent descriptions in order to ensure rigidity. The deep reply is that the world described is actually profoundly incoherent—it is like describing a world of bare particulars and asking how a description theory of names for *them* would work, since they have no properties to describe. There could not *be* any such bare particular world, as a matter of deep metaphysical necessity, so we need not trouble ourselves inquiring how a description theory of names for bare particulars might work. (Invoking bare particulars with names would have been a very quick and easy

[19] If it were possible so to separate genotype and phenotype, I would not say that the genotype determines the species identity of the animal. If you came across an animal that was phenotypically identical to a cat and yet had the DNA of a lizard (*per impossibile*), then I would say that you had come across a cat with the DNA of a lizard, not a lizard with the phenotype of a cat.

[20] I have moved somewhat quickly over these points about natural kinds, leaving the reader to fill in the details. Tricky cases can be produced, which call for delicate judgment. But I think the general principles are clear, especially the distinction between the appearance-based account of nominal essence and the objective-traits account.

way to refute classic description theories!) Similarly, a putative world in which objects and kinds of objects have no what-it-is-to-be—nothing that makes them what they are—is simply not a coherent world. It is therefore idle to wonder how such objects might be named. Naming and essence go hand in hand: naming requires descriptions, but the descriptions have to be rigid, so they must express essences— thus there are no names of objects without essences of objects. If you lack essence, you must remain nameless. In general, language can be about reality only because reality has what-it-is-to-be. Language *expresses* essence.[21]

[21] The right picture here is that things in reality have essences prior to linguistic representation—games, knowledge, husbands, individual people—and then language comes along and refers to these things by means of their essence, via concepts. Thus objective essences are "uploaded" into our concepts, fixing their content, and these are then fed into the meanings of our words (the essences may be simple or complex). The entire apparatus of reference in language is steeped in, and depends upon, objective essence in the world—reality being necessarily a certain way. Reference is essence-dependent. The what-it-is-to-be of things is the fulcrum by which reference is achieved (e.g., the nature of games is what underlies the ability of "game" to refer to games—since "game" expresses that nature by way of the concept associated with it). Reality creates reference (not vice versa). The positivists had it exactly wrong when they claimed that essence is an offshoot of meaning; it is meaning that owes its being to essence—meaning *tracks* objective essence. (I don't mean that *every* essence is expressed in language, only that *some* are. If the [or an] essence of water is H_2O, then that essence is not expressed by the word "water"—rather, the nominal essence of water is what is expressed by "water." But I do think that such a hidden [for us] essence *could* be expressed in language, and thus give rise to analytic truths: there could be speakers with enhanced perceptual and cognitive skills who know the chemical composition of water from the moment they start to speak, so that the corresponding conception enters their understanding of "water." Whether an essence shows up in language doesn't depend on the nature of the essence per se, but upon the epistemic talents of the speakers of the language. Some essences are a priori for us and some are not, but this pattern could conceivably be inverted for beings with other modes of knowing. My general point is that reference proceeds relative to some objective essence or other, but there may be essences that are not part of meaning—those that require special kinds of investigative methods not available to the ordinary speaker. The point I am making about essences such as water being necessarily H_2O is that such an essence is not *intrinsically* a posteriori, because we can conceive of speakers for whom it is an a priori matter that water is H_2O—those with direct and easy insight into the chemical composition of water. There is really only one kind of essence, but our epistemic relation to it can vary. I intend to develop this position elsewhere.)

9 Naturalism and Philosophical Method

The conceptual analyst adopts a distinctively philosophical method. As in any intellectual discipline, the analyst seeks knowledge—new knowledge. But the object of that knowledge is itself knowledge: the analyst seeks knowledge of knowledge. The knowledge that he seeks knowledge of is implicit knowledge; the knowledge that he seeks is explicit knowledge. He seeks explicit knowledge of implicit knowledge (which is to say, in practice, the human *umwelt*, our cognitive stance or slant). His explicit knowledge is thus second-order, and self-directed. But the implicit knowledge that he seeks to make explicit is first-order, so the second-order results have first-order content. Thus, for example, he seeks to explicate the concept *game*, where possessing this concept consists in knowing what games are; the explication of the concept is therefore knowledge of knowledge. But since that latter knowledge is knowledge of games, the theorist learns something about games themselves—not just about our first-order knowledge of them. The theorist thus presents us with an informative analysis of games in the process of saying explicitly what we know implicitly in knowing what games are. The new knowledge is knowledge of both knowledge and reality: it articulates our implicit knowledge and it *thereby* tells us the nature of a particular thing in reality, that is, games. We accordingly learn more about ourselves and more about the world by means of conceptual analysis. We learn about the world-as-conceived. The knowledge is double-edged, facing in two directions at once—at the human mind and at the external world. This seems like worthwhile knowledge to acquire.

But there are those who question such a method of acquiring knowledge: they view it as not properly "naturalistic."[1] Conceptual analysis, for them, is methodologically suspect. We must try to address their concerns, though we may find little to sympathize with in their suspicions (and less in some of their rhetoric). We may deplore their deploring. But let us proceed. It is customary, to begin with, to distinguish two notions of naturalism: metaphysical and methodological. Metaphysical naturalism is the thesis that everything real is natural: there is no room for the supernatural in nature—or anywhere else for that matter. Methodological naturalism is the thesis that only the methods of empirical science produce worthwhile knowledge, so these are the methods we must pursue if we seek knowledge; non-scientific methods of inquiry must be abandoned altogether and must be replaced by scientific methods. The question, then, is whether conceptual analysis is in conflict with naturalism of either variety, and if it is, whether that matters. I propose to be short and sweet (well, not so sweet) in dealing with these questions.

Naturalism in the metaphysical sense is hard to define satisfactorily. What is the criterion of the "natural"? Some say the natural is the causal, others the observable, others the lawlike, others the measurable, others the physical, others the mechanical, others the non-supernatural, others the objects of natural science, others what is not "queer," others what is "entrenched." I don't think any of these criteria work for different reasons, but I won't go though each in turn to establish that. The listed criteria tend either to rule out too much or too little, or are vague and poorly defined. So I see no sound positive metaphysical use of the word "natural," only an empty slogan tendentiously applied. I do, however, think it makes sense to be anti-non-natural, that is, to be opposed to those who peddle things proudly dubbed non-natural (partly because of a lack of clarity about the meaning of "non-natural").[2] But I doubt

---

[1] I would date the origin of the "naturalism" movement to Quine's saber-rattling 1969 paper "Epistemology Naturalized," but since then it has mutated and burgeoned considerably, covering a variety of positions. The latest is the "experimental philosophy" phalanx, though I do not find the meta-philosophy here to be well worked out, consisting mainly of slogans and tendentious philosophical history. Quine's proposal was stark and simple: stop doing traditional epistemology and hand the job over to empirical psychologists. I find it amusing that he himself ignored the actual work done by psychologists on knowledge acquisition, notably the work of Piaget on what he called "genetic epistemology." Nor did he have much time for the empirical work done by psycholinguists on language acquisition, preferring to conduct a priori thought experiments about how the child "must" learn the language. His own views about knowledge acquisition, emphasizing bombardments of the senses by stimuli, are stated without any reference to the scientific literature, stemming from his own philosophical predilections. He didn't bring empirical psychology to epistemology, only his own philosophical preconceptions—notably his strident anti-mentalism.

[2] The "transcendental naturalism" defended in my *Problems in Philosophy* is of just this form—a rejection of avowedly non-natural positions. I generally regard such positions as conceptually incoherent or semi-coherent (as I take the concept of God to be), but (as Wittgenstein says) they have a tendency to take root in the fevered philosophical mind. They give rise to the feeling that something "queer" is going on. This, for me, is the sole content that can be attached to the label "non-natural"— it is the label we reach for when our philosophical phenomenology gives us a sensation of queerness. Such feelings can occur in connection with meaning and reference, numbers, free will, consciousness,

there is any workable general notion of the metaphysically natural that entitles us to wield it in the exclusive way some philosophers seem to revel in. For example, it is quite unacceptable to declare the mind "non-natural" just on the ground that it cannot be reductively explained in "physical" terms (according to some undefined or wobbly notion of the "physical"). So am I saying that we can in principle accept the existence of things that are non-natural? Well, that surely depends on what things there actually are: if there *are* non-natural things, in some sense—for example, gods—then it is rational to accept their existence. We seek *truth* and if there truly are gods we should accept them—otherwise not. Truth trumps naturalism every time (whatever exactly "naturalism" means). Does science accept anything non-natural? It depends on your criterion of the natural, but physics was widely believed to have accepted the non-natural ("occult") when Newton first introduced gravity—this being a non-mechanical force. If to be natural is to be mechanical, according to Cartesian mechanism, then Newtonian physics is non-natural (ditto the physics of the electromagnetic field). But, if we use causality or measurability as our criterion, then gravity is natural (though its causal operation is mysterious by mechanistic standards). The question seems poorly defined and unhelpful when asked quite generally. Is conceptual analysis in conflict with metaphysical naturalism? Pending a better understanding of naturalism, it is difficult to say, but on the face of it the answer is "no." Are concepts somehow non-natural? They are psychological entities, as I understand them, so they are as natural as psychological entities in general, one would have thought. Are they physical? I don't know what that means, but if they are not, according to some precise definition of "physical," then I am not going to throw up my hands in horror. We have concepts, as we have knowledge and thoughts, and that is all I need to know; I am not going to get worked up over the question of whether they are "natural," whatever quite that means.[3] Are essences natural? Well, I think there are essences, so the question has no ontological cutting edge for me. I think things in nature have a what-it-is-to-be, so I suppose essences are natural in one way—they are part of nature. Are they non-natural in some other sense, say unobservable? (Necessity itself is not observable by the senses.) Maybe, but why should I care? The question seems pointless. So I see no interesting issue here as to whether conceptual analysis is metaphysically naturalistic. Nor do I suppose that many philosophers today would oppose conceptual analysis because of its alleged metaphysical non-naturalism—that is, on ontological grounds.

---

ethical values, laws of nature, the self, and other troublesome topics. What we must not do is project those feelings onto reality—positing an objective correlate for them (queer ontology). They are merely symptoms of incomprehension, not perceptions of eerie facts (no *fact* could be eerie—though feelings may be).

[3] Eliminativists, such as Quine and his latter-day disciples, would deny that we have thoughts and concepts, supposing that science does not "countenance" such entities, so that there is no possibility of analyzing them—there is nothing there *to* analyze. But I won't here discuss this kind of extreme stance (I criticize eliminativism in *Mental Content*, Chapter 2, and elsewhere).

The question of methodological naturalism is far clearer, and hence far easier to answer clearly. The method of the "natural sciences" consists of controlled observation, theory construction, empirical testing, mathematical methods (statistical and other), experiment, collaboration, and so on. The scientist is in his laboratory or out observing and recording nature, whether he is dealing with particles or people. He uses what we call the *empirical method*, summing up the list of activities that I just gave. But the conceptual analyst does not use the empirical method: she sits in her armchair, reflecting, cogitating, conducting thought experiments, devising necessary and sufficient conditions—engaging in what she calls "a priori investigation." And yet she claims to produce valuable new knowledge—knowledge of the world no less. Isn't this somehow a bogus activity, a kind of fraud? An armchair is not a good piece of research equipment! It is not a kind of observatory of the inner universe (where is the telescope?). Well, if the armchair is thus inadequate, the same accusation must be leveled at other chair-bound investigators: logicians, set theorists, geometers, game theorists, arithmeticians—that whole category of investigators we call "mathematicians." They too use a priori methods, in which definition plays an important part—so are they irresponsible frauds, too? That seems a little harsh: they simply do a different *kind* of work from that undertaken by empirical scientists. They are concerned with mathematical structures, as philosophers are concerned with conceptual structures. In fact, as I suggested in Chapter 7, the philosopher is best seen as a kind of logician—not in the narrow sense of the mathematical logician concerned with specific formal systems, but in the broad sense of trying to map the entailments that characterize our conceptual scheme. Her chief concern is *consequence*—what entails what, and why, and how things are logically related. Her characteristic thought pattern is: "If...then..."—chains of reasoning from one part of our conceptual scheme to another. Like the mathematician, she is obsessed with consistency and is on the lookout for contradictions and conceptual snarl-ups. She tries to fit things together conceptually. She isn't like someone who wants to know if it's raining outside but is too lazy or stupid to realize that she needs to get up from her armchair and have a look. Given what she is trying to do, the armchair is the ideal spot for doing it (as it is for the mathematician). It is quiet, meditative, and free of distractions from a buzzing world. You can *think* there. Philosophical inquiry is calmly conceptual, not busily empirical (yet the armchair can be an exciting place to be).[4]

---

[4] There is a very real issue, familiar to the practicing philosopher, as to where the armchair should be placed, with what surrounding sights and sounds. You don't want distraction, but you don't want complete sensory deprivation. You want a spot conducive to thinking, but not a silent and sealed room lacking any kind of view. Also, you need pen and paper, or some equivalent, to jot down your thoughts, so a writing surface is required—which means a table of some sort, and with it a suitable chair (armchairs are generally not so good for writing in). Some people write standing up, a few lying down. I use, boringly, an ordinary desk chair, with a ballpoint pen and blank sheets of paper. These constitute my professional equipment (along with books, of course). Most people like to have a nice view, preferably tranquil and not perpetually grabbing the attention: you need

The complaint might now be that the philosopher so characterized is inward-looking, introspective—while the empirical scientist is outward-looking, perceptive. The philosopher fixes his inner eye on his precious little concepts, his mental gems, dissecting them, polishing them, arranging them in neat rows, while his scientific colleague is out there taking in everything reality has to offer, enlarging her vision. Isn't the analytical philosopher stiflingly self-obsessed, while the scientist has a healthy interest in the world beyond herself? I think this image caricatures and over-simplifies the nature of the activities carried out by philosophers and scientists. First, as I have noted repeatedly in the course of this book, conceptual analysis is world-directed, not exclusively inward-looking: it is fundamentally concerned with properties and facts—with what certain things *are* (games, knowledge, perception, causality, etc.) Only a misplaced psychologism about concepts could make one miss this obvious truth. But second, and more interestingly, the putative contrast ignores an essential feature of scientific activity: that it too has its "inward-directed" side, its concern with the scientist's conceptual scheme as such. The scientist too must be "introspective" in order to do her work properly. There are two sides to this looking within. First, and most obviously, the scientist must be concerned about the definition and integrity of her concepts: she must be sure that the concepts of her science are clear and well defined, not vague and ambiguous, and this requires being as explicit as possible about their content. It was Einstein's insistence that the concept of simultaneity be clearly defined that led him to relativity theory. Clarifying the concept of "information" was critical to the development of cognitive science. The concept of the selfish gene was vital in coming to a better understanding of natural selection. Understanding the concept of continuity was essential in the development of mathematics; similarly, infinity. The scientist needs to fashion clear, precise concepts; so attention to concepts as such is part of the scientific enterprise. This is why some of the best scientists have a pronounced philosophical side to them. They don't just rush out and accumulate more data; they sit in their armchairs and think about the concepts they are using to organize the data. The scientist, in his attention to theoretical terms and his need for conceptual rigor, is not as far removed from the ways of the analytical philosopher as some people would appear to think.[5]

---

some space to gaze into, but not excessively lively. I look out over the ocean from a high position, which I find provides just the right degree of outside stimulation: just water and waves, the sky, no people, the odd boat. What is called (often derisively) the "armchair" is really the constellation of these ergonomic and environmental conditions. It is not so much the seating arrangements as the peace and quiet that characterizes the work environment of the philosopher. If the scientist in the lab or the field seeks sensory stimulation as a means of acquiring knowledge, the philosopher seeks sensory *under*-stimulation, the better to free the mind up for cogitation. In the "armchair" is where the ratiocinative faculties do their best work.

[5] This is particularly true of the psychologist, because of the conceptual challenges of the subject—hence the constant disputes about which concepts are scientifically respectable. You need to be sure that the concepts you are using are solid viable concepts, apt for scientific inquiry. For instance, if you are working on memory, you need to pay attention to the concepts you are using—so

Secondly, the process of confirmation and disconfirmation presupposes a kind of introspection—that is, knowledge of one's own beliefs. In order to be able to understand that a given piece of evidence confirms or disconfirms a held theory, the scientist needs to know what theory he or she holds. This is why the scientist will report that evidence E confirms theory T and not T'. There has to be a kind of reflective awareness of the theories that are up for test—the theories that the scientist regards as viable options. The scientist has to *know what she thinks* (or hypothesizes, or conjectures, or is inclined to accept), so that she can take her theory as a potential object of confirmation or disconfirmation. Merely thinking it is not enough. The attitude of confirmation, as a scientist has it, is a second-order attitude. This is why animals don't have an attitude of confirmation, though their beliefs may be refuted by experience: they don't reflect *on* their beliefs *as* their beliefs. But the scientist says, in effect, "I hold that such and such is the case, but let me see if that stands up to empirical test." So there is an essentially inward-looking component in the activity of scientific confirmation—a kind of introspection, if you like. The scientist must occasionally sit down in the armchair and make explicit to herself what it is she believes (or conjectures), because she needs to devise tests that are *appropriate* to what she believes; she needs to adopt the second-order attitude of confirmation. This is to look at one's beliefs (or suppositions) from the outside, to form a higher order view of them, not merely to have them in an unreflective style. The scientist is thus always *referring* to theories, not merely holding them. And this is a characteristically philosophical attitude: looking down on one's beliefs, suppositions, and so on—taking one's own cognitive temperature, so to speak. Moreover, the scientist must know what it is that she *really* believes if confirmation and testing are to work as they should: What is it *precisely* that I believe in holding to theory T? What does that theory *say*? That is necessary because otherwise it will be unclear what the implications of the evidence for the theory are. The scientist might even have to carry out a bit of conceptual analysis on the theoretical terms of the theory in order to clarify their content. For example, if you want to know whether energy is conserved in a certain experimental setup, you had better have a clear idea of what you take the concept of energy to be. Social psychology experiments on group conformity need to work with a well-defined notion of conformity. Studies of the growth of children's knowledge will benefit from an explicit definition of what knowledge is. Some attention to concepts themselves is presupposed in many areas of empirical

---

psychologists will distinguish different types of memory: echoic memory, short-term memory, long-term memory, procedural memory, symbolic memory, etc. The same is true for attention and vision as subjects of experimental study. (The psychologist will often try to "operationalize" his concepts, performing a conceptual reduction.) When I was a practicing experimental psychologist, as a student, working a good deal on visual search, I always found attention to concepts important in designing experiments and interpreting results—as with the distinction between heuristic and algorithmic search procedures (I was working on which of these was the more efficient, relative to an array, in the processing of colored shapes, presented tachistoscopically). Psychologists have always been conceptually sensitive, indeed self-conscious.

research (but this is obvious, is it not?). Questions of definition are almost never beside the point.

It might be said, peevishly, that the armchair philosopher's vice is being closed to any evidence apart from his own cogitations. He listens only to himself. He consults nothing but his own "intuitions." This is, however, not a very cogent criticism, unless offered as merely anecdotal commentary on the tendencies of this or that individual philosopher. First, the trained chair-bound philosopher is in as good a position as anyone to excavate his implicit knowledge—he should turn to his non-philosopher neighbor for this? Second, if he has any brains, he will consult colleagues and students as to the plausibility of any analysis that he comes up with, checking his intuitions against theirs—and being open to correction.[6] This is why dialogue, in addition to solitary contemplation, is so vital to philosophy; dialogue is, indeed, the crucial testing ground for conceptual analysis. Third, there is nothing to stop the analyst from enlisting empirical methods of conceptual exploration. Statistically analyzed surveys eliciting responses to conceptual questions might prove useful, and informal surveys of this type are common in the classroom. It is much harder to get reliable data in this way than many professional philosophers appear to suppose, having never been trained as empirical psychologists themselves (I myself used to *teach* experimental psychology), and the analysis of such data can be highly problematic—but I see no reason of principle why such data should be excluded. In addition, as I noted in Chapter 6, brain scans might in principle be employed, too: assuming that concepts have a cerebral signature, we can test for whether one concept includes another by observing whether the signature of one overlaps with the signature of the other. It is, however, very hard to believe that such neurophysiological evidence could actually overturn an analysis like Suits's analysis of games; but it could certainly have an empirical bearing on it. Still, I suspect the old tried-and-true method of solitary contemplation is unlikely to be ousted any time soon—and it is in itself a perfectly sound way to acquire the kind of knowledge we seek. It is much the same as the linguist consulting his own views ("intuitions") about what strings of his language are grammatical. How likely is it that your feeling that the string "about was hinder and at from dog it" is ungrammatical will be rejected by fellow English speakers?

Lastly, I must compose some weary words about the role of "intuitions" in philosophy. First, it is a bad word, if used indiscriminately, because of its connotations and

---

[6] When I was writing *Mindsight*, I was forever pestering people with questions about their intuitions concerning mental images, partly because my own imagery is rather poor (too abstract and verbal, I suppose). This supplied me with data to confirm or disconfirm what my own faltering intuitions had suggested. I would have thought this procedure to be plain common sense, hardly needing to be recommended—and I very much doubt that it is generally disregarded by philosophers working with intuitive verdicts of one kind or another. Overconfidence in one's own idiosyncratic intuitions strikes me as professional incompetence, likely to lead to professional embarrassment. A wise conceptual analyst will seek out the intuitions of others as a matter of course.

its other uses. Better to speak of one's considered judgments about actual and possible cases. Suppose I am wondering what the analysis of knowledge is. I now know, say, that it is sunny outside, but *would* I know this if either I did not believe it or it was false that it was sunny outside? I reflect for a few seconds and arrive at a judgment: no, I would not know it under either of those counterfactual circumstances. Why do I judge this? Because I have the concept of knowledge and my grasp of it tells me that you can't know things without believing them and you can't know things that are false. That is the use of "intuitions"—and it is hard to find fault with it. It is the same method that one employs in asking whether the laws of logic are necessary truths. Sometimes it is alleged that reports of intuitions vary from culture to culture or between the sexes or that they depend on the subject's mood or on what he or she had for breakfast.[7] Maybe so, but that could be for many reasons aside from the invalidity of the appeal to intuitions: people don't always pay close attention, some have more or quicker conceptual insight than others, concepts themselves can vary in unobvious ways between people, the question can be put in a biased fashion, and so on. Every social scientist knows that surveys are flawed ways of finding out about people's real beliefs; but people do have real beliefs—though their expression of them can be masked by a great many extraneous variables. As a researcher you learn to control for these variables, you don't abandon the idea that people have determinate opinions about things—not without a *lot* of rock solid evidence, anyway. In the same way, the vagaries of surveys about people's conceptual intuitions should not make one rush to abandon the whole idea that people have clear convictions about the proper application of their concepts and that there is strong underlying convergence. To entitle oneself to that negative claim, one would need to show that all other variables had been controlled for—a formidable task, and not one that has to my knowledge been accomplished. If two people have the same concept, that is, are in the same state of implicit knowledge, then it is inconceivable that their intuitions about possible cases could diverge wildly, *given* that those intuitions are sensitive to nothing other than the content of that implicit knowledge. This is really no more

---

[7] See Knobe and Nichols, *Experimental Philosophy*, for a representative selection of essays in this general vein. Of course, the title itself is a misnomer, even given the viewpoint of proponents of the movement: there *are* no experiments that could be devised to discover whether the will is free, skepticism is answerable, the mind is the body, and so on. The most that could be expected would be empirical investigations of what people think when they use certain concepts. The "experimental philosophy" label is pure false advertising, misleading rhetoric, and empty promises. The only way that the label could be justified is if we read it as "thought-experimental philosophy"—but that is quite contrary to the intentions of the devotees. What is the design of an experiment that we might perform on a human being to decide whether she has free will or knows there is an external world or is reducible to events in her nervous system or has objective moral reasons or harbors a persisting self or possesses a purely extensional language or refers to Meinongian entities? There is no such experiment, is the obvious answer—so why speak of "experimental philosophy," as if experiments could answer philosophical questions? The label is pure hype, catchy nonsense. Worse, it is *politics*—propaganda, ideology. It is calculated to advance an agenda, not capture the sober truth. (Note that I am objecting to the label here, not the work done under its banner, which may or may not have value.)

conceivable than the supposition that two people could share the same *explicit* definition of a concept and yet diverge wildly in their judgments about possible cases, *given* that the judgments reflect nothing but the explicit definition grasped equally by both (and not irrelevant variables like how hungry the respondent feels at the time of asking). For the definition *dictates* a particular answer to the question of whether the concept applies in a particular case.[8]

This chapter has been, I fear, a series of platitudes. But sometimes, apparently, platitudes are necessary. The next chapter will be anything but platitudinous.

---

[8] I suspect it is the assumption that people don't have determinate concepts that leads to the distrust of "intuitions"—that is, a kind of Quinean eliminativism about concepts. If there is no determinate concept in there, then intuitions have nothing to be faithful to. But if concepts have a clear determinate content, why should the faculty of intuition be unable to track that content? Why should we be blocked from knowing the entailments of our concepts, given that they have such entailments? Of course, we can be fallible here, as everywhere, but that is no reason to deny the possibility of well-grounded knowledge (experiments are fallible too, very fallible). It is only if concepts have no reality that our verdicts about them become free-floating and groundless, because then there is simply nothing to render one intuition rather than another correct or incorrect. But, of course, concepts do have a determinate inner nature—and so our intuitions have something solid to latch onto.

10 Philosophy as Play

Is philosophizing an intrinsically valuable activity? I expect the majority of my readers would answer with an indignant affirmative—of course philosophy is worthwhile! But I am not asking whether philosophy is a worthwhile subject. I chose my words carefully, so let me repeat the question with the right emphases: is *philosophizing* an *intrinsically* valuable *activity*? I shall approach the answer to this question circuitously, with the warning that the answer is by no means obvious.

In his classic study *Homo Ludens: A Study of the Play Element in Culture,* Johan Huizinga puts forward a general theory of the origin of civilization.[1] He wishes to find a bridge between biology and culture, between animal life and human society, and he suggest that play forms that bridge. Animals and children play, so play is biologically primitive, but it is also removed from the brute exigencies of survival; thus it has the right intermediate status to function as the transition between pre-civilized life and the institutions of modern civilization. This ludic theory contrasts with an intellectualist theory, according to which human beings simply formed the *ideas* of various institutions fully formed and then proceeded to build those institutions. The problem with the intellectualist theory is that it puts the cart before the horse and begs the central question: we could not have acquired the concepts of civilization without the external formations of civilization—the two had to develop together—

[1] The book was published in 1936, exciting a good deal of interest. It is not a book widely known to philosophers (except philosophers of games and sport), despite its relevance to the question of the nature of philosophy as an activity within culture. Page references are given in the text.

and so we have already presupposed the existence of civilization without explaining it. The play theory provides an external lever to start the process, by prefiguring the essential character of cultural formations without presupposing them. Play and culture, for Huizinga, have the same basic structure, the same motivation and dynamic. Play is the infancy of culture, its puerperal stage. When animal play and human intelligence met and fused, culture was the inevitable result: play evolved and human intelligence also evolved, and their convergence produced culture. Huizinga's book is a systematic working out and defense of this general theory, covering law, war, knowledge-games, poetry, myth, religion, art, *and philosophy*. In each area he identifies play elements, particularly ludic contest, and notes the trappings of play that surround these practices and institutions. Thus his third chapter is aptly entitled "Play and Contest as Civilizing Functions." After his detailed survey of a variety of cultural formations, late in the book, he sums up:

It has not been difficult to show that a certain play-factor was extremely active all through the cultural process and that it produces many of the fundamental forms of social life. The spirit of playful competition is, as a social impulse, older than culture itself and pervades all life like a veritable ferment. Ritual grew up in sacred play; poetry was born in play and nourished on play; music and dancing were pure play. Wisdom and philosophy found expression in words and forms derived from religious contests. The rules of warfare, the conventions of noble living were built up on play-patterns. We have to conclude, therefore, that civilization is, in its earliest phases, played. It does not come *from* play like a babe detaching itself from the womb: it arises *in* and *as* play, and never leaves it. (173)

It is easy to see that the practice of law, for example, is a kind of ritualized contest, bound by rules and conventions, with a performance element, the aim of which is victory and glory; it is a kind of game of words, with much taking of turns and arcane procedures, as well as "gamesmanship." It is as if each adversarial lawyer (the word itself is like "player") is trying to checkmate the other in a contest of wits and to take home the prize.

It is important to note right away that play need not always be frivolous or light-hearted; it can be deadly serious, sacred even. This is particularly evident in religious ritual, but solemnity is also present in other areas—war and law, obviously, but also poetry and myth. The player is not always smiling. He or she might be making an enormous effort, concentrating fiercely, taking substantial risks. Play is often no laughing matter. It is difficult to give a general definition of play, and Huizinga is no analytical Bernard Suits, but he does tell us what the general features of play are:

Summing up the formal characteristics of play we might call it a free activity standing quite consciously outside "ordinary" life as being "not serious," but at the same time absorbing the player intensely and utterly. It is an activity connected with no material interest, and no profit can be gained by it. It proceeds within its own proper boundaries of time and space according to fixed rules and in an orderly manner. It promotes the formation of social groupings which tend to surround themselves with secrecy and to stress their difference from the common world by disguise or other means. (13)

The *Oxford English Dictionary* defines "play" to mean "engage in games or other activities for enjoyment rather than for a serious or practical purpose." The intended contrast is between what Suits calls a "technical activity" and a "recreational activity": the former has clear practical goals and efficient means for achieving them; the latter is not concerned with mere practicality and aims rather at enjoyment in the activity itself. We play for the sake of playing, but we work for the sake of its payoff, not for its own sake. Playing is opposed to laboring, which has merely instrumental value. Thus play stands apart from the "ordinary life" of labor and practical achievement. For instance, we work in the office or in the factory and then we play on the tennis court or in the bowling alley—the former to earn a living, the latter for recreational purposes. We *have* to work—we do not do so of our own free choice—but we *choose* to play. In play we are free beings; in work we are in chains (keeping body and soul together). Often, we work *in order* to play. We dig ditches during the day so that we can play skittles at night. In play we are at our happiest; in work our attitude tends to be one of grim determination. We want work to be over, but we want the playing to go on forever. Play is escape, fulfillment, fun, freedom, self-expression, excitement, absorption, and purity. Sisyphus had to perform meaningless labor for all eternity, but there is no such thing as meaningless play—you cannot punish someone by condemning him to play for ten years. Hard labor is punishment, but "hard play" is not. This is why prisons are not play centers (no tennis courts or bowling alleys). Play has value irrespective of the practical outcome, and expects none, but work ("technical activity") derives its value *from* its practical outcome. In a sense, we take play more seriously than work: work matters to us not for itself but for what it can provide external to itself, so we disdain the activity per se; but we take play activity very seriously precisely because it has its own intrinsic value, its own inner point. We may despise what we do for a living, but we can never despise what we choose as recreation. "I hate my work" makes perfect sense, but "I hate my play" sounds peculiar.[2]

Human life is suffused with two opposing sets of attitudes, characteristic of work and play—grudging and welcoming, respectively. Huizinga's thesis is that play atti-

---

[2] One might hate training for a particular game (leg exercises for tennis), because that is an instrumental activity, but one cannot hate what one does *as* play—for then it would not be *play*. Play is something we voluntarily do for its own sake. If you "play" tennis solely to earn a living, you are not *playing*—any more than playing a violin for a living is a form of playing (it is a kind of working). To play at something requires a specific mental attitude, not merely performing certain movements, irrespective of the purpose. Notice that the movements of tennis, externally described, could constitute work instead of play, if the context was right. It is the *intention* that matters.

tudes underlie the structures of culture (as opposed, say, to industry). If we state his theory in the manner of a paleontologist, we can say the following: first there was the "pre-ludic period," in which life forms were too primitive to engage in play (bacteria, plankton, insects, maybe reptiles); then there came the "early ludic period," in which animals evolved that engaged in rudimentary play, mainly mammals, but also perhaps birds; this was followed by the "late ludic period," in which humans evolved and took play to a new level, exploiting those swelling frontal lobes. It was the late ludic period that eventually gave rise to culture and civilization, as play became ever more refined and structured, no doubt aided by language and other forms of representation. In this late ludic period of blossoming civilization, we find a great variety of activities that manifest the play spirit (though no doubt mingled with the work spirit)—and one of these is the activity of philosophy. Huizinga's Chapter IX, "Play-Forms in Philosophy," is devoted to this subject, and I recommend it to interested readers; it will change the way that you see your own discipline. Allow me to quote from it at length:

We can sketch the successive stages of philosophy roughly as follows: it starts in the remote past from the sacred riddle-game, which is at one and the same time ritual and festival entertainment. On the religious side it gives rise to the profound philosophy and theosophy of the Upanishads, to the intuitive flashes of the pre-Socratics; on the play side it produces the sophist. The two sides are not absolutely distinct. Plato raises philosophy, as the search for truth, to heights which he alone can reach, but always in that aerial form which was and is philosophy's proper element. Simultaneously it develops at a lower level into sophistical quackery and intellectual smartness. The agonistic factor in Greece was so strong that it allowed rhetoric to expand at the cost of pure philosophy, which was put in the shade by sophistication parading as the culture of the common man. Gorgias was typical of this deterioration of culture: he turned away from true philosophy to waste his spirit in the praise and misuse of glittering words and false wit. After Aristotle the level of philosophic thinking sank; emulation carried to extremes and narrow doctrinairism won the day. A similar declension was to repeat itself in the later Middle Ages, when the age of the great scholastics who sought to understand the innermost meaning of things was followed by one in which words and formulae alone sufficed. (151)

The general theme here is that philosophy begins in ancient riddle-games, played for sport, with winning and losing, glory and shame, and then devolves into a higher and a lower form: the higher form of Plato and Aristotle, and the lower form of the sophists and their ilk. Verbal contests can be played nobly and seriously, or they can be played basely and frivolously—but they are contests, nonetheless. We might thus describe philosophy as "the sport of reason." It consists of rivalries, teams, staged confrontations, skilled jousting, intellectual combat, agonistic struggles, victory and defeat. As Huizinga later remarks: "To beat your opponent by reason or the force of the word becomes a sport comparable with the profession of arms" (155). Philosophy originates in the competitive word game, the verbal battle of wit and tactics, and it still bears that agonistic mark in its later manifestations. However, the ludic dimension sits somewhat uneasily with the goal of attaining truth, and it can easily corrupt the pursuit of that goal—for victory in the game is not the same as rightness or real cogency. The dialogue form, always suited for the philosophical treatise, dramatizes the nature of philosophy as a kind of verbal competition—between people or between positions. Philosophy is historically a kind of athletic contest of the mind.[3]

And who can deny that this history marks the practice of philosophy up to the present day? We still have our staged confrontations, our verbal contests, in which truth and rhetoric uneasily combine—our combative dialogues and disputes. We speak of "winning" and "losing" arguments, of making "moves," of "cheating" and "evading." Some are admired for their polemical "skill" or "style," for their argumentative "prowess," for their "wit" and "brilliance"—as if they are star athletes of the podium and seminar room. We "train" our graduate students, we try to instill good "technique," and we encourage "competition." There are "gladiatorial" confrontations, "dirty pool" exchanges, good and bad behavior in "victory" and "defeat." We try to force our opponent to accept our position; we attempt to outmaneuver him; we paint him into a corner. When he is finally "beaten" in argument, we might even exclaim "checkmate!" All this takes place in ritualized settings and special locations, often with rules of engagement. There can be exhilaration or gloom, the thrill and anxiety of combat. For some practitioners, philosophy can resemble a deadly serious "blood sport"; for others, it is a mild recreational diversion. And notice that none of this is done for any "practical purpose": we are not seeking to gain territory or riches or to exact punishment or revenge for some evil act done. We engage in these intellectual contests for their own sake, like willing prizefighters, not for profit and material acquisition—victory is reward enough. The riddle-game is a contest played for its own sake; the philosophy-game is likewise a contest valued in its own right. We would do it even if we weren't paid (and often we are not paid). Philosophy is a lot like chess, with its moves, counter-moves, and strong positions—and its removal from practicality. As philosophers, we are athletes of thought, contesting rivals, ludic combatants. We are thus still caught up in the mentality of the verbal contests of old, reaching back to pre-history. Our *modus operandi* is competitive play, seriously

[3] The preoccupation of ancient Greek culture with heroes and superhuman figures (Perseus, Theseus, Achilles, Hercules, et al.) has its counterpart in the intellectual heroes of the age—and each has his commemorative statue and historical halo. There are heroes of the intellectual battlefield, as well as the military. Plato celebrates his distinguished upper echelon of "philosopher kings," beings above the common run of humanity. Hero worship is part of the culture of philosophy from the ancient Greeks to the present day: the select pantheon, the elevated few. We have our "star" philosophers, as sports enthusiasts have their "star" athletes. In both cases, our longing for heroes may well hide more subtle gradations and finer distinctions.

undertaken. We are more like professional chess players and football players than like farmers or factory workers. Our work is play and our play is work.

We must now turn again to Bernard Suits, the apostle of game playing. For Suits not only undertakes to define the concept of a game in *The Grasshopper*; he also attempts to establish a striking normative thesis—namely, that game playing is the only intrinsically valuable human activity. This is a startling contention: playing games is the *only* thing we do that has intrinsic value—everything else has merely instrumental value. The attempted proof of this thesis occurs in Chapter 15 of *The Grasshopper*, "Resolution," in a mere eleven pages. Suits begins by asking what would have to obtain in Utopia, where Utopia is defined as a mode of existence in which all our desires are satisfied without having to work. There is thus no need for any activity of an instrumental nature: we can do only what we find intrinsically valuable, not what we do for the sake of other things. Obviously, then, there is no need to build houses, grow and cook food, train for a moneymaking occupation, and so on. To obtain all these things, we simply press a telepathic button, without lifting a finger. All of our practical needs are automatically met. We don't have to do anything that we don't want to do. So what is there left to do? Answer: the activities that we value for their own sake. But what are they? We might naturally suggest the following: pursue art and literature, do scientific research, improve our own personalities, perform good deeds, have sex, think about philosophy, and play games. Suits then proceeds to argue that only the last of these would be pursued in Utopia. I cannot do justice to the richness and ingenuity of his discussion here, but will merely summarize it. There can be no good deeds to perform because there is no evil to rectify in Utopia, by definition. There is nothing in our personalities to improve, for the same reason (anyway, we could improve them just by mentally pressing a button). We will not do any scientific research, because everything has been discovered and we can always access this knowledge by means of the magic button. For the same reason, no one will think about philosophy (I will come back to this). Surely there will be sexual activity! But even here the Grasshopper argues thus:

> The obsessive popularity that sex has always enjoyed is, I suspect, inseparably bound up with man's non-Utopian condition. Sex, as we have come to know and love it, is part and parcel with repression, guilt, naughtiness, domination and submission, liberation, rebellion, sadism and masochism, romance, and theology. But none of these things has a place in Utopia. Therefore, we ought at least to face the possibility that with the removal of all these constituents of sex as we value it, there will be little left but a pleasant sensation in the loins—or wherever. (153)

Sexual relations will simply no longer be worth the effort, having lost their interest to us (we might just press the orgasm button when we feel the need). What about art and literature? Here the problem is that these activities center around the depiction of human aspiration, struggle, success and failure, moral challenges, human weaknesses: but there are no such things in Utopia—so art loses its rationale. The only activity left on the list is playing games—but why should that survive the erosive power of Utopia? The Grasshopper replies as follows:

What we have shown thus far is that there does not appear to be anything to *do* in Utopia, precisely because in Utopia all instrumental activities have been eliminated. There is nothing to strive for precisely because everything has already been achieved. What we need, therefore, is some activity in which what is instrumental is inseparably combined with what is intrinsically valuable, and where the activity is not itself an instrument for some further end. Games meet this requirement perfectly. For in games we must have obstacles which we can strive to overcome *just so that* we can possess the activity as a whole, namely, playing the game. Game playing makes it possible to retain enough effort in Utopia to make life worth living. (154)

Skepticus then adds: "What you are saying is that in Utopia the only thing left to do would be to play games, so that game playing turns out to be the whole of the ideal of existence" (154).

In game playing it is impossible to achieve the goal of the game, that is, winning or achieving a certain rule-governed result,[4] without *playing* the game; but in technical activities the goal is always logically separate from the activity, so you can obtain the goal without necessarily engaging in the activity. You can achieve your goal of having a house without needing to build it—you can just press the button. You can gain scientific knowledge without having to do scientific research—again, by pressing the button. But you can't achieve the goal of winning a tennis match except by *playing tennis*—the magic button won't do it for you. The activity cannot be sidestepped, with the goal achieved directly. So in Utopia you can't win games without playing games; this is one end that can't be satisfied except by engaging in an activity.[5] We will not compete with each other in Utopia for goods and services, because there is no scarcity of these resources; but we can compete in games because *winning* is a scarce commodity—someone has to lose. Therefore, only game playing will be pursued in Utopia. So Suits (or his playful Grasshopper) contends.[6]

[4] The reason for the disjunction is that not all games are competitive, as with patience (solitaire) or ten-pin bowling by oneself—so here we must speak of obtaining a certain result by means of following rules, not of winning. Of course, we could simplify by stipulating that in such solitary cases one is competing with the cards or the bowling pins.

[5] Likewise, you cannot really achieve a perfect 300 in bowling without following the rules of bowling and getting a strike on every ball (you can't just walk down the alley to the pins and whack them with the ball). You would find no satisfaction in simply pressing a button that knocked all the pins over while you just stood there watching. The goal of bowling is a *lusory* goal. Thus there is solitary bowling in Utopia, as well as competitive bowling. (Bowling conforms well to Suits's definition of a game, because it prescribes an extremely inefficient way to topple pins.)

[6] Let me observe here, parenthetically, that Suits's own book can be interpreted as a case of game playing: for he seeks to achieve a certain end, namely getting us to accept his definition of a game, but he does so by adopting an inefficient means, viz., by having a grasshopper engage in a

I agree with Suits that in Utopia games will still be played, and that this is a conceptual truth about games, and that it is a very important part of the reason that we find games valuable: but I think he is wrong that game playing (in the usual sense) is the *only* activity we find intrinsically valuable—that we will do nothing else in Utopia. Note that his reason for supposing that art and literature do not exist in Utopia is not that their goal is automatically met there, as is the case with science. His point is not that they aim at something, say amusement or knowledge of the human condition, which could in principle be achieved by a suitable machine, so that the end can be met without employing the means—as he claims for the case of science. His point is rather that the subject matter of art and literature will not exist in Utopia, so there will be nothing for these things to be about. It is not that they are a dispensable means to an end that can in principle be achieved otherwise. So they *may* have an end that is inseparable from the means, like game playing. And that is not so implausible: whatever the aim of art is, it is hard to see how it could be achieved except *through* art. The goal of art might be described as that of producing an aesthetic experience *of art*. A painting, say, aims to produce in the viewer an aesthetic experience of that painting, not just any old aesthetic experience—which might be producible in some other way (say, by pressing a button). Thus art objects (or their creators) have a *means-dependent* goal—the goal of producing a certain effect by that very means. *If* art had a subject matter in Utopia, then it would be

------

dialogue, ornamented by stories and fancies, the eventual upshot of which is our becoming persuaded of the rightness of the definition. (Since the Grasshopper, by his very essence, never does anything other than play, *his* engaging in a conversation with Skepticus *must* be a case of game playing—since he is constitutionally unable to work. And it is true that he never takes the shortest route to a conclusion.) Suits does not adopt the more direct method of simply laying the analysis out as in any standard philosophical work. He employs his mouthpiece the Grasshopper as his means of persuasion—and talking grasshoppers are not the most efficient means for getting people to accept philosophical conclusions. (Plato's dialogues can be seen as game playing by the same reasoning: using drama to convey philosophy.) Suits is playing a game called "Convince-around": getting people to believe something by choosing an inefficient means of persuasion. I am sure he was well aware of this ironic "meta-game"—secretly playing a game with the reader while overtly defining what playing a game is. I, on the contrary, am merely *working* in this book: choosing the most efficient means I can think of to get my point across. So here, by way of play relief, is my own stab at employing a woefully inefficient means:

> *Without analysis philosophy is in paralysis*
> *You have my license to seek essence*
> *By all means stare from your armchair*
> *Naturalism is un-naturalism*
> *Let the linguistic turn burn*
> *Let Aristotle out of the bottle*
> *Find your roots in Suits*
> *Hop like the Grasshopper.*

It may not be much of a poem, but you must agree that it is a *highly* inefficient way to persuade you of the position of this book—if only because you are unlikely to be convinced by such doggerel. Still, it counts as a philosophical verbal game.

indispensable in producing its effects, since these effects make reference to the art object itself—just as the goal of a game makes reference to the rules of the game. So it seems reasonable to argue. The novel, say, is not just one way the author might use to produce the effect she seeks; and the reader does not suppose that he could get the effects he desires from reading the novel in some more direct way. He values the means themselves—the activity of reading the novel. Suits never denies that this activity has intrinsic value, which is inseparable from its end; he merely points out that in Utopia novels won't have the interest that they have for those who live in a non-Utopian world.

The case of art is therefore quite different from that of science. The purpose of the scientific method is to produce scientific knowledge, but the knowledge is logically separable from the method (this again is a conceptual truth). This is why you can acquire scientific knowledge without doing the research yourself. Scientific research is a kind of labor, work, a technical activity; we wouldn't do it unless we had to, in order to obtain the knowledge. We have to make the observations, do the experiments, analyze the results, write up the research, publish it, taking up our valuable time the while. Why do these things if you could get the result you seek far more effortlessly? Why not give yourself more leisure time? Thus it is very plausible for Suits to say that in Utopia there are no scientific researchers: you might as well just press the button to acquire the knowledge you seek, without going to all the trouble of discovering it yourself. You just take the most efficient route to the knowledge— just as you do now by using the latest equipment or calculating devices. You don't pick defective equipment or unreliable calculators just to make things more challenging to yourself, as if you were playing a game with nature. You try to obtain the knowledge as efficiently as possible. (Don't say you might do it for self-improvement; there is no self-improvement in Utopia. Also, if that was your reason, you might achieve the self-improvement in some other way—which shows that you don't value the activity of scientific research *as such*). The value of the scientific method is instrumental, as the value of medical examination is instrumental or the value of scaffolding in constructing a building. Yes, we value scientific knowledge, sometimes for its own sake and not its practical benefits, and this valuing may be intrinsic; but that is not to say that we value scientific *activity* for its own sake—we value it only because it yields scientific knowledge. We would drop it if we could, as we would drop other forms of instrumental activity. If we could be given scientific knowledge for free, we would accept the offer. Why work for something if you can have it without working? Thus we can say that the aim of scientific activity is not a means-dependent aim: we don't aim to produce scientific knowledge *only as generated by a certain means*—namely, scientific research. The goal of obtaining scientific knowledge may be achieved without the knowledge being apprehended *as* produced by the means that actually generated it. It is the same with house building: the goal of house building can be achieved—someone having a house to live in—without the recipient apprehending the means by which the house was built. The value of the end is not *internally* related to its actual means of production (as the value of the end of winning a game *is* internally related to its means of production, i.e., playing by the rules of the game). The value of scientific knowledge is *detachable* from the means that produced it; the means were mere means.[7]

Now Suits maintains that philosophy is just like science in this respect. He says: "In Utopia, therefore, there are no scientists, philosophers, or any other intellectual investigators" (152). For, in Utopia, philosophical knowledge can be obtained at the press of a telepathic button, just like scientific knowledge or historical knowledge or geographical knowledge or mathematical knowledge. If your aim is just to obtain knowledge in these areas, why go to all the trouble of doing the experiments, combing through the archives, roaming the world, or constructing the proofs (in this last case we might begin to see a chink in the argument)? Why bother with philosophical reasoning, disputation, the process of conceptual analysis, the setting out of alternatives, or abstract reflection of any kind—why not just press the button and instantly get the philosophical answer you seek directly? Why not just skip the middleman, cut out the arduous philosophizing, and get the knowledge neat? Why bother with what *led up* to philosophical knowledge? Isn't that just so much unnecessary toil, when we could access the information we seek so much more effortlessly? For example, we could learn Suits's definition of a game just by asking the knowledge machine, "What is the correct definition of a game?" We need not read slowly through his entire text, following all his potential counterexamples, his reformulations, the twists and turns of his argument. That is just so much dispensable means— like doing time-consuming and difficult medical research in order to find the cure of a disease. Just tell me what the cure is!

I suspect that many of my readers will feel that there is something amiss with this way of thinking about the acquisition of philosophical knowledge. The activity doesn't seem as merely instrumental as this description suggests. I am on your side: I think that the instrumental perspective gives quite the wrong picture of the nature of philosophical understanding. I want to say, to the contrary, that the goal of philosophical activity is to produce philosophical knowledge by means of that very activity. That is, the goal has not been achieved unless the recipient of the knowledge appreciates that the knowledge was achieved by means of philosophical activity, or herself arrived at the knowledge by such a means. Philosophical knowledge consists of a certain known proposition—as it might be, an analysis of a particular concept—*and* what led up to the acceptance of that proposition—the procedure as well as the result. In fact, you can't detach the result from the procedure—as with games. But why is that? What is it *about* philosophy that makes it different from

---

[7] I think Suits here makes an important point in the philosophy of science, one that I have not seen made elsewhere—that scientific method (or methods) has only instrumental value. This distinguishes it from philosophy (according to me) and from the arts. Scientific activity is a species of *work*.

science and other instrumental disciplines? Here things become murky, because there are different conceptions of what philosophy is, and the question is a difficult one. On one well-known conception, philosophy is puzzle removal: "The results of philosophy are the uncovering of one or another piece of plain nonsense and of bumps that the understanding has got by running its head up against the limits of language. These bumps make us see the value of the discovery."[8] On this view, we have to be puzzled before we can appreciate the philosophical solution, so we have to go through the philosophical process in order to see the point of the results. The "bumps" are necessary for the discovery to be properly appreciated. Imagine asking the knowledge machine what the correct analysis is of sentences containing definite descriptions, and receiving back a statement of Russell's theory. That would be a substantive piece of knowledge, to be sure, but it would lack something essential unless it included mention of the puzzles that so troubled Russell—the temptation to introduce a Meinongian ontology in response to surface form. Russell's theory is significant *in relation* to those puzzles, not merely in itself. By contrast, the results of geography do not consist in the removal of puzzles generated by language or by the natural waywardness of our thought; they are simply self-standing facts. Nor is physics "a battle against the bewitchment of our intelligence by means of language" (109). But in philosophy we must experience the bewitchment and fight against it to see the point of the therapy that Wittgenstein recommends. However, this conception of philosophy is by no means the only one: there is also the idea that philosophy produces *theories* in response to *problems*. This brings it superficially closer to science. It is not quite the idea of discovering facts to remedy the mere absence of knowledge, as in the geography case, but it raises the question of why we can't just enunciate and absorb the true philosophical theories and leave it at that. Isn't belief in the true philosophical propositions all that matters in the end? So isn't the value of philosophizing purely instrumental?

I don't think so, but the reason is less clear. I think we get close to it by observing that philosophy is "essentially exclusionary" in its approach to knowledge production. What I mean by this phrase is that the significance of a particular philosophical theory lies in its excluding other rival theories, not merely in its own self-standing truth. Each theory exists within a space of options, each exercising some type of attraction, and philosophical knowledge consists in accepting one theory *as opposed* to the other theories. For instance, consider idealism, materialism, and dualism: to accept one of these is to *reject* the others—to reject them despite their appeal. If I ask the knowledge machine which of these theories is true, having never thought through the options myself, and receive the answer "dualism," I have a piece of propositional knowledge; but I have no *philosophical* appreciation of the answer— for that I have to grasp the way in which the three options compete and why someone

---

[8] Wittgenstein, *Philosophical Investigations*, 119—and there are many other remarks to the same effect.

might adopt one or the other (by hypothesis) false views.[9] I must grasp not merely that the world contains two fundamentally different kinds of substance, but also that it is *not* wholly material or wholly mental. Thus the knowledge is "essentially exclusionary": it makes essential reference to a range of excluded positions. In the case of science (geography, etc.), the knowledge is not *essentially* exclusionary: to be sure, one theory supplants others in response to evidence and other considerations, but you don't need to grasp the supplanted theories, as well as their attractions, in order to have scientific knowledge. You don't need to compare and contrast the geocentric and heliocentric theories of the solar system in order to know the truth of the heliocentric theory, and you don't need to grasp the phlogiston theory of heat in order to grasp the kinetic theory—any more than you need to know old discredited geographical theories in order to have perfectly respectable geographical knowledge. In philosophy, by contrast, we always have a kind of thesis-antithesis structure: to accept one theory *is* to reject the others, to see its *comparative* merits. Often, indeed, we have little reason to accept one theory as opposed to others *except* that we reject all the others and there are no more options.[10] In a sense, philosophical knowledge is inherently negative—it is all dissent and disavowal. To arrive at a positive view, one has to go through a process of option evaluation, trying out one thing and then another, until the truth emerges (or seems to): without this, the final result is empty, unmotivated, pointless. The arguments for a position, and against other positions, are thus at least as important as the position itself; they are not detachable from that position. In principle, you could grasp the entire scientific truth about the world and know nothing of the way in which this truth was acquired or what the live theoretical options once were; but in philosophy, the procedure and the options are integral to understanding—conditions of its possibility. This is, indeed, why in one case we are more apt to speak of straightforward positive *knowledge,* while in the other case we speak of *understanding:* in the former case we select a position and discard its rivals, producing knowledge of a given proposition; but in the latter case we understand the *issue* and *favor* one *view* over others. As we might say, philosophical knowledge is "contextual"—relational, situated. The object of philosophical inquiry is to obtain such contextual understanding, as well as a definite choice of position—

[9] Actually this is not the best example, because, as I argue in the next chapter, these classic doctrines are not capable of coherent formulation—so there *is* no answer as to which of them is correct. So pick your own favorite example of a philosophical problem. I myself would dearly love to know whether Meinong's ontology was right and whether space is absolute and whether W. D. Ross's pluralist theory of morality is correct (as I strongly suspect it is).

[10] My discussion of the DIME shape in *Problems in Philosophy* illustrates the dialectical structure of a typical philosophical problem: we are always being asked to choose between a Domesticating solution, an Irreducibility solution, a Magical solution, and an Eliminative solution. To adopt a particular position is to choose one of these options *over* the others, once their attractions have been duly registered. It is always a kind of forced choice, not an untroubled acceptance of the clearly correct position. The characteristic state of mind of the philosopher is: I am inclined to think this, *despite* that. The philosopher is chronically *ambivalent* (and hence subject to cognitive dissonance and its contortions).

but this involves appreciating what led up to the final view. The situation is not so different from that of mathematics: the object of the exercise is not merely to discover which mathematical propositions are true; it is also to arrive at *proofs of theorems*. You can't cut out the proofs and retain the mathematical knowledge. Similarly, in philosophy it matters how you got there, not merely where you arrived. This is why in teaching philosophy we proceed by laying out all the possible theories, evaluating each in turn, and then attempt to select one as better than the others. In science that would be deemed a waste of time (and rightly so).[11]

This is also why history matters in philosophy and why false ideas can retain their relevance. We need to know how ideas and theories develop, how one idea is replaced by another, in order to understand the content of a given idea or theory. Philosophical positions always exist in relation to other positions, mirroring them or contrasting with them, and history displays this contextual structure most dramatically. Aristotle rejected Plato's theory of Forms, rationalism rejected empiricism (and vice versa), Frege rejected psychologism, Russell rejected Meinong, the positivists rejected metaphysics, the later Wittgenstein rejected the earlier Wittgenstein, Nietzsche rejected traditional Christian morality, and almost everyone came to reject idealism. Philosophical history is essentially a history of rejection, repudiation, and replacement. But this is not simply a process of falsification, as exists in science, because the rejected theories live on to breathe life into the accepted theories. That is why we still teach idealism, Plato's theory of Forms, Meinong, and so on: not necessarily because we accept these theories, but because they are the indispensable *context* for understanding the theories that we do accept. And, of course, to speak of "false ideas" here is horribly oversimplified, because once-rejected ideas enjoy recrudescence, regain favor, while others once widely accepted fade into the background. There is never a definitive refutation, accepted by everyone, so that an idea or doctrine is put completely out of its misery once and for all (even Meinong has made a spirited comeback).[12] Philosophy as it now exists is a kind of quilt of ideas and theories, standing in tension with each other, shedding light on each other, but never tearing off a part and consigning it eternally to the flames. To accept a subset of these

---

[11] In philosophy we often spend a lot of time showing why what we take to be false *is* false, before coming to what we take to be true. The reason is that the view we favor exists in a space of alternatives with which it necessarily competes. But the scientist doesn't spend precious time totally demolishing the geocentric theory of the solar system before moving on to the heliocentric theory—instead just giving the evidence for the latter theory directly. The physicist doesn't bother refuting the views of the pre-Socratics before presenting the modern atomic theory. In contrast, philosophers will often expound and criticize (say) Plato's theory of universals while conducting a class on the meaning of predicate expressions and the nature of generality. Falsity matters more to the philosopher than to the scientist (or historian, geographer, or etymologist): we may not know what is true, but we are pretty sure we know what is false—and we are apt to dwell on that.

[12] I talk about the merits and benefits of nonexistence in my "The Objects of Intentionality." Meinong is by no means as refuted (as opposed to rhetorically ridiculed) as many contemporary philosophers fondly suppose.

ideas and theories, one has to have an appreciation of the whole quilt and its inter-relations. Philosophical understanding is tracing a path across this quilt, not merely occupying a square in it. The journey matters as much as the destination. Perhaps this is why scientists are apt to be impatient with philosophy: instead of simply arriving at a piece of information and incorporating it into the store of human knowledge, philosophers seem obsessed with their own history, their tortured dialectics, the perpetual dance of ideas, the wreckage of past intellectual edifices. Philosophers seem caught up in their own process, neurotics lost in a maze of options, defensive and uncertain. Why can't they just spit it out and get it over with? Why all the agonizing?[13]

I can summarize all this quite simply as follows: it is not the purpose of the scientific method to produce scientific knowledge *by* the scientific method, but it is the purpose of the philosophical method to produce philosophical knowledge *by* the philosophical method. That is: the goal of science can be achieved simply by acquiring scientific knowledge, possibly by way of the knowledge machine; but the goal of philosophy cannot be achieved simply by acquiring philosophical knowledge (i.e., knowing which philosophical propositions are true), possibly by way of the knowledge machine. You have to acquire philosophical knowledge by *philosophizing*—by employing philosophical method. So, granted that philosophical knowledge has value, philosophizing has value, because you can't really possess the former without doing the latter. To really know something in philosophy you must have *philosophized*. You must have followed philosophical procedure. Thus *philosophizing* has *intrinsic* value as an *activity*—to return to my opening question. (But scientific researching does not have intrinsic value as an activity, but only instrumental value as producing a certain goal state—like other kinds of honest labor.) The reason is that in philosophy the goal is not separable from the method: philosophical knowledge *is* knowledge gained by philosophizing—as scientific knowledge is *not* knowledge gained by following scientific method (ditto for

---

[13] It is this no-nonsense attitude on the part of scientists that makes them prone to be such bad philosophers when they turn their amateurish hand to it (mainly in retirement). They don't understand, because of their training and scientific practice, the inescapably dialectical structure of philosophical issues. They see only the isolated pockets in the quilt, not the quilt itself. They thus think they know what is obviously the correct solution to a problem and they charge into the china shop intent on promoting that solution, failing to appreciate the complexity and subtlety of the issue (I am thinking particularly of those who see free will in quantum indeterminacy or consciousness in neural synchrony or morality in biology). Their naïveté consists in not grasping the matrix of options that define the issue: they accordingly don't understand what has to be done to establish a philosophical position. In a sense, philosophical issues are always more *complex* than scientific problems—more fraught and frustrating, more hemmed in, more *torn*. This is why the honest philosopher can often find herself tossed hither and thither across the philosophical quilt, as one option after another seizes her allegiance. The intellectual life of the scientist is calmer, less conflicted, more firmly committed. The facts speak more for themselves in science than they ever can in philosophy. (This is why Frege's theory of sense and reference, for example, could never have the status of Darwin's theory of evolution.)

geography and history). We must *define* philosophical knowledge by reference to the means for acquiring it—this is the *essence* of philosophical knowledge—but it would be wrong to *define* scientific knowledge by reference to the methods used in acquiring it. This is why in Utopia we can gain scientific knowledge by pressing a button, but we cannot do the same for philosophical knowledge; in the latter case, we must put in the requisite effort. Structurally, the situation is the same as with playing games: we can't achieve the goal of a game without playing the game, as we can't achieve the goal of philosophy without "playing" philosophy. Thus there *will* be philosophical activity in Utopia (contrary to Suits's suggestion, or at least the Grasshopper's), alongside game-playing activity.[14] If we define "work" as "engaging in a technical activity," that is, putting in some means-oriented effort in order to achieve a logically separable goal, then philosophizing is not work, since it is integral to the goal of the activity. The means are *part* of the goal, as playing a game is part of the goal of winning at a game, so that the goal cannot be achieved without the means being employed: but those means are precisely engaging in philosophical activity. And now, if we define "play" as "the opposite of work," we can derive the result that philosophizing is a form of play—it is an activity that we value for its own sake, intrinsically, not something we value merely because it is the only way we have to achieve a logically separable goal. We value scientific method instrumentally, as we value medical method instrumentally; but we value philosophical method intrinsically, as we value "lusory method" intrinsically. We philosophize for the sake of philosophizing, as we play games for the sake of playing games (though we may have other subsidiary goals in both cases, such as to make money). Philosophizing is not work in the sense that we would dispense with it if we had the chance, as we would "technical" forms of labor—but of course that doesn't mean it involves no effort or training or self-sacrifice or skill. Putting it very intuitively, philosophizing is "playing with ideas"—and we will want to do that even if the "philosophical truth" is obtainable at the touch of a button. We want to arrive at the truth *by* playing with ideas, that is, reasoning, reflecting, devising necessary and sufficient conditions, thinking up counterexamples, and so on. But in science we have no particular desire to arrive at the truth by playing with lab instruments, telescopes, calculators, and so on—any more than we want to cure diseases by undertaking costly and effortful medical research. In these cases we would welcome the

---

[14] I hate to disagree with the astute Grasshopper, who is generally preternaturally wise in most matters, but I suppose that no Great Thinker is *completely* infallible. Still, it is not child's play (!) to develop an account of philosophy that makes its continued existence in Utopia possible. The consolation for the Grasshopper is that his reflections on games will be of interest to people in Utopia—he will not be rendered obsolete by a knowledge machine that simply prints out his final conclusions (assuming them to be correct). People will want to listen to his tale and follow the intellectual journey that he lays out—because only then can they really know (*philosophically* know) what a game essentially is and why games are played in Utopia. Contrary to his own self-abnegating message, I am saving him for a useful existence in Utopia—as an instigator of intrinsically valuable philosophical activity.

Utopian knowledge machine, but in the philosophy case such a machine leaves us cold. We may be tempted to resort to it when our philosophizing gets jammed and frustration mounts, but we know it will produce only a thin and unsatisfactory simulacrum of the epistemic state we seek; for that we need to do the "work" ourselves. Anything less is *cheating*. (We may be similarly tempted to resort to a "game-winning machine" when we seem in danger of losing at a game, but again that will not produce the goal we seek, namely winning by the rules of the game.)[15]

We can see the asymmetry in relation to the different role of experiments in science and philosophy. Ordinary empirical experiments are just a means to acquiring knowledge, something we need to go through to get what we want—they can be forgotten once they have served their instrumental purpose. But thought experiments in philosophy are not like that: they are integral to knowledge. When teaching a class on the analysis of knowledge or games, you don't just state the analysis for the students and tell them to memorize it; you take them through the intuitive steps that lead up to the analysis—you make them perform the thought experiments over again for their own edification. Only then do they have the knowledge that you seek to impart. They cannot grasp the full import of the analysis unless they see how it handles a range of possible cases, and for this they need to do some mental experiments of their own, with you as guide. In a sense, then, all philosophical learning is lab work—thought experiments in the laboratory of the intellect (this is the place where *modal* questions are settled). But you could teach science (the content of it) while never having your students set foot in a lab. In the search for necessary and sufficient conditions, everyone is a lab worker, an experimental scientist, performing those inexpensive internal experiments of thought. Philosophy is *already* "experimental." In short: you don't fully understand an analysis unless you have done the thought experiments yourself. Again, the means are integral to the ends. And these really are experiments—controlled setups in which hypotheses are tested. Your hypothesis is that knowledge is true belief (say) and you want to test that hypothesis. You imagine possible cases in which these two conditions are met and ask yourself whether there are any counterexamples among them; if so, you have falsified your hypothesis and must devise a new one. You didn't prejudge the issue or ignore counter-evidence; you conducted an inquiry in an open-minded spirit and you accepted the verdict delivered by the data—there *were* cases in which there was true belief without knowledge. You violated no rational rules of inquiry and you came up with

---

[15] The idea of a game-winning machine is really an incoherent idea, because you can't skip directly to the victory without playing the game—that wouldn't be *winning at* the game. Similarly, the idea of a philosophical knowledge machine is incoherent, because there is no real philosophical knowledge without philosophical activity preceding it. In both cases, the goal is "backward looking" or "means sensitive": the goal must be achieved in a certain way—that *is* the goal. In philosophy we want to achieve the goal of believing the truth *by* sound and correct philosophical reasoning—which involves (*inter alia*) the weighing of alternatives. We want the whole sequential package, the entire philosophical rigmarole, not just its terminal stage. We want to climb the mountain ourselves.

a justified result, namely that true belief is insufficient for knowledge. You looked for counter-evidence to your initial hypothesis and you found it. You did what any responsible experimenter would do, except that you did it in your own head. (And it was fun, too, like playing a mental game.)[16]

If philosophizing is like playing a game, at least in one respect, and unlike doing scientific research, some interesting consequences follow. First, in an important sense, philosophy is discontinuous with science, not only in being a priori, but also in that it is an intrinsically valuable activity. Science is instrumentally valuable, like most other human activity, but philosophy has value *qua* the activity it is: so these are not the same *kind* of enterprise. The two have a different motivational structure.[17] Philosophy cannot, then, consist of questions that science eventually appropriates; there is a sharp line between the two, methodologically, motivationally, and in the form of the knowledge they seek. Philosophy cannot be just very general science or pre-science or sloppy science—any more than playing is continuous with working. Second, science might come to an end some day, but philosophy never will, in the following sense: advances in technology might make scientific activity redundant—we might invent the universal knowledge machine or be made a gift of it by well-meaning aliens—but this would not make philosophical activity redundant, because of the internal relationship between philosophy and philosophizing. Science ends when all the knowledge it can acquire has been acquired—and that can happen in a finite time; but philosophy (the activity) remains valuable eternally. Just as we will keep playing games in Utopia, so we will keep on doing philosophy. Riddles and word games will survive in Utopia, and so will philosophical discourse. Philosophy is in its essential nature eternal, but science is in its nature finite. Even if we come up with all the answers in philosophy (whatever that may mean), we will still want to engage in the activity, because the answers embed the activity—the product and the process are inseparable. (I think the same is true of art and literature, to revert to an earlier topic, because you cannot separate the aim of art from artistic means. We will still be going to the opera in Utopia.) Third, as Suits points out, playing games affords us a glimpse of Utopia, since game playing will be central there (he thinks it will be our sole occupation). This is surely part of the reason that we like to play games: we are thereby liberated from the world of instrumental labor, fear of the future, work slavery. Playing games is what we would do if we were totally

---

[16] Thus there is no equivocation on "experiment" in "thought experiment"—the term was aptly chosen to describe a particular intellectual exercise. Thought experiments are *literally* experiments. Nor is the thought experiment suspiciously "non-empirical": you tested your theory by gathering data involving your intuitive verdicts about possible cases—and the data were new pieces of information intentionally acquired and rationally evaluated. The data comprised thoughts, not perceptions, but they were data nonetheless. The procedure was, in one clear sense, perfectly "empirical."

[17] None of this is to deny that both science and philosophy are dedicated to the pursuit of truth and are rational inquiries. It is merely to point out that the means employed in the two cases have a different kind of value—instrumental and intrinsic, respectively.

free to do anything we want. It is the ideal state of being. But equally, if philosophizing is also something we would do in Utopia, it too affords us a glimpse of that ideal state of being: it makes vivid and real to us what we only dimly imagine and devoutly wish for—a life without labor and anxiety, a life of ease and plenty, of safety and security. In philosophizing it is *as if* we already exist in such an ideal state, since it is one of the things we would choose to do in that state. Philosophy makes us *feel* Utopia, live it here and now. This is what we wish life consisted of—wholly, purely. Philosophy is freedom—life without necessary work. Fourth, the perspective here adumbrated must influence the attitude we take toward our philosophical exertions: they are not undertaken in a spirit of work, but of play, for their own sake, not for the external goods they bring (though they may bring such external goods). When you are working on philosophy, you are not *working*—your exertions have intrinsic value. Philosophy is not an *industry*. That is, the procedures you follow are integral to the result you wish to achieve. You should not resent these exertions, as you may resent the exertions of digging a ditch or filing your tax returns—just as you do not resent your exertions when playing a game of tennis or chess. You can't achieve the goal of tennis or chess without exertions, that is, attentively playing by the rules, and in the same way you can't achieve the results of philosophy without using the methods of philosophy. You can't resent having to perform the *action* if the action is part of the desired object. Thus your attitude to philosophy will change for the better if you begin to see it for the intrinsically valuable activity that it is. It is no more an unnecessary burden imposed by an inconvenient universe than hitting tennis balls is an unnecessary burden in trying to win at tennis (or looking at art objects is an unnecessary burden in the pursuit of aesthetic experience).

Huizinga considers the role of play in our contemporary world in Chapter XII of *Homo Ludens*. He believes that the role of play in civilization has receded since the industrial revolution of the nineteenth century, combined with the rise of the "protestant work ethic." Play came to be something frowned upon, and confined to the margins of life, once the hard day's work has been done. Living was no longer playing—it was laboring. This downgrading of play has led, he thinks, to some distortions of contemporary culture, in two opposing directions. First, the work attitude has entered the traditional domain of play—as with present-day professional sports. Sport has become an industrialized moneymaking enterprise, and the play element has been muffled and stifled: it is now apt to be grimly serious, joyless, and mechanical. Capitalism has taken the play out of play, at least to some degree. But, on the other side, work activities have paradoxically taken on a play-like aspect, as business people cast themselves as players in a game, with competition, winning and losing—athletes of the boardroom and stock market floor. Hedge funds resemble gaming casinos, with high-risk players placing big bets, victory and defeat, even league tables, and the famous names of "major players." Thus there is widespread confusion and uncertainty in our culture about what is a game and what is not. Accordingly, people are confused about what they are doing: are they working or are they playing? I think this confusion has infected academic life, with science taken as the worthy work paradigm and every other discipline judged by comparison to science. Philosophy has felt this force, pulling it toward science; and the self-conception of the philosopher has followed suit. Philosophy has been distorted as a result: that is, professional philosophy, as an institution and cultural formation, has been distorted—not the intrinsic character of philosophy as an intellectual inquiry. The instrumental model has taken hold. As sport has become too close to business, philosophy has become too close to science, and so the essential nature of philosophy has been misunderstood (the same is true of sport). One of the aims of this chapter has been to try to correct this misunderstanding. Philosophy is a distinctive type of intellectual activity, not to be assimilated to other types, worthy though they may be. It should not lose sight of the spirit of play that animates and sustains it. Philosophers don't have *jobs*.[18]

---

[18] If you meet a professional poker player or tennis player and ask them what they do for a job, they are apt to reply, "I don't have a job—I play poker/tennis for a living." Similarly for the philosopher: *qua* philosopher, he has no job—he does philosophy for a living. This is not to say that philosophers don't have to do jobs as part of their occupation—because not all of being a professional philosopher is philosophizing. Grading papers, going to meetings, and doing admissions—these are all jobs, i.e., instrumental activities performed for the sake of an extrinsic goal. But the activity of philosophizing itself, for which one is (luckily) paid, is not a merely instrumental activity, because the activity is valued for its own sake. Thus being a philosopher, as such, is not a job. Teaching philosophy may be a job, but the activity of philosophizing is not. There are no jobs *in* philosophy, only jobs surrounding it.

11 The Possibility of Ontology

The world—the sum total of what there is—contains things of many kinds: (1) tables and chairs, plants, animals, mountains, galaxies, electrons, quarks, magnetic fields, radio waves, gravity, neurons, space, time; (2) beliefs and desires, sensations, perceptions, memories, images, emotions, thoughts, language, traits of character, intellectual and athletic abilities; and (3) numbers and geometrical figures, sets, properties, propositions, functions, moral and aesthetic values, nations, universities, laws, patterns, systems, theories, colors, novels, and symphonies. The split by semi-colon in this list is intended to evoke the customary metaphysical division into three exclusive and exhaustive categories: the "physical," the "mental," and the "abstract."[1] We start with more specific categories, drawn from common sense and science, as illustrated by the words on my list, and then we find (allegedly) that these categories divide neatly into three very broad groups. The ontological question then becomes which of these is basic, and which real. The "physicalists" hold that everything belongs to the first group. They may be reductive or eliminative. Everything that exists is analyzable as physical. The "idealists" hold that everything belongs to the second group, claiming that everything that exists is analyzable as mental. The "abstractists," a rare breed, hold that everything belongs to the third group: every-thing that exists is analyzable as something abstract (the Pythagoreans perhaps,

---

[1] Note that the third category grows increasingly tenuous as it lengthens, as if attempting to find a home for all the things that don't fit in elsewhere—hence its rag-tag character.

Plato on one interpretation).[2] Correspondingly, the "dualist" denies that everything mental is physical. The "Platonist" denies that abstract entities are either physical or mental (or lack existence altogether)—while the "nominalist" maintains that there are no abstract entities (that are not reducible to physical or mental entities). Each of these familiar doctrines presupposes that the general terms in question are well defined—that we know what we mean by "physical," "mental," and "abstract." But do we?

Note, first, that these are not terms derived from ordinary language or empirical science, at least not as they are used in these debates. They are philosophers' appropriations, employed far more capaciously and absolutely than ordinary uses of the words (they are what I called "category terms" in Chapter 7). Bodily pain is not ordinarily described as "mental"; magnetic fields are not usually (or historically) designated as "physical" or "material"; the word "abstract" is commonly used to characterize certain kinds of ideas, not in an ontological way (*OED*: "theoretical rather than physical or concrete"—as in "abstract art"). Philosophers, however, think that each item in my three groupings has something in common with the others, which they describe by the appropriated terms in question, despite the superficial variety. Each item can be analyzed, they suppose, either as physical or mental or abstract: this is what we see when we look into their metaphysical essence. The three ontological categories constitute the ultimate genus essence of things, of which each item on the list is a species. What is striking, however, is how difficult they have found it to define these traditional terms of art—that is, to say what the alleged common feature is. This is by now an old story, so I won't labor it; it is the significance of the difficulty that I want to focus on. The effort to find a "criterion of the mental" has not met with notable success: intentionality is neither necessary nor sufficient, the idea of qualia is both controversial and wrong in scope, and privileged access won't do the job.[3] These concepts, themselves philosopher's inventions, may apply to subcategories of the supposed general category, but they fail to capture everything that traditional philosophers have wanted to include. The notion of the "physical" has likewise proved difficult to pin down, especially since the demise of seventeenth-century mechanism: fields and forces are not easily included, or space itself, and current physics seems to flout many of the principles

---

[2] The "abstractist" may accept that not all *appearances* are abstract while insisting that the underlying *reality* is abstract. Thus Plato regarded the changeable empirical world as mere appearance and the unchangeable world of Forms as true reality. An atomist might take the same kind of view with respect to the observable world and then claim that the atoms are mathematical in character. On certain views of physics, the physical is held to be abstract in some sense.

[3] This has been convincingly urged by Rorty, *Philosophy and The Mirror of Nature*, chapter one. He views the customary philosophical use of "mental" as stemming from a particular historical tradition rooted in Descartes and depending on his (now rejected) views. The notion of family resemblance is often wheeled in here to try to unify what is evidently not unified (see below).

previously held to define the physical (such as definite spatial location and causal determinacy).[4] The idea of the "abstract" has always seemed most like a philosopher's term of art, and efforts to define it have generally been halfhearted and unsatisfactory. The usual proposal is that abstract entities have no causal powers and exist outside of space and time. But these are wholly negative characterizations, giving us little by way of positive ontological content. In addition, the lack of causal powers seems insufficient to secure the desired extension: epiphenomenalism about the mental would make it qualify as abstract by this criterion.[5] The idea of existing outside space and time, deriving from Plato, raises the question of what other kind of medium they might reside in; and it is not clear that space and time themselves exist *in* space and time. What about God, or Cartesian immaterial substance, or moral reasons—are they "abstract"? Isn't "outside" itself a spatial term? What does it *mean* to speak of something existing neither in space nor time? The notion of the abstract seems largely to be understood as what does *not* belong to the other two categories—what is left over when they are exhausted. So, in each case we have nothing satisfactory to pin down the general categories into which we are trying to sort the types of things we ordinarily talk about. And, indeed, it is customary in philosophy to proceed with the use of these terms without even acknowledging that there are questions of definition to be addressed. The standard procedure is to offer some alleged paradigms and then say "and things like that."[6] This must raise the question as to whether those supposed categories are really well founded: might they be philosophers' inventions with no clear definable content? Certainly, their viability lacks the authority of either common sense or science—so one would

[4] Chomsky has long doubted the integrity of the concept of the "physical": see the entry by him in *A Companion to the Philosophy of Mind*, ed. Guttenplan. Crane and Mellor attack the very idea of physicalism in "There is No Question of Physicalism." Hempel long ago skewered the concept *physical* on what came to be called "Hempel's Dilemma" (too narrow if restricted to current physics; empty if expanded to ideal physics): see his "Reduction: Ontological and Linguistic Facets."

[5] On some views, only basic physics specifies properties with genuine causal powers—all the special sciences are causally epiphenomenal. Whether plausible or not, we surely don't want to conclude that everything except physics is abstract! And couldn't God by fiat remove the causal powers from a physical object? What about gerrymandered properties like being *either* a wedding *or* an explosion? These don't seem causal, but neither do they seem abstract. What should we say about the property of *not* being electrically charged? Lack of causal powers seems insufficient for being abstract. On the other hand, reference to numbers occurs in causal explanations—so do numbers have causal powers in some sense? If we were persuaded that they do, would we then automatically deny their abstractness? The causal criterion doesn't get to the heart of the intuitive traditional conception: "abstract" doesn't *mean* "non-causal." Then what does it mean?

[6] The problem with this, of course, is that no similarity standard has been specified: things like that *in what respect*? Suppose the paradigms were some items of furniture: then "physical" as introduced in reference to those things might mean "furniture" or "stored in a warehouse" or "brown in color" or "shabby." We need to say that something counts as physical just if it resembles the paradigm items *in being physical*. But the definitional circle is then obvious—that very concept is what we were trying to explain. The general point is that similarity relations to chosen paradigms are far too abundant to tie down a notion like "physical."

think that philosophers have a special obligation to explain their intended meaning. Yet they are strangely mute on the question, suspiciously so. What exactly *is* the physical-mental-abstract distinction? Might this be a dogma of metaphysics, a historical excrescence, manufactured to keep the enterprise going? Might the alleged distinction come to nothing in the end?

The difficulty, evidently, is that there is too much heterogeneity within the alleged classes to permit any workable general definition. Energy and elementary particles, electricity and galaxies; thoughts and emotions, volitions and linguistic understanding; numbers and propositions, geometrical shapes and properties: this is a very motley enumeration, and there is nothing to guarantee that the items in each group can be unified with other items in that group. In some respects, indeed, space resembles geometrical figures (points in space seem especially abstract); energy can seem volitional; capacities like the ability to play the violin seem to straddle the physical and the mental. Where do *persons* fall? Are they mental, physical, or abstract? Or are they none of the above? Strawson took persons to be a primitive ontological category—which is to say, not a conceptual compound of the mental and physical, and not each alone.[7] How much *sense* is there in the question of whether the self is mental, physical, or abstract? One wants to say all three, as different aspects of the self take prominence in one's thinking about the self; or none, as the dissimilarities with other things so designated become apparent. What about the butterflies that a mathematician may feel in his stomach when he thinks he is about to prove a new theorem? A feeling, so mental; in the stomach, so physical; about numbers, so abstract: it seems artificial to confine it to one category to the exclusion of the others. Not everything can be slotted neatly and naturally into one or other of these pre-arranged philosopher's categories. They start to seem contrived and artificial. My question is what this difficulty *shows*.

It might be maintained that the problem is superficial; we should be able to come up with better definitions in the end. But that seems doubtful, given the energy that has gone into defining these terms hitherto; and they are not concepts that wear their integrity on their face—they are borrowings pressed into technical service. They have a history, but it is unclear whether they have an analysis. It is unclear, that is, whether their alleged extensions share a common essence. It might alternatively be claimed that the concepts are primitive—that nothing can be said to elucidate

[7] Strawson, *Individuals*, Chapter 3. That is, Strawson did not regard the concept of a person as reducible to either mental or physical concepts—so the property of being a person is neither sort of property. Persons therefore belong in a distinct ontological category, neither mental nor physical (and not a combination of the two). Older traditions have likewise implicitly taken the concept of the self or ego as ontologically distinct from the mental or physical: certainly not physical (because not extended), but also not mental (because mental items are *contents* of consciousness, not the non-introspectible *subject* of consciousness—the subject is conceived as a kind of transcendent entity, unlike mental phenomena). Such views challenge the alleged exhaustiveness of the "mental" and the "physical," which start to seem increasingly procrustean (without the merit of clarity).

them any further, and they can be safely taken as they are. That too seems highly doubtful, since they are terms of philosophical art, not basic concepts we bring to the world; and the manifest variety in their putative extensions invites skepticism about their integrity. They are nothing like "red" or "good" or "not" or "exists"—arguably primitive terms. It therefore seems a real possibility that we do not have well-defined concepts here at all. The words have been ripped from their usual context of use and applied in an extended and undefined sense (Wittgenstein had a lot to say about this habit of philosophers), and it is far from clear that they connote anything meaningful in their new use. Compare the philosopher's use of "natural," discussed in Chapter 9: it is not at all clear that there is an intelligible concept here. Or consider the use of the word "Spirit" (always capitalized) to denote everything from human consciousness to physical energy to divine presence in the world. What about the "Absolute" as used by a certain type of idealist?[8] We may thus be victims of a kind of linguistic illusion: we mistakenly think that there are real thoughts lying behind these dubious appropriated terms. In fact, they express pseudo-concepts, insidiously planted in us by our philosophical upbringing. It is perfectly easy to talk mumbo-jumbo if one has been schooled to do so, and these terms are part of our philosophical schooling (compare religious schooling and the terms of religion, e.g., the concept of the "Trinity" or "transubstantiation"). We should look with suspicion on the obscure trinity of the "mental," "physical," and "abstract," and the metaphysical package that they imply. Should we allow ourselves to talk that way, given the difficulty of saying what we mean?

In reply to such skepticism, it might be retorted that there is something further we can say that serves to delimit the intended categories: namely, that there are characteristic ways of *knowing* about items from each category. Thus we know the physical by means of sensory perception (plus inference), we know the mental by means of introspection, and we know the abstract by means of reason or "intellectual intuition." So we can define each category in epistemic terms: the physical is what is known perceptually, the mental is what is known introspectively, and the abstract is what is known by pure reason. Now this proposal certainly encounters problems extensionally (is the mental always known introspectively, even in the first-person case?), but let us assume that it works to delimit the categories in the intended way. Then the problem is that this mode of definition is precisely epistemological; it is not ontological in form. It does not tell us what the entities are like in themselves, but only how human minds know about them. It is not properly *intrinsic*. Surely there has to be something about the entities *themselves* that qualifies

[8] A more controversial example would be the concept of absolute motion. When Newton introduces the notion we do not immediately jib—we appear to know what he means. But further reflection can convince us that the idea is actually devoid of intelligible content: we just don't know what it would *be* to move through absolute space without reference to any physical coordinate. Concepts can appear intelligible (sometimes for centuries) and yet not be, because of confusions with other concepts, the prop of putative paradigms, obsolete theories, and the sheer difficulty of definition.

them as belonging to one category or the other, not merely their relations to know-ing subjects. But, again, what is that? In fact, I suspect that the epistemological tri-partite division is what fuels the philosophical conviction that we have three distinct *ontological* categories here. We have a more or less workable epistemic sorting—three ways of knowing about reality—and then we convert it (illicitly) into an ontological partition. We project our epistemic faculties onto the world, in effect. But such an ontological conclusion simply doesn't follow from the premises: heterogeneity of faculty does not imply heterogeneity in the subject matter. If this were all there is to it, then reality might itself be utterly homogeneous, exhibiting no such grand tripartite partition. It is like assuming that because sight and touch are so different, their *objects* must be. But what we need is an account of reality such that the epistemic division *follows* from it: it is *because* something is physical that we know it perceptually, *because* something is mental that we know it introspectively, and *because* something is abstract that we know it by pure reason. The epistemic division cannot be what the ontological division *consists in*. The admitted genuineness of the epistemic division cannot then ground the solidity of the ontological division.[9]

A final attempted salvage operation must be considered: the suggestion that we are dealing with family resemblance concepts. That position has been maintained for the word "mental," but it is less popular for "physical" and "abstract." The thought is that conceptual unity is compatible with extensional variety. The concept *game* is a unified respectable concept, some say, even though there is nothing in common bet-ween all the activities in its extension. I doubt that this would meet the needs of the typical physicalist or idealist or Platonist, because of the monistic urge that prompts such doctrines. Everything is uniformly physical, say, but there is nothing in *common* between all the things that are physical. Then why insist so strongly on the ontological leveling? What is the point of maintaining that everything is uniformly physical when the physical itself is hopelessly non-uniform? That would be a very peculiar form of reductionism. The reduction base would itself exhibit irreducible ontological variety with no common factor. But anyway, the whole family resemblance story about concepts is shot through with error and confusion, as I urged in Chapter 2; so this way of salvaging the integrity of our three suspect category concepts will not serve the turn. And even if it did, it would invite the following obvious response: but if only family resemblance unifies the categories, can't we find other dimensions of

---

[9] The deep-seated tendency to confuse metaphysics with epistemology is a standing foible of the human mind: we can't help thinking that reality must somehow be constituted by our ways of apprehending it. Thus we commit projective fallacies, imposing our methods of knowing onto the world. Just because we have distinct faculties of knowledge, we reify an objective metaphysical cor-relate and give it a name: we know the world by means of epistemic faculty E so there must be a class of objects M such that M objects are known by E. For instance, E is sense perception and M is the class of "physical" objects. When the M class threatens to outrun what can be detected by E, we start muttering about paradigms and similarity, supposing that we have identified a genuine ontological category. But we have merely confused metaphysics with epistemology.

similarity that recommend other metaphysical divisions—as it might be, resemblances between energy and volition or between geometrical objects and space or between thoughts and speech? Family resemblance comes cheap, and cannot ground the traditional unwavering tripartite division. Thus it has always been assumed, tacitly or otherwise, that our problematic terms express "common-property" concepts. But we can't say clearly (or even unclearly) what the common property might be. If everything dubbed "physical" were mechanical, then we could define the physical as the mechanical. If everything called "mental" were a state of consciousness, then we could define the mental as the conscious (assuming this latter notion to be well defined). If everything designated "abstract" were numerical, then we could define the abstract as the numerical. These are well-defined *definiens*, of sufficient clarity and integrity in their own right. The trouble is that nothing like this will work to define the problematic terms in the way they are traditionally employed. Perhaps the terms started their semantic lives in some such way, with a clear restricted definition (mechanical, conscious, numerical), but then the world proved richer and more various than anticipated; instead of retiring the terms, people just kept using them in extended, metaphorical, and ungrounded ways. The result is a trio of rogue terms reluctant to accept that their time is up.

I conclude, then, that there are ample grounds for skepticism about the traditional grand categories of metaphysics. What follows? Suppose we abandon them altogether: what is left? The first casualty is that many traditional doctrines can no longer be meaningfully formulated: physicalism, dualism, idealism, Platonism, nominalism, three-world-ism.[10] For all these doctrines rely upon genuine content in the notions of the "physical," the "mental," and the "abstract." We can no longer affirm, "Everything is P" or "Not everything is P," where "P" is one of these three terms. But does that mean that old-fashioned ontology is no longer possible? Is there *nothing* to the old doctrines, merely empty noise? In other words: what does metaphysics look like when we drop the tripartite grouping? It might be tempting to sweep it all away: metaphysics is meaningless! Not for the positivist's verifiability reasons, but for more mundane reasons: the key terms lack *ordinary* meaning (they are unverifiable because meaningless, rather than vice versa). But that would,

---

[10] By "three-world-ism" I mean to refer to the general metaphysical position of Frege and Popper: the physical world, the mental world, and the abstract world. Popper further strains the division by claiming that the third world contains the products of the human mind—such as novels and scientific theories. Somehow these things originate in human psychology but fight free of it to reside in a third separate realm. Does Popper also think that human superstitions belong in the third world along with scientific theories? What about prejudices and ideologies? He might have done better to postulate a fourth world, so as to distinguish products of the mind from traditional abstract entities like numbers or propositions or geometric forms. On some views, indeed, the social world exists separately from both the mental and abstract worlds, as an ontological realm in its own right. (Actually, this proliferation of "worlds" strikes me as a step in the right direction, not the wrong direction: it is an incipient acknowledgment of irreducible pluralism. But we should really drop the loaded talk of "worlds.")

I think, overstate the upshot: we can still formulate more restricted theses of ontological interest. We can't say that mental states are physical (this is doubly empty), but we can say that sensations and thoughts are identical to specific states of the nervous system—as it might be, neurons firing. We can't say that (so-called) material objects are all mental, but we can say that tables and mountains and molecules are reducible to sense impressions (though we might need to be more specific about which sense impressions). We can't say that abstract entities are mental (or physical), but we can say that numbers are identical to numerical concepts (or marks on paper). That is to say, we can formulate something *like* "physicalism," "idealism," and "nominalism" without using the suspect general categories, restricting ourselves to more specific categories. Likewise, "dualism," "realism," and "Platonism" can each be formulated by denying such restricted claims, instead of using the suspect general terms. Much of traditional ontology can therefore go forward as before, debating the pros and cons of these restricted theses. All the concepts here employed are perfectly *kosher*.

But notice that the shift, though seemingly subtle, is actually quite significant. For the various positions start to seem either implausible or trivially true once the emendation is made. If "physicalism" is simply the claim of identity between sensations and thoughts and electrical firings of neurons, it starts to seem implausibly dogmatic: Why should *these* brain states, in particular, be the only ones that sensations and thoughts can reduce to? What if we are wrong about the actual brain correlate of pain, say? Don't we really want to say that "the mental" is reducible to *some physical states or other*? We don't want to be limited to a specific type of physical state—but to allow any type of physical state. But this uses the suspect general category again. It isn't *metaphysically* interesting if pain turns out not to be identical to C-fiber firing, so long as it is identical to *some* physical state. And dualism can seem trivially established if it merely denies such a specific identity, since the retort will be: But might not mental states still be reducible to *some* sort of physical state? Then the dualist will have to affirm the more general denial to maintain interest, thus trading in the suspect category of "the physical." It is a little better for the idealist, since she always has in mind a specific type of "mental state" as her favored reduction base, namely, sense impressions (as opposed to thoughts and emotions, say). But even here there is a problem of unwanted narrowness: for *which* sense impressions are to constitute objects? It can't be just a subset of human sense impressions, leaving out taste and smell, say (though in practice it is sight and touch that are favored by idealists such as Berkeley). But even if we include all of the human senses, there is the more fundamental problem of favoring the *human* senses. What about Martians and material objects: Are objects on Mars constituted by *their* distinct types of sense impression (whatever weird senses they may have)? But then these differ from ours, and whose is to be preferred? Indeed, what really *counts* as a "sense impression" once we start to use the concept with the generality necessary? What of beings who have only thoughts in response to stimuli—are objects for them constituted by their thoughts? It is only when we restrict ourselves to the actual human senses, or a subset of them, that we have a well-defined thesis; but then it looks implausible through extreme arbitrariness. Again, what the idealist really wants to say is that everything is definable as *some* sort of mental state, and not be tied down to a specific kind ("the universe is mind/spirit"): but then we have the suspect general concept intruding again. And equally the realist thesis—that objects are not reducible to human sense impressions—starts to seem too obviously true: *of course* objects cannot be constituted by just *those* sense impressions. The realist wanted to say that objects are not constituted by *any* kind of mental fact (or any kind of sense impression)—but there is the suspect general category popping up again. The metaphysical idealist, such as Berkeley, really aches to proclaim quite generally that reality is inherently "spiritual"— that spirits are the only substances and ideas the only accidents—while the metaphysical realist wants badly to deny any such claim.[11] The restricted theses don't match their intentions at all; they need the general categories. That is when the metaphysical water starts to boil, but the restricted theses are tepid and inconsequential or too obviously false. The trouble is that such general (and exciting) claims cannot be formulated if we prohibit use of the general categories traditionally used to formulate them. And much the same is true of the metaphysics of the abstract. When the nominalist tells us that numbers are really mental (or physical) he seems to be saying something philosophically interesting and possibly true—just as the Platonist seems to have a stirring thesis when she declares that numbers are abstract and *not* identical to anything mental or physical. But if the nominalist is confined to the more restricted formulations, his view starts to seem implausible right off the bat. For again, *which* numeral ideas or marks do the constituting, and why ideas in *human* minds or marks *on paper* instead of a more general range of numerical symbols? Is it to be specifically human ideas and not Martian ideas, and must they be expressed in a certain kind of notation; and what sorts of external numerical signs will be included? Why symbols and signs at all, whether "mental" or "physical"?

---

[11] Even this formulation in terms of "ideas," itself a philosopher's invention, is too narrow to capture the full range of idealist doctrines, because too closely allied to perception. What if, like Schopenhauer, we thought that the world consists of Will? Then volitions would be the ultimate ontological category, not ideas. We accordingly need an overarching concept that applies to both ("mental") in order to state the general doctrine of idealism. And Berkeley's own final theory—that so-called material objects are ideas in the mind of God—goes well beyond the limited range of merely human ideas. Presumably, ideas in God's (infinite) mind are nothing like ideas in our (finite) mind, if only because God's knowledge is not perceptual. But then we are trading in a notion of "idea" that outstrips anything that we can pin down by reference to our own sensory states. What *is* this generalized notion of "idea" that Berkeley is trying to foist on us? Is it just "whatever exists in God's mind"? But what is that, and what do we mean by speaking of God's "mind"? Intelligibility gets bleached out once we reach for the generality we need: we are then just moving words around.

Some nominalists wish to claim that numbers are material objects or collections of them—and they want to claim this quite generally, not just with respect to some specific kind of object (as it might be, pebbles and biscuits).[12] The metaphysical nominalist wants to say, "No, the claim is that numbers are identical to *some* kind of mental or physical entity, not any specific kind"; they don't want to commit themselves to a particular kind, for fear of excessive narrowness and arbitrariness. So, again, they are caught trading in the prohibited locutions, trying to beef up the metaphysical content by wielding the suspect terms. However, if we stay honest, using only the approved specific categories, we fail to get anything with the right content to capture our ontological intentions. And the problem, for the skeptic about the traditional categories, is that such intentions are actually incoherent. Slipping and sliding between the ordinary and legitimate categories, on the one hand, and the technical and illegitimate categories, on the other, is what keeps the traditional metaphysical enterprise afloat—giving us an illusion of sense. The *interest* evaporates once we disavow the traditional categories—though we can keep up an appearance of philosophical substance by limiting ourselves to the narrower categories. In fact, the old ontological issues *need* the traditional categories to sustain them, and these categories are at risk of vacuity (or are thoroughly saturated with it). They simply don't stand up to analysis. The corresponding predicates are impostors, mere sounds without sense.[13]

What remains of ontology if we cease to ask the kinds of questions that require the suspect categories? What picture of the world results from expunging these questions? What results, clearly, is a kind of systematic *pluralism*: there are sensations and thoughts, emotions and decisions, as well as mountains, galaxies, and magnetic fields, and even numbers, properties, and propositions—*but there is no general grouping of these into broader categories.* When we speak of psychology, physics, and mathematics as academic disciplines, we are using a necessary institutional convenience, not "limning the most general traits of reality," as Quine would put it. This is why a psychologist knows about the nervous system and a physicist

---

[12] I am alluding to Frege's criticism of Mill's theory of arithmetic in *Foundations of Arithmetic*: Mill tries to analyze numbers in terms of the material objects—pebbles and biscuits—that are numbered (he is an "object-nominalist" not a "sign-nominalist").

[13] I know this makes me sound like a positivist, which is the last thing I want to sound like. My position has nothing to do with the lack of verifiability of sentences containing the suspect terms. In fact, I think Carnap's introduction of the notion of a pseudo-concept to characterize dubiously metaphysical debates trades upon doubts about meaningfulness that are quite independent of considerations of verifiability. Religious sentences, for example, are dubiously intelligible independently of their unverifiability (in fact, I would say that there is no logical bar to verifying a sentence that is actually lacking in sense); and Heidegger's infamous "Nothingness nothings" is meaningless even before we get to the question of its verifiability. In general, nonsense language is not nonsense *because* it is unverifiable; it is unverifiable because it is (already) nonsense—as with "Twas brillig and the slithy toves...," etc.

can be interested in the relation between the world he studies and the way it appears to the human mind (the subject of psychophysics)—and why there are such people as mathematical physicists. Philosophers have in effect reified these academic distinctions, supposing that everything that exists must slot neatly and naturally into one or other of the big three categories—even though they have been unable to define these categories satisfactorily. We can go on discussing the specific items in the list, wondering about their interrelations, but we cannot ask whether the general category exemplified by some of them subsumes all the rest—affirming *or* denying this. The result will be that we shall be less inclined to ontological leveling: we won't lust for uniformity and excessive generality. Reality has an irreducible variety. Monism of any kind is out of the running. But note that the resulting pluralism does not resuscitate dualism or Platonism (or even realism about material objects), because these doctrines too rely upon there being coherent concepts of the "mental," the "physical," and the "abstract." We can meaningfully say, for example, that sensations of red aren't the same as these specific neurons firing in this specific pattern, but we can't go on to add, "and nothing like that either—nothing physical." We can't even say they are distinct from whatever their correct physical correlates turn out to be—because we have used that suspect general concept again. The reductionist thinks he can get by with one (or possibly two) of the three general categories, with at least one reducing to the others; the anti-reductionist thinks that we must assert the existence of all three categories of entity. But the pluralist, seeing that both the reductionist and the anti-reductionist are up to their ears in pseudo concepts, holds merely that numbers aren't ink marks and pains aren't C-fibers firing and tables aren't visual impressions. If asked whether the first items in these pairs might be identical to *other* things drawn from the general classes of the mental, physical or abstract, he declines to go on with the conversation. He sees only disguised nonsense ahead.

And there is a further disappointment to the ambitions of the traditional metaphysician. He wanted his propositions to be distinctively *philosophical,* as opposed to scientific or empirical. The permissibility of the general categories of the mental, the physical, and the abstract allowed him to fulfill that ambition; the methods appropriate to debating the questions so formulated were distinctively philosophical. But if we limit ourselves to the kinds of restricted theses that I have mentioned, it is not clear that this remains the case: the views start to look like empirically refutable scientific or commonsense claims. Pain may not identical to C-fibers firing because actually the true correlate is D-fibers firing; the table isn't the same as the visual impression of a table because it is there when other types of sense impression are registered; the number 2 isn't the same as this numerical mark for it because of all the other numerical marks for 2 that exist or might come to exist. It is only when we allow ourselves the general categories that the claims attain the condition of philosophy; without them we are left with empirical matters of fact to debate or settle. Metaphysics, *as philosophy*, disappears. The concepts were originally introduced to frame philosophical debates, and without them the philosophy implodes on itself.[14]

It isn't easy giving up the general categories and resting content with pluralism. We are not just abandoning the doctrines of one particular philosophical school; we are abandoning the framework of debate of all philosophical schools (physicalists, dualists, idealists, realists, Platonists, nominalists). We have to stop ourselves from thinking in terms of these overarching metaphysical categories, limiting ourselves to the specific categories that exist in our thought and talk (commonsense and scientific) before traditional metaphysics gets to work on them. We have to curb our ontological enthusiasm. It is not that these three conceptual categories indisputably exist and the question is whether the world contains instances of each of them in unreduced form. Rather, the categories themselves lack coherence, so there is no question to begin with. It simply makes no *sense* to ask if reality is fundamentally physical or fundamentally spiritual or fundamentally abstract; and the denials of such doctrines are as ill defined as the doctrines. There are tables, mountains, and magnetic fields; there are sensations, thoughts and feelings, there are numbers, properties, and propositions: but we cannot ask whether these things are physical, mental or abstract. To do so is to use these last three terms in extended metaphysical senses that they cannot bear. This is not an easy pill to swallow; it goes against the intellectual grain. Even now I feel an undertow toward the old categories—they still have a deep hold on me. They have been part of my philosophical thinking for decades. I was brought up on them. Their attraction is undeniable. They satisfy our "craving for generality" (to use Wittgenstein's phrase). Maybe they will inevitably crop up in the minds of any intelligent beings that start to think philosophically; they are natural to us as thinkers, arising spontaneously, gripping the mind. They are mesmerizing (which is to say hypnotic: we are hypnotized by them). Repetition drums them in. Maybe our ordinary concepts necessarily produce them as pathological offshoots (they don't feel entirely gratuitous or imposed). We just can't help ourselves. And we feel lost without them, bereft. There is grief at their passing. (Did the positivists ever feel such grief at the death of metaphysics, as they saw it? Apparently not, but appearances may be misleading.) I certainly feel a wistful nostalgia toward them, sadness at their implosion. They are like old (but untrustworthy) friends, steady (but hazy) companions. It is hard to believe they are gone—that they never were.

---

[14] A neuroscientist investigating the cerebral correlates of pain has no use for the concept of the "physical." She is not trying to find out if "physicalism" is true. The concepts she uses are specific to neuroscience: *neuron, dendrite, axon, action potential, neurotransmitter,* etc. She wants to know what the correlate of pain is using *those* concepts; she has no need of the philosopher's notion of the "physical." She may even declare that pain *is* such and such a state of the brain, speaking in the vocabulary of her special science; but she has not thereby committed herself to "physicalism." For she may stand ready to revise her stated position in the light of further neurophysiological discoveries. At no point, as a scientist, has she ever claimed that pain is a "physical" state: that is a distinctively philosophical proposition, which employs a concept that she can do without.

But they did create a lot of trouble in the past, generating much heat and passion, much squabbling and denouncing—as slogans and ideology often will. Maybe, then, their demise is a blessing in disguise. Still, their expulsion must be tinged with regret.[15]

---

[15] One wonders whether the very emptiness of the terms is what has kept debates involving them going for so long. It certainly helps to explain why such debates are so hard to resolve. The vacuity of a concept has never been much of an obstacle to disputants engaging in heated and lengthy debates involving it. Just think of the explosive *furors* of religion concerning angels, the Trinity, the nature of godhood in man, God's powers, and so on: their conceptual emptiness did not stop people from burning each other at the stake for having the "wrong" opinion. Likewise, debates about the truth of "physicalism" have divided philosophers into warring factions, with much molten rhetoric and denunciation on both sides (at one time, the same was true of debates over "idealism"). Questions of tribal allegiance and intellectual integrity have been insinuated. Sometimes the less well-defined a doctrine is, the more dogmatic people become in its defense. The old advice to "define your terms" might have spared us a lot of this kind of thing. And yet, as I remark in the text, the human appetite for such hot and hazy debates is hard to quell. We are drawn to them like a moth to the flame—even against our better judgment. We love to defend big airy claims, even when their sense proves elusive.

12 The Concept of Instantiation

What is the most basic concept in our conceptual scheme? Which concept is the most general? These are natural philosophical questions. The concept with the strongest title to that accolade is surely *instantiation*. Instantiation is simply a being's being a certain way—having a certain mode of being. It is the being of a thing to be thus and so—to have properties, possess attributes. Nothing has being unless it is some way or other. Instantiation is even more basic than existence and identity: it is not obvious that everything that instantiates exists, as with fictional and other non-existent objects; and identity is a relation instantiated by an object. Even being an object is instantiated by an object. Moreover, instantiation appears in every definition, since a definition attributes properties to things—anyone who has knowledge, for example, instantiates belief, truth of belief, and a non-fluky way of having truth in belief. Hence instantiation cannot be defined without circularity, since it crops up in every definition—including a purported definition of itself. It is utterly basic and completely general—and the root of all reality. To be is to instantiate.

Instantiation accordingly has no decompositional analysis—no set of non-circular necessary and sufficient conditions. It has no more primitive parts, being itself primitive. What has to hold for an object to instantiate a property is simply that the object *instantiates* the property—has it, exemplifies it. There are synonyms for "instantiates" but they provide no conceptual breakdown, no constituent analysis. But this doesn't mean that it has *no* kind of analysis; there might yet be significant non-trivial conceptual truths governing it. It might have an essence, capable of being revealed by conceptual inquiry: there could be analytically true statements concerning it—even if they are not of the dismantling kind. In fact, the basic laws of logic look to contain just such an essence. It is of the essence of instantiation that the following three laws hold of it: (1) if x instantiates P, then x instantiates P (the "law of tautology"); (2) if x instantiates P, then x does not instantiate *not-P* (the "law of contradictory exclusion"); (3) every object x either instantiates P or it does not instantiate P (the "law of alternation"). In other words: instantiation implies itself, instantiation excludes its non-instantiation, and everything must either instantiate a property or not instantiate it. These are all analytic truths concerning instantiation. They arise from (or underlie) the basic logical laws. The application of those laws to objects and properties depends on the essential characteristics of instantiation—what it is in its very nature.

It is a further characteristic of instantiation that it is *pleonastic*. When we say "x instantiates P" we can paraphrase that statement simply as "x is P" or "Px."[1] The relational term disappears, being absorbed into simple predication. In this respect, instantiation is like truth, though truth is a property of propositions, not a relation between objects and properties. When I say, "Socrates argues," I could have more long-windedly said "Socrates instantiates the property of arguing": the latter has the same content as the former. The latter might even be regarded as an analysis of the former, since it is syntactically more complex and has the appearance of an articulating paraphrase, bringing out hidden structure. In any case, the predicate "instantiates" is pleonastic in the sense that it adds nothing to the sentence it expands. The same redundancy can be seen at work in the natural counterparts to instantiation at the level of concepts and words. Strictly speaking, objects instantiate only properties, but we have other terms for the relations between objects and concepts and predicates: falling under, being subsumed by, exemplifying, and satisfying. Thus an object can fall under the concept *square* and it can satisfy the predicate "x is a square." In both cases, we can paraphrase the corresponding statements simply by dropping the relational term—as with Tarski's famous, "an object x satisfies 'square' if and only if x is square." The satisfaction relation is absorbed into the simple subject-predicate statement; no trace of it remains. So we can say that instantiation (and its counterparts at the level of concepts and predicates) are essentially pleonastic.

These points, in one form or another, are familiar and widely recognized (though I have consciously formulated them in such a way as to raise hackles in some quarters). In this final chapter, I want to inquire whether there are other essential truths about instantiation that can be extracted by analysis. I want to know, that is, whether this most primitive of primitives can be subjected to analytic investigation. This is

---

[1] In the two quoted sentences, "P" has a different logical role: it must be functioning as a singular term denoting a property in "x instantiates P," but in "Px" it occurs as a predicate expression. When we introduce the relational "instantiates" in the paraphrase, we need to nominalize the predicate. In logical notation, we could express this by Church's lamba abstraction—a term-forming operator on open sentences. (We could use a semantically parallel operator to form terms denoting concepts from predicates expressing concepts.)

therefore to be an essay in analytic metaphysics of the most blatant and unrepentant kind: What is the metaphysics of instantiation as revealed by a priori investigation of its conceptually revealed essence? Thus I seek to exemplify the general methodology advocated in this book in this particular case. I think there are real questions here with highly non-trivial answers—questions about the most fundamental structure of reality (not about words and concepts). My aim is to discover the nature of this aspect of the real by analyzing our concepts of it—thus engaging in the very kind of philosophy defended earlier. (Remember, though, in case the subject seems heavy, that it is undertaken in a spirit of play.)

The world is the totality of instantiated properties, to paraphrase the Wittgenstein of the *Tractatus* ("The world is all that is the case"). Whether everything that instantiates a property is properly described as an *object* is a delicate question—numbers, events, selves, regions of space, and so on—but the universality of instantiation itself is not in question. *What* is instantiated—whether it is universals or predicates or concepts—is also controversial, but that there is instantiation is not. Yet surprisingly little is ever said about the nature of instantiation itself—about its distinctive features. What can we say about the metaphysics of instantiation? What is its abstract character?

The first feature I shall discuss is what I shall call *unionism*, using the term in a technical sense.[2] The intuitive idea of unionism is that what may appear to be independent and separable is not: there is an inevitable clustering, a refusal to exist in splendid isolation. You can't have one thing without the other, despite their undeniable distinctness. Unionism will come in degrees, naturally, depending on how *many* things must be united; but the essence of it, as a philosophically useful term, is that there are subtle and surprising interdependencies among the items in question—there is no possibility of deep division. My unionist thesis about instantiation is, then, simply this: properties cannot be instantiated singly but only in clusters. There cannot be a case in which a particular (let us use this familiar term) instantiates just one property: a plurality of properties must always be instantiated together. The instantiation relation is necessarily one-many. I mean this as a hard metaphysical necessity. We are familiar with the point that a single property is apt to have many instances, but it is doubtful that every property *must* have more than one instance—though it is plausible that every property *could* have multiple instances (except for such odd properties as being identical with Venus). It is, at least, in the nature of properties potentially to spread themselves around, whether they actually succeed in so proliferating or not. I am claiming that it is in the nature of particulars

---

[2] I considered using the over-used "holism" to express the concept that I had in mind, but decided it had too many irrelevant connotations to be tolerable in the new sense—and it is simply too hackneyed as a term of art. Still, it is helpful to bear it in mind here, sticking to its literal meaning and abstracting away from familiar theses about mind and meaning. I think "unionism" works well enough, technical neologism that it is, but "collectivism" would also be apt.

to attract a cluster of properties: there cannot be a particular that limits itself to a single property. So, though symmetrical, the two claims differ in modal status: properties are necessarily *potentially* one-many with respect to particulars, but particulars are necessarily *actually* one-many with respect to properties. You can't have a particular that is wedded to one property alone; polygamy is the rule.

I must immediately ward off a triviality charge. Suppose a particular instantiates *red*.[3] Then, whatever else might be true of it, it also instantiates *colored* and *not-green* (all over) and *has a property*. That is, it instantiates any property entailed by *red*. But this is trivial, a simple consequence of the logic of entailment—not a deep ontological truth. So let me refine: the unionism attaches to *logically independent* properties. For example, if something is red, then it must also have certain properties of shape and size and location and so on The clustering is non-trivial, not the result of simple entailment. An object's color does not determine *what* shape it has, but an object has to have *some* shape—some determinate from within the range of the corresponding determinable. These properties are not logically related—it is contingent what shape something has, given its color—but there is a necessity to this contingency, since *some* shape has to be instantiated. So the thesis is far from the trivial truth that properties always entail other properties. The thesis says that it is impossible to have *any* property without having *many* (logically unrelated) properties. Let me put it this way: in Plato's heaven the universals are laid out like knives in a box, waiting for selection by particulars. There is clustering among the universals in virtue of logical relations of entailment, but no clustering as between contingently related universals. But when particulars make their selection (or universals make theirs), clustering eventuates: suddenly the universals form into families, converging in particulars. There is none of the unionism I am talking about in Plato's heaven, but the unionism comes into force once the universals make their descent into the sublunary world. It is the particulars that impose the union—they refuse to harbor just a solitary universal. They adopt a whole family of universals *en bloc*, pressing the hitherto isolated universals into composite units or teams. In other words, instantiation is always one-many.

The thesis, though intuitively compelling, might be disputed, at least as a metaphysical necessity. Ingenious counterexamples might be proposed (and I have no objection to such a procedure—this is conceptual analysis). What about nature's simplest particulars—electrons or quarks or strings? Aren't these defined by a single attribute? Significantly, they are not. Particles have mass, position, and charge, not just one of these; and even elementary strings have extension and location, as well as vibrating in a certain frequency. Nothing is entirely *simple*—not in the sense of having no parts, but in the sense of possessing a single property. Every particular, even

---

[3] Here I use italics to form the name of property—not a concept, as in the rest of the book. This is a mere typographical convenience, not an admission that concepts and properties are indistinguishable—which I emphatically reject.

one with no proper parts, is complex with respect to its properties. Nothing encountered in nature violates the unionism that I have identified. And the same is true of
events as is true of continuant particulars: every event exemplifies a plurality of
properties that are not instantiated merely by entailment. At a minimum, every
event has location and duration, in addition to sortal properties like *explosion* and
wedding.

I think, further, that the unionism applies to *intrinsic* properties, not merely
relational ones. It is easy to generate relational properties—such as *existing in a
world in which Mount Everest exists*—which apply to every particular in the actual
world: so the unionism is less interesting when we include such properties. But it
seems to me that reality encourages the stronger thesis that multiple *intrinsic* properties must always be instantiated by particulars. I know of no counterexample even
to that stronger thesis. If it were not so, then the unionism would not imply the
notion of a complex nature for every particular—and this notion is what the initial
intuition surely suggested. When the unionist thesis is first stated, we naturally interpret it as claiming that particulars cannot be one-dimensional in their nature, but
that requires a multiplicity of intrinsic properties, not merely relational ones.

What if someone does not share this intuition or wonders what it demonstrates
metaphysically? I entirely sympathize with them. It is certainly not enough simply to
observe that empirical reality offers no counterexamples to the unionist thesis and
that it is intuitively compelling. The thesis is meant as a hard necessity concerning
objective reality, so it must apply to all possible cases of instantiation, and the intuitions must have some solid ground. But, so interpreted, it lacks simple self-evidence,
or (as yet) a logically secure foundation. Couldn't there be a possible world that was
one-one in its pattern of instantiation—one property for every object and one object
for every property? Isn't a *non*-clustering world possible? Nothing in logic seems to
preclude it. And yet it seems fantastic, a mere play with words. It is not *logically*
impossible, in the narrow sense, so what makes it metaphysically impossible? Surely,
we feel, it does not just *happen* that our world contains no counterexamples; it is
built into the very nature of particulars that they conform to unionism. But why do
we feel that? We can't envisage the one-dimensional particular, any more than we
can make sense of the bare particular—the particular with *zero* properties. Intuition
seems firm on the point, but intuition is so far bereft of articulate backing. *Why* is
the unionist thesis true?

I think that the reason goes deep: it rests on the very distinction between properties and objects, universals and particulars. Since instantiation depends on the
robustness of that distinction, it is built into the very structure of instantiation. It is
this: without unionism, the distinction between a particular and its properties
becomes moot, nugatory, and baseless. Suppose that a putative particular *x* instantiates a single property *P*, so that there is nothing more that can be said about *x* other
than that it is *P*. Then how is *x* to be *distinguished* from *P*—what constitutes it as
ontologically separate? Since the whole nature of *x* is to be *P*, it is unclear how *x* can

be anything other than *P*. *P* can be distinct from *x* because other particulars can instantiate *P*, but *x* seems absent of anything to make it stand apart from *P*: it collapses into *P*. What, indeed, makes it a *particular* at all? But if particulars have multiple properties, there is no danger of collapsing into any one of them, since the other properties certainly don't so collapse. If there are no co-instantiated properties, however, the ontological distance between object and property vanishes. Genuinely to be an instance of one property requires that other properties be co-instantiated; in the absence of that, the notion of instance loses purchase. Not for nothing did earlier theorists identify objects with *bundles* of qualities, not qualities singly, since otherwise there is simply no distinction between the two. The bundling was a good thought, even though it is a mistake to identify particulars with mere sets of qualities.[4] Look at an ordinary physical object: Why do you distinguish it from any one of its qualities? Because there are many of those and only one of it, so that no ontological collapse is possible—no quality alone can swallow the particular up, so to speak. But for a putative particular with just one quality no such basis for distinction exists, and the particular finds itself squeezed into the mold of that single quality. There is nothing for its distinctness from that quality to consist in. Consider the (alleged) possibility of two particulars instantiating only the same single property, for example, *red*: how could they be distinct from each other? There is nothing to distinguish them, since by hypothesis they have just that single property (not even spatial location, since that too is a property). They both collapse into the same property, and hence are the same, which reduces the original supposition to absurdity.

I hope that jogged or shaped your intuitions somewhat. We are dealing here with elusive questions that resist resolution into others more graspable (i.e., we are doing philosophy). My thought above is just that instantiation requires the particular/property distinction, but that distinction rests upon the unionism that I have alleged. So instantiation is essentially union forming. It is not that properties in themselves have this kind of mutual affinity—they are not so unionized in Plato's heaven—but when instantiation gets its teeth into them, they are compelled to join hands. To make a world of particulars, they have to submit to forced unionization. They cannot create particulars without teaming up. I might even say, yet more metaphorically, that instantiation transforms properties from their natural individualism into a forced collectivism. For without the collectivism, particulars cannot enjoy their own

---

[4] The standard objection to such a view is that it renders material things abstract, like sets in general. That uses the notion of the "abstract" in ways we should be wary of (see Chapter 11). A better thought is that properties are not *members* of the particular that exemplifies them, as they would have to be if particulars were sets of properties. Exemplification (instantiation) is not the same as set-membership: these are relations of an entirely different order. In addition, co-membership in a set is nothing like co-instantiation: a set of properties can include properties not co-instantiated in any particular—and indeed, necessarily not co-instantiated (e.g., the set containing the property of being even, the property of being odd, and the property of having a headache).

distinctive mode of being. Particulars must pitch their tent where properties gather; they cannot exist in a state of property monogamy (to switch the metaphor).[5]

The transformative power of instantiation takes me to another feature of it. Let us assume, for expository ease, that Plato was right about universals: they originally exist in a timeless unperceived pre-instantiated state, awaiting descent to the world of changing particulars. Then it becomes irresistible to distinguish universals and particulars ontologically, by saying that universals are "abstract" and particulars "concrete"—at any rate, they are beings of a totally different ontological order. Many philosophers then become puzzled about this abstract Platonic realm, suspecting it even of not existing. But it seems to me that the really hard problem occurs once we have happily accepted Plato's abstract realm: for how can the here-and-now concrete particular and the remote abstract universal ever succeed in meeting in an intelligible nexus? Structurally, the problem resembles Descartes' problem of mind-body interaction: once we buy into his radical dualism, with its contrasting essences, how do we explain the way in which mind and body interact, forming a unified causal nexus, a *person*? Similarly, once we buy into Plato's radical dualism of concrete particulars and abstract universals, how can we explain their "interaction"—the fact, that is, that the *nature* of concrete particulars is constituted by those removed abstract universals? The chasm between them is too great; the required ontological blending is too bizarre. We get pushed toward the reduction of universals to particulars (Aristotle and many others of "nominalist" stripe) or the reduction of particulars to universals (as with those "bundles of qualities" theorists). The really difficult thing is to maintain Plato's dualism, which has much to be said for it, while managing to allow for that "participation" that Plato deemed so essential to creating an empirical world. How can such disparate entities contrive to "participate" together in anything, let alone that most intimate of relationships—instantiation? That is the deep metaphysical puzzle raised by Platonism, not the alleged problems of the "abstract" per se. How can instantiation reach up from the sublunary world of grubby distributed particulars to the transcendent world of shining self-subsistent universals? How can heaven and earth be brought together into the propertied particular with which we are so familiar?

I have no solution to the puzzle, but I think it shows something interesting about instantiation—that it must be transformative. If it brings about the grouping of universals that I mentioned above, then it also brings about a more internal transformation in the being of universals—it renders them "concrete." It gives them, in

---

[5] In these remarks I am letting my philosophical imagination have free rein (always a risky procedure), following it where it leads me. I do so in the belief that timidity about indulging in such flights of fancy can inhibit the gaining of insights. We need the philosophical thought police to maintain law and order, yes, but we shouldn't let them interfere with legitimate intellectual adventure. Thus I am trying not to hold anything back, to let it all out, despite the danger of courting absurdity (and maybe absurdity, too, can have its philosophical uses). The only question is the *spirit* in which one indulges one's imagination—as exploration or as dogmatic conviction.

Shakespeare's memorable phrase, "a local habitation and a name." They descend from the elevated Platonic realm and come to qualify humble spatiotemporal particulars. One of the ways in which this happens is that they lose some of their prior inner unity: they come to be instantiated in various distributed particulars, becoming dispersed around the universe, like so much wind-blown pollen. Before, they existed in total self-contained unity, not being spread far and wide by multiple instantiation; but with instantiation they divide into a multitude of instances—into shards of their former being. To "participate" in the empirical world they must take on some of its nature, losing their unadulterated purity, their pristine unity. (It is impossible here not to think of the gods—indeed, Plato's whole system is clearly modeled on the relation between gods and mortals). The Form of the Good, say, must be transformed into individual good acts, blending seamlessly with the empirical world, and being muddied and stained in the process (think of god becoming man). Whatever underlying ontological reality these Platonic metaphors evoke, it is clear that instantiation does not leave universals unaltered—somehow they must make the transition from the "abstract" to the "concrete." An obvious symptom of the transformation is that we cannot *perceive* them when they reside solely in the Platonic realm—they are creatures only of intellectual apprehension there—but they become perceptible once instantiation gets a grip on them. The same is true of their causal powers: they are causally idle when existing in their pre-instantiated state, but they become causally potent once instantiation performs its magic. I want to say, then, that instantiation makes alterations *in* universals, bends and shapes them: they go from independent to collective as unionization takes hold, and they go from "abstract" to "concrete"—imperceptible to perceptible, non-causal to causal. Instantiation has this transfiguring power: it reconfigures the realm that it invokes—and particulars come to be what they are in virtue of such transformations. I regard this as a conceptual truth about instantiation—part of its a priori analysis. The metaphysics issues thus from the analysis—and it is a stirring and substantial metaphysics (which is why I suspect that most of my readers will recoil from it).[6]

Can instantiation come in degrees, or is it essentially all-or-nothing? Is there such a thing as *partially* instantiating a property, as there is such a thing as being partially immersed in water or being partially blind? I think not: instantiation only comes in two strengths—total or not at all. I would therefore reformulate the law of excluded middle as follows: an object either has a given property totally or it totally lacks that

---

[6] Philosophy is often like a contest between letting one's hair down and keeping it brushed neatly back. We find ourselves wanting to say things that we feel embarrassed to say—things that sound quirky or bizarre or even slightly mad. But if we keep our hair rigidly and flatly in place, we risk missing interesting intellectual experiences—not learning all there is to learn. The upshot of these conflicting impulses is apt to be a kind of halfhearted and over-qualified semi-lunge. I am striving here for extreme candor, the icy exhilarating plunge, the extravagant gesture—I am letting my philosophical unconscious have its say. (And don't think my philosophical super-ego is not made uncomfortable.)

property; there is no such thing as partially having a property or partially lacking it. We cannot view instantiation as subject to a scale that allows for differences of degree, all the way from zero to one hundred percent. This means that we can't say that one thing instantiates a given property *more* than another thing does, or that one thing instantiates a property *twice as much* as another.

We must be careful about what exactly this claim amounts to. It is not the denial of vague properties. The property of baldness comes in degrees, as do many properties, so that it is not an all-or-nothing matter; but we need not suppose that *instantiating* baldness likewise (and in addition) comes in degrees. What we have here is the all-or-nothing instantiation of a property that is not all-or-nothing. Suppose that A is bald to degree d and that B is also bald to degree d: it doesn't make sense to suppose that one of them, but not the other, *instantiates* baldness of degree d to degree d'. What could that mean, except that one is balder than the other?—and we stipulated that A and B agree on that. Baldness comes in degrees, to be sure, but once the degree is fixed, there is no room for further variation in the degree to which the vague property is instantiated. To suppose otherwise is to introduce two levels of variation where one suffices. All the variation is taken care of by the vague property itself, not by variations in its degree of instantiation. If we consider a precise property, such as having exactly one thousand hairs (of such and such length), then we can see that there is no room for variation in the degree of instantiation—someone either definitively has that many hairs or not. Similarly, in the vague case, the variation is all within the property and does not afflict the instantiation relation per se. Someone either totally has the vague property of being bald or not—which is to say that he has (*tout court*) a property that comes in degrees. You may be someone who totally has that property in a small degree or totally has it in a large degree or even totally has a borderline case of it; but you are never in a state of partially instantiating the property, if that means you can instantiate partially the property of being (say) *very* bald. Once the degree of baldness is fixed, there is no possibility of varying the degree of instantiation *of* that degree of baldness. You can't make a person more bald by first fixing his degree of baldness and then adding the extra condition that he instantiates this property to a high (or low) degree. The variation takes place inside the property, so to speak, not externally to it in the instantiation relation. The correct analysis of "I am very bald" is "I instantiate the property of being very bald," not "I very much instantiate the property of being bald." If we add another "very" to this last sentence before "bald," we get something either meaningless or trivially equivalent to the first paraphrase. These modifiers of degree attach to the predicate, not to the instantiation relation itself.[7]

---

[7] By way of contrast, modal modifiers *do* attach to the instantiation relation (they are copula modifiers, not predicate modifiers), as in "John necessarily-is a human being": see my *Logical Properties*, Chapter 4. But these modifiers do not admit of degree and do not produce grades of instantiation. What we don't want to allow is that things can actually instantiate properties (whether necessarily or contingently) to a greater or lesser degree, as temperature comes in degrees (absolute

It might alternatively be suggested that it makes sense to suppose that an object can *approximate* to the condition of instantiating a property but not quite get there—as someone might approximate to being a genius by merely being very clever. Don't they *somewhat* instantiate being a genius? Isn't there such a condition as *almost* instantiating a certain property—as when someone almost comes in first in a running race? But in these kinds of cases, the object does fully instantiate some *other* property related to the given one in a certain way—say, being very clever or coming in second in the race. The object thus totally fails to instantiate the given property but also totally instantiates a property related to it in a certain way—there is nowhere in this that partial instantiation of a property needs to be recognized. It is not that the object actually does instantiate a property but less than totally: it either does or it doesn't. The properties of an object are either present in it or not; they cannot hover in the vicinity of the object, being instantiated by it only tenuously or marginally. There cannot be two levels of participation in the realm of universals—being fully involved with them or only halfheartedly involved. Properties are either right there in objects or not there at all—they cannot qualify objects to one degree or another. A particular cannot be partially immersed in a property, so to speak. If a property is a property of a particular, then it is fully a property of it; it cannot be a property of it and yet have some way to go before it is fully instantiated. All the properties a thing has it has to the same degree, that is, completely.

I hope the sense of my claim is now clear. It should strike you as a self-evident truth, once certain distinctions are made (it may have struck you that way at the beginning). But it has some powerful consequences, relating to questions of indeterminacy. Epistemic indeterminacy is unproblematic, of course, since we can clearly have degrees of certainty as to whether an object instantiates a property; it is the ontological kind that is troubling—the idea that it is objectively indeterminate or probabilistic whether a certain property is instantiated. This idea frequently comes up in connection with quantum theory: there is no "fact of the matter" about the exact position or velocity of a particle. Such indeterminacy claims are very difficult to understand. They cry out for conceptual analysis. It can't be that the particle has each of *many* positions or velocities, since these are all determinate facts; nor can it be that the particle has none of them, since that is equally determinate. The only (non-epistemic) way to interpret such claims, so far as I can tell, is to invoke an apparatus of partial instantiation: the particle *partially* instantiates being at location l and *partially* instantiates being at location l'. That does supply a full-blooded notion of ontological indeterminacy, since it is not an all-or-nothing matter whether a certain property is instantiated on this model. The trouble is that the notion of partial instantiation is incoherent, a logical monster. It makes no sense to suppose that the particle is *somewhat* at a certain location, if that means anything other than

---

zero is not having the property at all, being very hot is having the property powerfully, and being warm is having the property in an intermediate way). This is really just nonsense.

that it is *near* that location. Things have properties or not; they don't have them to a certain degree. We can't then suppose that an object has a property other than determinately, since it can't *have* a property in any other way: one thing can't have a certain property any more or less than another thing has it, if both have it. It can't be that one thing has location *l* in the all-or-nothing way but another has that same location (at another time) in a qualified way: for what would it mean to *have* a location in anything other than a complete way? To have it is to have it completely, determinately. A particle can't really, truly have a location but have it only slightly or minimally or uncertainly (in a non-epistemic sense).[8]

The all-or-nothing nature of instantiation implies that we cannot make sense of the idea of an object *probably* instantiating a property, that is, the idea of ontological probability, where this is construed as some sort of partial instantiation. There are various acceptable notions of objective probability, but none of them is the notion of an object *having* a property with a certain (non-unity) probability: that phrase can only mean that we are in a certain epistemic state with respect to a state of affairs—it cannot be a feature of the state of affairs itself. That is, we cannot interpret objective probability in terms of partial instantiation, identifying degree of probability with degree of instantiation. There is presence or absence of a property, not a range of probabilistic instantiations. An object can *possibly* have a property, but it cannot, ontologically, probably have one, if that is taken as a mode of *actual* instantiation: there is no such state of affairs as an object actually having a property to a degree less than unity. Degrees of probability cannot be degrees of instantiation. They might represent relative frequency in a population, but that is not a matter of the objects in that population instantiating properties to different degrees—just a matter of the relative frequency of things instantiating the property *simpliciter*. In the single case, the object either has the property or not; it cannot *probably-have* it (where "probably" here modifies the instantiation relation).

Instantiation is thus all-or-nothing, unionist, and transformative. These are its essential features (or some of them), as disclosed by conceptual analysis. It is also primitive, in the sense that it cannot be dismantled into conceptual parts. Nor could anything more basic bring it into existence. For suppose we tried to find a reality more fundamental to bring about its existence, something anterior to instantiation. That would have to involve the having of properties of some sort by something, in which case it would presuppose instantiation. Anything causal or explanatory or foundational would have to consist in the instantiation of properties, so nothing could be more basic than instantiation. There is logically nothing that instantiation

---

[8] It is still unclear to me, having read many accounts of quantum indeterminacy, whether some theorists are advancing a notion of partial instantiation to describe the phenomena. The degree of unclarity about the nature of the indeterminacy claim makes it very difficult to tell what the "Uncertainty Principle" in physics is saying. I may be tilting at windmills here, excoriating the notion of grades of instantiation; but it is as well to be clear. If they don't mean that, then what *do* they mean?

could *come from*—no genesis or prehistory or deep structure. Even God could not create it, because he himself is precisely a system of instantiated properties (benevolence, omnipotence, omniscience, say). God could not create instantiation because he is created *by* instantiation. It has no explanation; it is metaphysically ultimate. With instantiation we reach bedrock. All conceivable being rests on instantiation (and all inconceivable being, too). Many things are optional across the space of possible worlds, but instantiation isn't one of them. Reality just *is* the instantiation of properties. There is nothing else it *could* be. This is the conceptual truth of all conceptual truths. And it is why no one has ever sought to deny that instantiation is real—as they have denied almost everything else. The general is exemplified in the particular: that is the ultimate essence of the world. We philosophers have discovered that essence by conceptual analysis alone, and have even managed to say a few things about its general structure. When we analyze the concept *reality* we find that it resolves into the general, the particular, and the instantiation of the general by the particular. That is the a priori essence of reality (the thing), as revealed by the activity of conceptual analysis—undertaken in the spirit of play (that is, for its own sake).[9]

---

[9] The grand division of the world into the particular and the general was one of the first achievements of conceptual analysis—any fact in the world must be breakable down into its particulars and its universals, as an a priori necessary truth. Here is a dualism that is far from untenable, and the concepts used to characterize it are unexceptionable (though maximally general). The nature of the duality is indeed a matter of controversy, but it is a rare philosopher who can see nothing in it (in Quine the distinction between individual variable and predicate is sacrosanct). This is something that philosophy has indisputably discovered! It is so familiar to us now that we probably underestimate how blindingly revelatory it must have been for the first human beings to grasp and articulate it. Was it perhaps one of the first achievements of abstract reflective thought? Did it initiate philosophy as a distinctive area of inquiry? Was it the earliest demonstration of the awesome power of conceptual analysis?

References

Aristotle. *Metaphysics, Topics,* in *The Basic Works of Aristotle,* ed. Richard McKeon. New York: Random House, 2001.

Beaney, Michael. *The Frege Reader.* Oxford: Basil Blackwell, 1997.

Burge, Tyler. "Disjunctivism and Perceptual Psychology," *Philosophical Topics* 33 (1): 1–78, 2005.

Crane, Tim, and D. H. Mellor. "There Is No Problem of Physicalism," *Mind* 99 (394): 185–206, 1990.

Davidson, Donald. "Freedom to Act," in *Essays on Actions and Events.* Oxford: Clarendon Press, 1980.

Frege, Gottlob. *The Foundations of Arithmetic,* Evanston, IL: Northwestern University Press, 1953.

Geach, Peter. *Mental Acts.* London: Routledge and Kegan Paul, 1957.

Grice, H. P. "Meaning," *Philosophical Review* 66 (3): 377–388, 1957.

Grice, H. P. "The Causal Theory of Perception," *Proceedings of the Aristotelian Society,* Supp. Vol. xxxv, 121–153, 1961.

Griffin, Nicholas. "Wittgenstein, Universals and Family Resemblances," *Canadian Journal of Philosophy* 3 (4): 635–651, 1974.

Guttenplan, Samuel. *A Companion to the Philosophy of Mind.* Oxford: Basil Blackwell, 1996.

Hempel, Carl. "Reduction: Ontological and Linguistic Facets," in *Philosophy, Science, and Method,* eds. S. Morgenbesser, P. Suppes, and M. White. New York: St. Martin's Press, 1969.

Huizinga, Johan. *Homo Ludens: A Study of the Play Element in Culture.* Boston: Beacon Press, 1950.

Jackson, Frank. *From Metaphysics to Ethics: A Defence of Conceptual Analysis.* Oxford: Oxford University Press, 1998.

Kant, Immanuel. *Critique of Pure Reason,* translated by J. M. D. Meiklejohn. New York: Barnes and Noble Books, 2004.

Knobe, Joshua, and Shaun Nichols. *Experimental Philosophy.* New York: Oxford University Press, 2008.

Kripke, Saul. *Naming and Necessity.* Cambridge, MA: Harvard University Press, 1980.

Locke, John. *An Essay Concerning Human Understanding.* London: Penguin Books, 1997.

McGinn, Colin. "Mach and Husserl," *Journal for the British Society of Phenomenology,* May 1972; "A Note on the Essence of Natural Kinds," in McGinn, *Knowledge and Reality: Selected Essays,* Oxford: Clarendon Press, 1999; *The Character of Mind,* Oxford: Oxford University Press, 1982; *The Subjective View,* Oxford: Oxford University Press, 1983; "Sartre," in *Oxford Companion to the Mind,* ed. R. L. Gregory, Oxford: Oxford University Press, 1987; "The Concept of Knowledge," in *Knowledge and Reality;* "The Mechanism of

Reference," in *Knowledge and Reality; Mental Content*, Oxford: Basil Blackwell, 1989; *Problems in Philosophy*, Oxford: Basil Blackwell, 1993; *Logical Properties*, Oxford: Clarendon Press, 2000; *Mindsight*, Cambridge, MA: Harvard University Press, 2004; "The Objects of Intentionality," in *Consciousness and Its Objects*, Oxford: Clarendon Press, 2004; *Sport*, London: Acumen Publishing, 2008.

Moore, G. E. *Principia Ethica*. Cambridge: Cambridge University Press, 1993.

Plato. *Theatetus, Meno*, in Plato: *Complete Works*, ed. John M. Cooper. Indianapolis: Hackett Publishing, 1993.

Quine, W. V. "Two Dogmas of Empiricism," in *From a Logical Point of View*, New York: Harper and Row, 1963; *Word and Object*, Cambridge, MA: MIT Press, 1960; "Epistemology Naturalized," in *Ontological Relativity and Other Essays*, New York: Columbia University Press, 1969.

Rorty, Richard. *Philosophy and the Mirror of Nature*. Princeton: Princeton University Press, 1981.

Russell, Bertrand. *The Problems of Philosophy*. New York: Oxford University Press, 1997.

Sartre, Jean-Paul. *Being and Nothingness*. London: Methuen, 1957.

Soames, Scott. *Philosophical Analysis in the Twentieth Century*. Princeton: Princeton University Press, 2005.

Strawson, P. F. *Individuals*, London: Methuen, 1949; *Analysis and Metaphysics*, Oxford: Oxford University Press, 1992.

Suits, Bernard. *The Grasshopper: Games, Life and Utopia*. Toronto: University of Toronto Press, 1978; reissued by Broadview Press, Ontario, 2005.

Thomasson, Amie. "Phenomenology and the Development of Analytic Philosophy," in *The Southern Journal of Philosophy* XL, 2002.

Unger, Peter. "An Analysis of Factual Knowledge," *The Journal of Philosophy* 65 (6): 157–170, 1968.

Urmson, J. O. *Philosophical Analysis*. Oxford: Clarendon Press, 1956.

Williamson, Timothy. *Knowledge and Its Limits*. Oxford: Oxford University Press, 2000.

Wittgenstein, Ludwig. *Tractatus Logico-Philosophicus*, London: Routledge and Kegan Paul, 1961; *Philosophical Investigations*, Oxford: Basil Blackwell, 1958; *The Blue and Brown Books*, Oxford: Basil Blackwell, 1958; *Remarks on Color*, Berkeley: University of California Press, 1978.

Index